Social Interaction in the Prehistoric Natufian

Generating an interactive agency model using GIS

Carla A. Parslow

BAR International Series 1916
2009

Published in 2016 by
BAR Publishing, Oxford

BAR International Series 1916

Social Interaction in the Prehistoric Natufian

ISBN 978 1 4073 0399 4

© C A Parslow and the Publisher 2009

The author's moral rights under the 1988 UK Copyright,
Designs and Patents Act are hereby expressly asserted.

All rights reserved. No part of this work may be copied, reproduced, stored,
sold, distributed, scanned, saved in any form of digital format or transmitted
in any form digitally, without the written permission of the Publisher.

BAR Publishing is the trading name of British Archaeological Reports (Oxford) Ltd.
British Archaeological Reports was first incorporated in 1974 to publish the BAR
Series, International and British. In 1992 Hadrian Books Ltd became part of the BAR
group. This volume was originally published by Archaeopress in conjunction with
British Archaeological Reports (Oxford) Ltd / Hadrian Books Ltd, the Series principal
publisher, in 2009. This present volume is published by BAR Publishing, 2016.

Printed in England

BAR titles are available from:

        BAR Publishing
        122 Banbury Rd, Oxford, OX2 7BP, UK
EMAIL   info@barpublishing.com
PHONE +44 (0)1865 310431
FAX   +44 (0)1865 316916
        www.barpublishing.com

ABSTRACT

The Levant (Israel and Jordan) has a long history of human occupation. Archaeological sites in the region demonstrate this history as one of continuous change. The focus on understanding this history of change is most pronounced in the overriding interest in the transition from a mobile hunting and gathering economy at the end of the Pleistocene (Ice Age), to a settled agricultural economy in the Holocene, less than 10,000 years ago. This transition from the Late Pleistocene to Holocene is the period when the Natufian culture flourished (approximately 12,800 BP to 10,300 BP).

Forty years of research on the Natufian has led to further understanding of their technology and their place in time. Although the technological patterns are quite similar, the documentation of material culture and features from various Natufian sites throughout the Levant reveals variability across time and space. Traditionally, interpretation of variability is based on chronology and its relation to the ecological setting. I hypothesize that this variability reflects, not only the ecological setting in which Natufian populations were located, but also the social groups formed over time and space. The acceptance of new technology, techniques, and ideas depends on the frequency and intensity of interaction with other groups, both near and distant, throughout the region. The more frequent and intense the interaction, the greater the amount of information, or innovation, that is likely to occur.

This thesis addresses some of these issues by demonstrating that the ecological environment does not bind past populations. Both social and ecological structures play a role in the dissemination of knowledge through communication. The sharing of information acquires a spatial context through the construction of an interactive-agent model detailing three spheres of interaction: (1) within-group interaction; (2) between-group interaction; and (3) competitive interaction. Both archaeological interpretive methods (collection of site data and analysis of materials) and geographical information science (GISc) (least cost path analysis) are used to show that Natufian groups had the opportunity to interact with one another and that these interactions occurred in defined locations where potential paths cross.

ACKNOWLEDGEMENTS

The decision to take on such a research project, and to see it through to the end, is not a task that one can complete alone. Foremost, I would like to thank Dr. Michael Chazan, for his support, advice, and enthusiasm. This support extends both academically and financially. Michael takes a positive approach to graduate students, and has always encouraged me to discuss my ideas and take my research an extra step. Furthermore, he has also supported my decisions to undertake projects that were, at times, outside of the Natufian. This has made me a well-rounded archaeologist for which I have Michael to thank.

I would also like to thank those who have reviewed and commented on this research: Dr. Ted Banning, Dr. Ezra Zubrow and Dr. Max Friesen. Extended thanks go to Dr. Margaret Conkey, for finding the time during her relentless schedule to read this manuscript. Her comments and suggestions were invaluable. I wish to express special gratitude to Ted Banning for his support, both academically and financially. Ted first introduced me to archaeology in the Near East by bringing me to Jordan to work on the Wadi Ziqlab project. Ted is also notorious for his "Red Sea" of ink editing, which is always appreciated. I also would like to acknowledge Ezra for his time and encouragement through the process of writing this research and for always "being on board" when I asked for his participation outside of advising responsibilities.

This research was supported by University of Toronto Open Fellowships, the Andrea and Charles Bronfman Award for Israeli Studies, the Halbert Fund through grants to Michael Chazan and Ted Banning, and the Social Sciences and Humanities Research Council of Canada, through grants to Michael Chazan and Ted Banning.

TABLE OF CONTENTS

CHAPTER 1 — 1-3
INTRODUCTION: QUALIFYING AND QUANTIFYING SOCIAL INTERACTION
Preamble — 1
Research Objective — 1
Theoretical and Methodological Perspective — 2
Research Outline — 2

CHAPTER 2 — 4-10
THE AGENT AND THE ARCHAEOLOGIST: AGENCY IN ARCHAEOLOGY
Introduction — 4
Bourdieu – Putting rules into practice, the art of 'doing' — 4
Giddens – practical consciousness, I know why I 'do' it — 5
Agency and Archaeology — 6
Social Agency – A Critique — 7
Misinterpretation and misrepresentation — 8
Eclecticism and Redlining — 8
Neo-Darwinian uses of Agency — 9
Summary — 9

CHAPTER 3 — 11-18
TIME, SPACE, AGENCY AND THE NATUFIAN
The Natufian in Context — 11
Chronology – Time and the Agent — 11
Core and Periphery – Site Catchment and the Agent — 12
Cultural Ecology and Evolution – Structure and the Agent — 14
The Natufian Agent — 15

CHAPTER 4 — 19-30
DATA PART I: ARCHAEOLOGICAL SITES AND MATERIAL CULTURE
Introduction — 19
Archaeological Sites — 19
Natufian Sites in the Mediterranean Forest — 20
Natufian Sites in the Saharo desert — 22
Natufian Sites in the Irano-Turanian hills — 23
Sites not included in the study — 23
Material Culture — 26
Classification - Dunnell — 26
Types of Classification — 27
Variables and Attribute in Relation to Classification — 27
Encoding the Data — 28
Summary — 29

CHAPTER 5 — 31-39
METHODS PART I – CLUSTER ANALYSIS
Introduction to Clustering — 31
Proximity Matrix - Similarity measures for binary data — 32
Association Coefficients — 32
Choice of Similarity Coefficient — 34
Clustering Methods — 35
Hierarchical Clustering Methods — 36
Number of Clusters — 37
Validation Techniques — 38
Summary — 38

CHAPTER 6		40-46
	RESULTS PART I – ARCHAEOLOGICAL SITES AND MATERIAL CULTURE	
	Introduction	40
	Calculating the Proximity Measure and Applying the Clustering Method	40
	Number of Clusters	44
	Validation of Clusters	44
	Chipped Stone Data	45
	Summary of Results	46

CHAPTER 7		47-55
	DATA PART II – SPATIAL DATA	
	Introduction	47
	What is a Geographical Information System?	47
	GIS in Archaeology	47
	Archaeological Data as Spatial Data	50
	Elevation Models and Their Off-Spring	51
	Present Day Ecological Data	53
	Data Produced through Remote Sensing	54
	Summary	55

CHAPTER 8		56-62
	DATA ANALYSIS PART II – CREATING SPATIAL DATA MODELS	
	Introduction	56
	History of Cost Surface Analysis and Models	56
	Cost Surface Analysis	57
	Critique of Cost Surface Analysis	59
	Cost Surface Analysis in Archaeology	59
	Cost Surface Analysis – Methods for this research	61
	Summary	62

CHAPTER 9		63-76
	RESULTS PART II – SPATIAL ANALYSIS	
	Introduction	63
	First Level Analysis – Least Cost Paths for Each Cluster	63
	Second Level Analysis – Least Cost Paths to Each Cluster	68
	Other Possible Considerations	71
	The Chipped Stone Data	73
	Summary of Results	76

CHAPTER 10		77-
	CONSTRUCTING A MODEL OF SOCIAL INTERACTION FOR THE NATUFIAN	
	Introduction	77
	Progressive Group Splitting and Displacement	77
	Year-Round Settlement in the Mediterranean Forest	77
	Semi-Sedentary Groups and Nomadic Groups	78
	Semi-Sedentary Occupation of the Large Settlements and Logistical Organization	78
	Models and Chipped-Stone Data	79
	Interactive Agency Model	79
	Within Group Interaction Sphere	79
	Between Group Interaction Sphere	79
	Conflict Interaction Sphere	80
	Applying the Model to the Natufian	80
	Alternative Interpretations	81
	Final Remarks	82

CHAPTER 11		83-85
	CONCLUSIONS	
	Bridging Theory and Method in Archaeology – Building Models	83
	Socializing the Natufian	83
	Implications for the Interactive Agency Model	84

REFERENCES CITED		86-95
APPENDIX A		96-103
APPENDIX B		104-105
APPENDIX C		106-120

LIST OF TABLES

Table 3.1	Hypotheses tested in this research and potential alternatives	18
Table 4.1	Kinds of archaeological classification and their purposes.	27
Table 4.2	Variables and attributes defined for research.	28
Table 5.1	Section of the data matrix coded with qualitative data - 1 for present, 0 for absent.	32
Table 5.2	A two-by-two table giving the number of 1-1, 1-0, 0-1, 0-0 matches from the data matrix shown in Table 5.1.	32
Table 5.3	Summary of similarity coefficient equations as well as the calculated similarity distance for the data matrix in Table 5.2.	35
Table 5.4	Summary of hierarchical agglomerative clustering methods considered.	36
Table 5.5	Results of Hands and Everitt's (1987) study on hierarchical clustering methods using binary data.	37
Table 6.1	Possible cluster membership solutions for (a) Simple Matching and (b) Sorenson's similarity measures.	40-41
Table 6.2	Proximity measures used to test accuracy of Simple Matching and Sorenson's measure.	42
Table 6.3	Cluster membership for all similarity measures based on five clusters.	42
Table 6.4	Outcome of Pearson's r correlation coefficient.	43
Table 6.5	Cophenetic correlations between values in the original (Sorenson's) similarity matrix and the implied matrix (dendrogram measures).	44
Table 6.6	Nonparametric cophenetic correlations between values in the original (Sorenson's) similarity matrix and the implied matrix (dendrogram measures).	45
Table 6.7	Comparison of proximity measures tested for chipped-stone data.	45
Table 8.1	Expressions used in map algebra equation for cost surface analysis.	62

LIST OF FIGURES

Figure 1.1	Geographical location of the study area.	3
Figure 3.1	Year-round sedentism model proposed (Perlès and Phillips 1991).	17
Figure 3.2	Progressive group fusion and displacement model proposed (Perlès and Phillps 1991).	17
Figure 3.3	Semi-sedentary groups and nomadic groups model proposed (Perlès and Phillips 1991).	17
Figure 3.4	Semi-sedentary occupation of the large settlements and logistical organization model proposed (Perlès and Phillips 1991).	17
Figure 4.1	Conceptualization of data at the site, variable and attribute level.	19
Figure 4.2	Location of Natufian sites used in this research.	25
Figure 4.3	Scatterplot correlating area of Natufian sites with number of Red Sea Dentalium recovered.	29
Figure 5.1	Graph of the number of clusters against the fusion or amalgamation coefficient.	38
Figure 6.1	Plot of number of clusters versus Fusion Coefficient, Sorenson's Similarity Measure and Average Linkage solution.	44
Figure 6.2	Plot of number of clusters versus Fusion Coefficient, Squared Euclidean Distance Measure and Average Linkage solution for chipped-stone data.	46
Figure 7.1	Three vector formats: (a) point; (b) line; (c) polygon.	49
Figure 7.2	A simple raster (a), and corresponding data file (b).	49
Figure 7.3	Natufian sites in their geographical context.	51
Figure 7.4	Original digital terrain elevation data (DTED).	52
Figure 7.5	Digital elevation model (DEM) for the study region in 100 m intervals	52
Figure 7.6	Slope values for the study region.	53
Figure 7.7	Aspect values for the study region.	53
Figure 7.8	Ecological zones (biomes) for the study region.	54
Figure 7.9	Ecological biomes for the study region.	54
Figure 7.10	SPOT image for the study area.	55
Figure 7.11	LandSat image for the study area.	44
Figure 8.1	Hypothetical site catchment model for Natufian sites.	57
Figure 8.2	Tessellation of Natufian sites through Thiessen polygons.	57
Figure 8.3	Representation of hypothetical walking velocity compared to slope.	58
Figure 8.4	Graphical representation of Tobler's hiking algorithm.	58
Figure 9.1	Geographical location of clusters of Natufian sites in the study region.	63
Figure 9.2	Geographical location of lithic clusters of Natufian sites in the study region.	63
Figure 9.3	Calculation of Tobler's Hiking Algorithm (walking velocity) calculated from slope of study region.	64
Figure 9.4	Cluster 1 (a) cost distance, (b) cost direction, and (c) least cost path.	64-65
Figure 9.5	Cluster 2 (a) cost distance, (b) cost direction, and (c) least cost path.	65
Figure 9.6	Cluster 3 (a) cost distance, (b) cost direction, and (c) least cost path.	66
Figure 9.7	Cluster 4 (a) cost distance, (b) cost direction, and (c) least cost path.	66-67
Figure 9.8	Combined least cost paths.	67
Figure 9.9	Identified areas where least cost paths intersect.	68
Figure 9.10	Cluster 1 second level least cost paths.	68
Figure 9.11	Cluster 2 second level least cost paths.	68

Figure 9.12	Cluster 3 second level least cost paths.	69
Figure 9.13	Cluster 4 second level least cost paths.	69
Figure 9.14	Identified areas where second level least cost paths intersect.	69
Figure 9.15	Cluster 1 nodes and potential site networks.	70
Figure 9.16	Cluster 2 nodes and potential site networks.	70
Figure 9.17	Cluster 3 nodes and potential site networks.	70
Figure 9.18	Cluster 4 nodes and potential site networks.	71
Figure 9.19	Second level intersections as extension of first level paths.	71
Figure 9.20	First level least cost paths for Early Natufian sites.	72
Figure 9.21	First level least cost paths for Late Natufian sites.	72
Figure 9.22	Second level least cost paths for Early Natufian sites.	72
Figure 9.23	Second level least cost paths for Late Natufian sites.	72
Figure 9.24	Combined least cost paths, chipped-stone data.	73
Figure 9.25	Identified areas where least cost paths intersect, chipped-stone data.	73
Figure 9.26	Combined second level least cost paths, chipped-stone data.	74
Figure 9.27	Identified areas where second level least cost paths intersect, chipped-stone data.	74
Figure 9.28	Identified clusters of Natufian sites based on chipped-stone data in relation to terrestrial biomes.	74
Figure 9.29	First level least cost paths for Early Natufian sites based on chipped-stone data.	75
Figure 9.30	First level least cost paths for Late Natufian sites based on chipped-stone data.	75
Figure 9.31	Second level least cost paths for Early Natufian sites based on chipped-stone data.	75
Figure 9.32	Second level least cost paths for Late Natufian sites based on chipped-stone data.	75

CHAPTER 1
INTRODUCTION: QUALIFYING AND QUANTIFYING SOCIAL INTERACTION

Preamble

My introduction to the Natufian culture is the result of weekly visits with a professor (and later my advisor) who just completed his first year of excavation at Wadi Mataha, a Natufian site in southwestern Jordan, near Petra. After our visit, I usually left with an article to read on the Natufian. I would go home, read the article, and then come prepared the following week to discuss what I read. What made our discussions different from published discussion on the Natufian is that I had no previous knowledge or perceptions of the variability of Natufian sites and their assemblages. I came from a North American tradition of hunter-gatherer archaeology where the focus is on seasonal settlement and subsistence. I therefore believed that there must be some *pattern* of settlement for the Natufian and that it could only be understood through a shift in analysis – from searching for variability to concentration on similarity.

During this time, I also started to expand my thoughts on past hunter-gatherer behavior. I became increasingly dissatisfied with the North American tradition because it was detaching itself from the anthropological aspects of archaeology. Familiar with Clive Gamble's 1986 book, *The Palaeolithic Settlement of Europe*, and in agreement with Gamble's interpretations on the concept of region, I eagerly read his 1999 book *The Palaeolithic Societies of Europe*. I expected his latest manuscript to be a revision of his first book, and was surprised and delighted to be wrong in my assumption.

Gamble's 1999 contribution to archaeological theory and analysis marked a turning point in my own perceptions of past human behavior. *The Palaeolithic Societies of Europe* first introduced me to social agency and particularly Anthony Giddens' Structuration Theory. Gamble (1999:16) reiterates what Kuper (1988) originally asserts: "It took many years for Europeans and North Americans to acknowledge that hunters and gatherers had a social life and for its systematic investigation to begin." I find this statement very powerful. It addresses the problematic issue I have faced since my introduction to archaeology.

With my new interests in the Natufian culture and social agency, I venture into an area of archaeological research where I acknowledge that past populations had a social life and that this social life influenced all aspects of their behavior.

Research Objective

The objective of this research is to develop a model of social interaction for the Natufian culture in Southwest Asia through interpretation of environmental and material-culture variability. I accomplish this objective through the development of rigorous systematic grouping and spatial analysis of artifacts. The Natufian culture (approximately 13,000 or 12,800 BP to 10,500 or 10,300 BP based on radiocarbon dates) is critical to our understanding of the transition from mobile hunter-gatherers to sedentary hunter-gatherer-farmers (Sellars 1998). They are thought to represent one of the final periods of archaeologically known hunter-gatherers in Southwest Asia, preceding the advent of cultivation and agricultural economies.

The people who we classify as Natufian are situated in the Levant, which now encompasses Israel, Jordan, Syria and Lebanon (Figure 1.1). I limit the focus of this research to those Natufian sites situated in what is now modern day Israel and Jordan. Within this region, three ecological biomes are identified – the Mediterranean forests, the temperate grassland savannahs and shrublands of the Irano-Turanian, and the Saharo-Arabian desert and xeric shrublands.

Characterization of the Natufian is primarily based on the chipped-stone technology, most notably lunates, bladelets and multipurpose cores. Other distinctive characteristics include material culture of ground stone, marine shell, and bone as well as architecture, bedrock mortars, and burials.

The documentation of material culture and features from various Natufian sites throughout the Levant demonstrates variability across time and space. Although the technological patterns are quite similar, there is typological variability within each class (Belfer-Cohen 1991a). Traditionally, this variability is interpreted chronologically and in relation to the ecological setting.

One suggestion to account for the observed variability is that the Natufian culture had two types of sites: base camps and transitory camps. Base camps are larger and richer in material culture and are located in the Mediterranean core. Transitory camps are used for a short period, usually during procurement activities, and have limited material remains. Although these transitory camps can occur in the core area, they are believed to be primarily located in the peripheral Irano-Turanian and Saharo-Arabian desert zones. Because the ecological setting and function of base and transitory camps differ, it was logical to conclude that the material culture recovered from the individual sites would also differ.

There are also suggestions that Early Natufian sites are restricted to the core area (Mediterranean) while Late Natufian sites are found in both the core and periphery (Irano-Turanian and Saharo-Arabian). The hypothesized reason for this expansion is deterioration in the size of the Mediterranean core area. This deterioration led to a reduction in resources, mainly vegetational resources, and a need to expand the resource base (Bar-Yosef 1998; Gorring-Morris and Belfer-Cohen 1998; Henry 1981, 1995).

Other suggestions, resulting from further research outside of the core area indicate that the extent of the Natufian culture, particularly the Early Natufian, is greater than first thought. Early and Late Natufian sites, including both base and transitory camps, are now represented in the periphery area. This discovery is interpreted as a result of micro-environmental variability. Regardless of these discoveries, variability still existed and interpretations remain heavily steeped in the ecological tradition. I discuss hypotheses developed from past research in detail in chapter three.

With the exception of recent burial studies (Belfer-Cohen 1995; Boyd 2001), the primary basis for interpreting Natufian distribution in the Levant is ecological. It is also clear that Natufian sites are investigated individually or in small groups and hence treated as distinct entities existing in their own micro-environment. What is left to explain is the fact that, although there is variability at both inter- and intra-site levels, there remains a general homogeneity of Natufian material culture throughout the entire Levant.

At a more general level, I pose the question: are some sites more similar to each other than to others? At a more specific level of questioning, I question and attempt to answer the question: if there is a degree of homogeneity, how can one illustrate it in a way that not only identifies this similarity but also defines it, particularly in a geographically diverse archaeological region? This research takes on these questions from an agency approach rather than from the cultural historical and ecological approaches of past research.

Theoretical and Methodological Perspective

The history of hunter-gatherer social interaction is profoundly entrenched in economic and ecological theories (Bettinger and Baumhoff 1982; Binford 1980; Higgs and Vita-Finzi 1972; Jochim 1976, 1998; Kelly 1995; Sahlins 1972; Steward 1937). This tends to leave the human aspect somewhat detached from the interpretation of hunter-gatherers in prehistory. Archaeologists are now seeking alternative paradigms to explain why and how past individual hunter-gatherers interacted with one another. Use of the social agency perspective is now prevalent in archaeological research. In particular, research on prehistoric hunter-gatherers is the fastest-growing sector in archaeology to employ this approach.

A social agency perspective assumes that human thoughts and actions are structured through relationships. These relationships are with other humans as well as with their surroundings. These relationships are associated with fields of discourse or communication. In this sense, we may regard archaeological sites and their artifacts as fragments of the practices of social discourse (Barrett 2000:27) or as residues of past communication. By employing an agency approach, we no longer view archaeological sites or their material culture as static entities representing a past population or their life ways.

In the case of the Natufian, previous research demonstrates how this culture interacts with and embeds itself in the ecological structure. However, we know little about the social structures that the Natufian culture creates and transforms through action. We also know little about the interaction between social and ecological structures. To reveal these social structures, we must examine Natufian action and agency through analysis of Natufian technology and artifacts.

Although this analysis includes all artifact types, the focus is on material culture related to exchange and artistic activities. There are three reasons for limiting analysis to these material culture classes: they are present throughout the Levant and demonstrate variability through time and space; they signify the knowledge and actions of individuals; and it is possible to show that they interacted with both the ecological and social structures of the Natufian. Those materials of interest related to exchange and artistic activities include all non-lithic artifacts as well as features.

The methods for this research include two components: systematics and spatial analysis. I address the systematics component on two levels: the level of the artifact and the level of the site. Acknowledging the current taxonomic grouping for Natufian artifacts, I measure the similarities between artifact collections in different sites through cluster analysis. The spatial component involves input of the data into a GIS to perform various forms of analyses, most notably least cost path analysis. Recognizing that human interaction takes place over space, it is possible to use artifact evidence to calculate what sites interact with each other the most and thus, may have had the strongest social ties. It is also possible to suggest the possible routes used to facilitate this interaction. The main advantage of using a GIS is that, through implementation of artifact grouping in a GIS, it is also possible to account for ecological variability. In this way, social and ecological structures are addressed simultaneously. The results illustrate similarities and interrelationships of sites over the landscapes that, in turn, demonstrate the probable social relations of populations that once inhabited these sites.

Research Outline

This research has four parts. The first part, chapter two and three, addresses the theoretical paradigm and its role in this research. In chapter two, I explore the origins of agency theory and review the history, albeit short, of agency-centered research in archaeology. It becomes apparent that there is more than one way to interpret and apply agency to archaeologically driven research. It also becomes apparent that the approach I take for this research is one in which agency theory is viewed as a *temporary construct which takes shape for and by empirical work*. Chapter two discusses the theoretical perspective applied for this research.

In chapter three I discuss the vibrant history of research on the Natufian. The lines of interpretation used to understand Natufian settlement and subsistence have followed different schools of thought over the years yet they all share a common background. The characterization of this background is both culturally variable and ecologically inspired. In this research I test these hypothetical models using an agency theoretical perspective using several Natufian sites found throughout the archaeological region. As well, I propose and test a behavior model that centers on social agency.

The second part of this research, chapters four through six, introduces the archaeological data used in this research as well as the first stage of analysis. Chapter four examines the Natufian sites and data available for this research as well as the limitations encountered in the process of data collection. Following this, in chapter five, I define and discuss the methods I use to identify similarities among Natufian sites, cluster analysis. I recognize that there are many methods that can be used for this but, given the data available as well as the format of the data, the choice to use one method, average linkage cluster analysis using Sorenson's proximity measure, over all others becomes clear. Chapter six presents the results of this first stage of analysis.

The third part of this research, chapters seven through nine, directs attention to the second stage of analysis: spatial analysis. In chapter seven, I present the data used in this analysis and discuss issues pertaining to the precision and accuracy of some spatial data. The results of the first stage of analysis are included in the dataset. The method used to conduct the second stage of analysis, least cost path analysis using a constructed cost surface through GIS, is illustrated in detail in chapter eight. I also review and critique previous archaeological studies using this method. The conclusion of part three, chapter nine, presents the results of the spatial analysis.

I dedicate the last part of this research, chapter 10, to the testing of these previous hypotheses. I also outline the construction of an agency-centered model based on the information provided in the second stage of analysis. I call this model the *interactive agent model*.

Although I am aware that the inclusion of all available data for Natufian sites in Southwest Asia is preferable for a robust model, the purpose of this research is not to construct an all-inclusive model to account for the spatial arrangement of Natufian sites. Rather, the objective is to construct a model proposing social relations for a prehistoric population. This is demonstrated in the discussion of practical applications of the social interaction model.

In this research I attempt to incorporate a social agency dimension into Natufian research. It is not my overriding purpose to contradict past interpretations of the Natufian culture based in culture history or ecology. Rather, the ultimate goal is to complement this past research and to illustrate an alternative interpretation available for research on past human life. To this end, the research I now present achieves this goal.

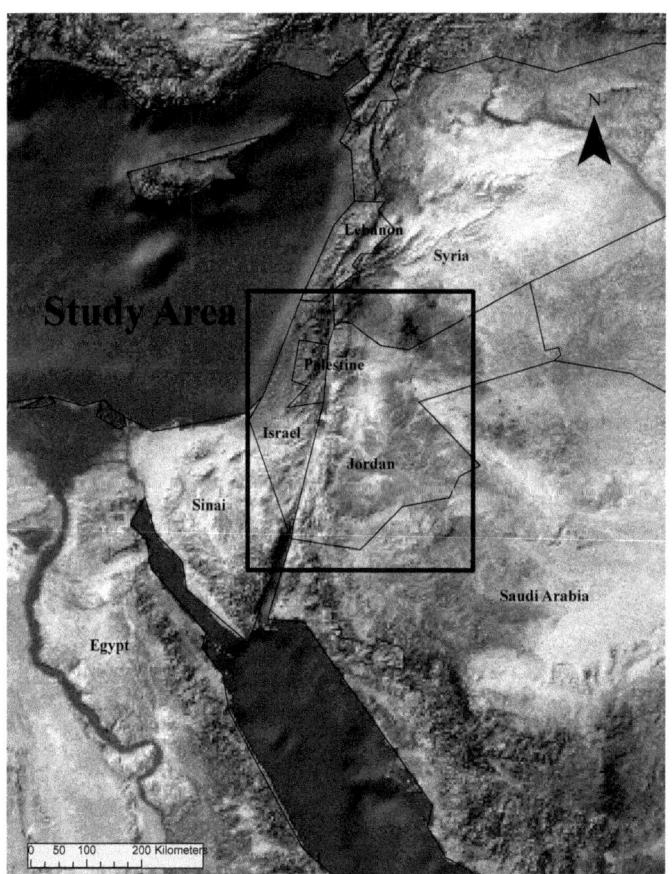

Figure 1.1: Geographical location of study area.

CHAPTER 2
THE AGENT AND THE ARCHAEOLOGIST: AGENCY IN ARCHAEOLOGY

There is no doubt a theory in my work, or, better, a set of thinking tools visible through the results they yield, but it is not built as such...It is a temporary construct which takes shape for and by empirical work.
-Pierre Bourdieu, 1989

Introduction

The purpose of this chapter is to introduce the theoretical perspective, or better yet, the set of *thinking tools*, directing this research. This perspective, or set of tools, is known under several labels: action theory, practice theory, structuration, constructivist structuralism, social theory, agency theory and social agency. In keeping with the spirit of the above quote by Bourdieu, it is not my intention in this chapter to list all aspects of these perspectives. Rather, the objective is to demonstrate the development of the construct of agency. I argue that the construct of agency results in an understanding of the development of early social relations, particularly those of the Natufian.

In the first part of this chapter I examine practice theory and structuration. It is imperative to understand the background leading to the conception of these constructs from a historical and *theoretical* perspective because they have shaped what is now commonly known as social agency in archaeology. The second part of this chapter is devoted to the introduction of agency in archaeological research and how it shapes and is shaped by archaeological empirical methods. Included in this discussion on agency in archaeology is an ongoing critique of the role agency plays in archaeological research.

Bourdieu – Putting rules into practice, the art of 'doing'

Pierre Bourdieu's thoughts on society and culture have had a profound effect on all disciplines in the social sciences. A philosopher, as well as an anthropologist and sociologist, Bourdieu developed a complex set of *thinking tools* through ethnographic research, mainly among the Algerian and French populations. He is also known for practice theory and his epistemological critique of research practice and sociological knowledge. Although rejecting the notion of *Grand Theory*, common in French sociology, he, along with other prominent social theorists, including Levi-Strauss, Althusser and Foucault, followed the structuralist perspective of Saussure. One of the most constant themes in Bourdieu's work is the endeavor to understand the relationship between 'subjectivity' – individual social being as it is experienced and lived – and the 'objective' social world within which it is framed and towards the production and reproduction of which it contributes (Jenkins 2002:25).

Knowing this, it would be wrong to assume that Bourdieu was a structuralist. His main critique of structural theory is that it outlines rules of how structures are organized in society, a recipe of how to 'do' things, but, in reality, it does not necessarily explain how things 'get done' with any real organizing intention – the practices (Bourdieu 1977; Jenkins 2002:35). This frustration with the structuralist approach to understanding society and culture led Bourdieu to develop an alternative approach, one that incorporates practices and experiences. This is known as practice theory.

Practice theory is defined as a "model of social practice in which what people do is bound up with the generation and pursuit of strategies within an organizing framework of cultural dispositions (habitus)" (Jenkins 2002:38). According to Bourdieu (1977:72), habitus are "systems of durable, transposable dispositions...the principle of generation and structuring of practices and representations". Jenkins (2002:76), further explains that habitus encompasses social performances and that these performances "are produced as a matter of routine, without explicit reference to a body of codified knowledge, and without the actors necessarily 'knowing what they are doing' (in the sense of adequately being able to explain what they are doing)." This codified or both conscious and unconscious knowledge is one's disposition. Bourdieu, in the notes for chapter two (structures and the habitus) in *Outline of a Theory of Practice* (1977:214), clarifies the use of the term disposition:

> The word *disposition* seems particularly suited to express what is covered by the concept of habitus (defined as a system of dispositions). It expresses first the *result of an organizing action*, with a meaning close to that of words such as structure; it also designates a way of being, a *habitual state* (especially of the body) and, in particular, a *predisposition,* *tendency,* or *inclination*. [Bourdieu's emphasis]

While this does clarify the concept of disposition, Jenkins (2002:76) further adds that disposition includes the "spectrum of cognitive and affective factors: thinking and feeling."

If habitus is defined as a system of dispositions *and* dispositions are the result of an organizing action, then how does the concept of structure fit into practice? According to Bourdieu (1977:72), structures are representative of a particular type of environment. Environment, in this sense, refers to class – the material conditions of existence characteristic of a class (Bourdieu 1977:72). This is where Marxist influences on Bourdieu are evident. Bourdieu (1977:95) further argues that habitus both produces and is produced by the social world. In this regard, people internalize external structures, and they externalize things they have internalized through practices.

In summary, Bourdieu's Practice theory seeks to connect agency (the individual) and structure (society). Concern is directed towards the subjective, the individual, and the unconscious disposition – *habitus* – that structures human action.

Giddens – Practical consciousness, I know why I 'do' it

Following the lead of practice theory, structuration is a direct reaction to deterministic, evolutionary thinking in the social sciences during the late 1970s and into the 1980s. According to Giddens (1984:236), "human history does not have an evolutionary 'shape', and positive harm can be done by attempting to compress it into one." Giddens further argues (1984:239-242) that there are four dangers that evolutionary thought entertains: (1) the tendency to compress general information into the specific - unilineal compression; (2) to imagine that there is homology between the stages of social evolution and the development of individual personality - homological compression; (3) to identify superior power, economic, political or military, with moral superiority on an evolutionary level - normative illusion; and (4) the tendency for evolutionary thinkers to assume that history can only be written as social change, that the elapsing of time is the same as change - temporal distortion.

Structuration theory, as Anthony Giddens (1984:376) defines it, involves "the structuring of social relations across time and space, in virtue of the duality of structure." Like practice theory, structuration develops from other theoretical perspectives, including functionalism, structuralism, hermeneutics, interpretivism, and systems theory. In essence, structuration manages to incorporate the more pertinent aspects of these perspectives to answer questions about human behavior, society, and culture. The emergence of structuration comes not only as a reaction to evolutionism's determinist thinking but also as a reaction to Bourdieu's theory of practice, particularly his focus on the unconscious and his historical materialism. To fully understand structuration, it is essential to define some of the terms used. The following terms are used consistently in the framework of structuration as well as social theory in general: agent, agency, structure, system, and duality.

An agent is usually a human being. The term *actor* or *material agent* is also synonymous with agent. In structuration theory, it is assumed that humans operate with a certain amount of knowledge and understanding of the world around them therefore, they are knowledgeable agents. In this sense, it is also assumed that humans are purposive agents. Purposive agents are ones who have reasons for 'doing the things that they do' and, if asked can report on these reasons. According to Giddens (1984:3), being a purposive agent does not comprise of a series of intentions, reasons or motives. Rather, purposive action occurs as a *durée*, a continuous flow of conduct. In other words, to be a purposive agent means to have both discursive and practical consciousness. Discursive consciousness refers to what agents are able to say about social conditions and their own actions whereas practical consciousness consists of what agents know (or believe) about social conditions as well as the conditions of their own action, but cannot express discursively (Giddens 1984:374-375). An agent is a human being who is knowledgeable of his or her world, is purposive in her or his actions, and has both discursive and practical consciousness within the understanding of those actions.

Agency refers to any actions of the agent, the process of doing. It does not refer to the intentions or motivations of the agent, but rather the capability of action (Giddens 1984:9). Through this line of reasoning, Giddens (1984:9) argues that an agent is also considered a *'perpetrator'* because, at any given time in the process of action, the agent can choose a different course of action, leading to a different result. This is the essence of agency, the fact that the actions of agents will produce different outcomes. What is important to understand about agency is that there needs to be separation between the agent and the intention.

At the very core of structuration theory is the notion of structure and the duality of structure. According to Giddens (1984:17-23), structure refers to organized sets of rules and resources, the properties that make it possible for social practices to exist across time and space and, in essence, give these social practices systematic form. Rules are what we do naturally, they are not conscious, but are the routines we produce to transform things. In this sense, they are evident in our day-to-day life, and regulate our sleeping, eating, and general living habits. Rules are both normative elements and codes of signification. Resources are also of two kinds: authoritative resources, which derive from the co-ordination of the activity of human agents, and allocative resources, which stem from control of material products or of aspects of the material world (Giddens 1984: xxv-xxvi). Rules and resources, which make structure, are viewed as the social-cultural makeup and ecological means of a population.

Structure is both the medium and outcome of the conduct it organizes. The structural properties of social systems do not exist outside of action but are chronically implicated in its production and reproduction (Giddens 1984:374). These structural properties and their implication are known as duality. Duality also asserts that structures are not external to individuals. Agents can transform structure, although not necessarily as the agent intends. There is interaction between agents and structures, and agents are embedded in structures.

Reviewing the initial definition of structuration - the structuring of social relations across time and space, in virtue of the duality of structure – it is crucial to understand what Giddens is talking about when he incorporated time and space into the theoretical model. The incorporation of time and space into social relations is a direct attack on social theory. According to Giddens (1979:201):

> ...neither time nor space have been incorporated into the centre of social theory; rather, they are ordinarily treated more as 'environments' in which social conduct is enacted.

On the subject of space, Giddens (1979:201) further states:

> The importation of the term 'ecology' into the social sciences has done little to help matters, since this tends both to encourage the confusion of the spatial with other characteristics of the physical world that might influence social life, and to reinforce the tendency to treat spatial characteristics as the 'environment' of social activity, rather than as integral to its occurrence.

In contemplating the role of space and time with regards to social life, structuration theory introduces two concepts: time-space edges and time-space distanciation. Time-space edges refer to connections, whether through conflict or symbiotic relation between societies of differing structural types. Time-space distanciation refers to "stretching of social systems across time-space, on the basis of mechanisms of social and system integration" (Giddens 1984:377). In other words, the greater the time-space distance of social systems, the more resistant they are to manipulation or change by any individual agent (Giddens 1984:171).

The inclusion of space and time in social theory is particularly important for the advancement of social theory in archaeology. The fundamental issue that links all archaeological research is the question of human behavior over space and time. The notion that space and time have a role in the interaction between populations as well as in the maintenance or continuation of social or cultural practices allows agency approaches to be applicable to archaeological research.

Agency and Archaeology

Bourdieu's practice theory and Gidden's structuration provide a foundation for a new perspective in understanding past human behavior. This perspective is labeled, in the broadest sense, as *agency*. This broad labeling begs the question: what exactly is agency-based archaeological research? In this section, I discuss the basics of agency in archaeology. Detailed discussion on the history of thought with reference to agency and archaeology appears in other publications (Dobres & Robb 2000; Pauketat 2001).

Agency involves the structuring of social relations and the ongoing production, maintenance, and transformation of societal institutions across time and space (Clark 2000; Dobres 2000; Dobres and Robb 2000; Pred 1986). According to theories of agency in archaeology, individuals make decisions that are based on their sociocultural and ecological surroundings (i.e., structure), and they, not their technology or artifacts, are the active agents of prehistory (Dincauze 2000; Dobres 2000; Gamble 1999). If this is so, what can we say of technology and artifacts? How can archaeologists, who rely on artifacts as the basis of their interpretation, understand social agency in a culture? Since agency consists of decision-making and actions, it is logical that the development of technological knowledge and skill is part of decision and action. This is where the term agency becomes more operational.

According to Dobres and Robb (2000), those who believe that agency is about intentionality also argue that the material world is created and manipulated by agents. Therefore, artifacts can be viewed as "inactive traces, residues, or correlates of particular kinds of human activity and agency" (Dobres and Robb 2000:12). It is possible to take this one step further by suggesting that material culture, including artifacts, represent not only the world within which people act, but also the people themselves (Dobres and Robb 2000). If such is the case, then it is possible to understand social relations and agency through investigation of artifact variability through time and space. According to Wobst (2000), artifacts are the material products and precedents for human action and, thus, can be identified as "material interferences". Wobst (2000:42) refers to artifacts as "interferences" because they interfere with the natural variables (i.e., the raw materials used to make the artifact) and they interfere with humans (i.e., social interactions). This view finds wide support (Dobres and Hoffman 1999; Sassaman 2000; Sinclair 2000). Todd and Christine VanPool (2003:90-91) believe that most agency-based archaeological research shares seven basic premises.

These premises are:

1. The rejection of any approach that reduces human behavior to a 'behavioral system,' 'adaptive response,' or 'evolutionary lineage.'
2. Viewing social structures as the products of behavioral relationships between individuals created during day-to-day material production, hence; social institutions and formalized relationships are the products of these interactions among individuals within a group.
3. Rejection of the concept of free-will because humans do not choose the social and material contexts of action. Therefore, they are constrained in their behavior. This is due in part to the influence of the social structure within which they operate.
4. Structural institutions and conditions are considered to be the product of material contexts and relations.
5. Structural institutions that make up a social structure create a material world observed by individuals, thus affecting their behavior.
6. Social history is an important factor shaping human behavior and social structure.
7. Humans are actors whose behavior can only be understood in terms of their motives expressed within their social contexts.

Although the use of an agency perspective in archaeology is new, several views and approaches are already in use.

According to Dornan (2002), there are five approaches to agency in archaeology. These coincide with the development of agency in archaeology (time), as well as what Schiffer describes as conjoiner perspectives. These approaches are as follows: (i) collective agency; (ii) individual intentionality; (iii) a rational-actor approach; (iv) unintended consequences of social struggle; and (v) practical rationality as manifest within social struggle.

Collective agency was one of the first approaches to appear on the archaeological scene. This approach is illustrated most effectively through the work of Michael Shanks and Christopher Tilley (1992). According to Shanks and Tilley, "Archaeology is unavoidably social not only in the sense that it is produced by men and women in and outside institutions but because its data are the products of social practices" (1992:116). Drawing heavily on Gidden's concept of structuration, Shanks and Tilley assert (1992:128-129):

> People act knowledgeably in terms of intensions and choices upon which social structures or unintended consequences of action depend. People are knowledgeable with the capacity to define themselves, and practice is open to discursive and practical consciousness; knowing *that* and knowing *how* to act. [Author's italics]

Shanks and Tilley also rely on the work of Bourdieu, particularly the notion of *habitus* in that they argue that all social action is over-determined by structures. This meaning structure, above all else, decides social action. This is clearly demonstrated in Shanks and Tilley's points on agency (1992:124):

1. All action is social action.
2. The primary characteristic of such action is a realization of goals (action is purposive).
3. All social actions are determined actions because (i) some actions may be forced by violence or its threat; (ii) most actions have a habitual basis; (iii) some actions are influenced and promoted by ideology; and (iv) actions that seem to be free in the sense that they involve a choice on the part of the subject involve interests and values.

Contrasting collective agency is individual intentionality. This approach, initiated by Ian Hodder, focuses on individual lives and treats individuals as real historical agents (Dobres & Robb 2000:11). Hodder (2000:22) argues "that there is a need to shift from agency and the construction of social beings, to individual narratives of lives lived and events." He argues that focusing on the role of small-scale events and processes within the long term is insufficient, constructionist, and inadequate for dealing with archaeological data (2000:22). The focus on the individual (subjective) event in archaeology is important to Hodder for two reasons: the indeterminacy of levels (micro/subjective and macro/objective) and the fact that it is at the individual scale that "contradictions and conflict are worked out, lived through and resolved" (2000:26).

The third approach, the rational-actor approach, is an attempt to connect agency theory to methodological individualism (Doran 2002:311). This approach asserts that collective actions and shared structures are the result of decisions and actions of individuals. It is the ideas, decisions, and actions of individuals that explain change and any change that is not predicted is usually unintended (Bell 1992:39). This approach further asserts that archaeologists do not have access to information on an individual's intention. Therefore, we must focus on "the realm of human activity where the ideas and motives are widely shared" (Dornan 2002:312). Intentionality is purposive and can be best examined in terms of shared human activity. However, we must also realize that a purposive action can create both intended and unintended outcomes. This is the basic principle of structuration.

The fourth approach, which focuses on the unintended consequences of social struggle, states that people's actions and representations (practices) are reproducible. According to Pauketat (2001:74), "practices are historical processes to the extent that they are shaped by what came before them and they give shape to what follows." In this sense, this approach is more appropriately identified (by Pauketat) as historical processualism. In this approach, behavior (abstract, goal-oriented human activity) is not practice (homologous actions and representations that vary between contexts or events even if the routinized forms seem to remain the same) (Pauketat 2001:86). Rather, all processes, considering that they are historical, must be understood "through detailed and large-scale studies of who did what when and how" (ibid.).

The final agency approach, practical-rationality manifest in social struggle, is proposed by Arthur Joyce (2000; Joyce & Winter 1996) in his research on the role of commoner resistance and social negotiation in the founding of Mount Albán in the Oaxaca Valley. Joyce and Winter (1996:33) examine behavioral strategies in relation to the "biophysical and sociocultural environment" and they further asserts that "people pursue particular behavioral strategies to acquire and use resources, including information." Furthermore, Joyce and Winter (1996:35) maintain that population-level phenomena, such as social organization and subsistence patterns, are the outcome of these behavioral strategies and that the strategies are both enabled and constrained by the biophysical and sociocultural environment. In this sense, Joyce's approach to agency parallels Giddens' structuration.

Dornan (2002:314) states that Joyce relies on a more contextual notion of rationality comparing this perspective to the rational-actor approach. This approach also allows attribution of goal-orientated motivated actions to past agents running parallel to Pauketat's historical processualism.

Social Agency – A Critique

The application of social agency paradigms is increasingly popular in the social sciences and, particularly, in the field of archaeology. In this section I examine some critiques of theories of social agency from an archaeological perspective. What is unique to critical appraisal of social theory in archaeology is that the majority of the critiques come from those applying a social agency perspective to their work. It becomes clear that, while some critical issues are warranted, many other issues archaeological researchers have with regard to social agency are based on misunderstanding of some of the concepts fundamental to this theoretical paradigm. Furthermore, it is only through the magnifying glass of the 'critical eye' that application of social agency can become more robust and find its place in the field of archaeology.

Misinterpretation and misrepresentation

In 2001, Jonathon Robb presented a paper at the Society for American Archaeology meetings titled *Social agency and anti-social agency: archaeology in the grey zone*. The purpose of this paper is to discuss the tendency to emphasize individual agency, and to associate it with the 'rational pursuit of goals'. One problem he addresses concerns the concept of motivation and how misuse of this concept endorses an individual's proximate goals of attaining power or prestige. As Robb indicates, when motivation reduces human action to such a general level, concepts such as "power" and "prestige" have little explanatory worth. In reexamining Giddens' theory of structuration, agency refers "not to the intentions people have in doing things but to their capability of doing things in the first place" (1984:9). This is where agency implies power. According to Giddens (1984:14), "To be able to 'act otherwise' means being able to intervene in the world, or, to refrain from such intervention with the effect of influencing a specific process or state of affairs".

A second issue that Robb addresses, relating to motivation, centers on the question of relating intention and action at the individual level with social reproduction at the systemic level. Giddens also addresses this issue in his discussion of intentionality and action. According to Giddens (1984:11), "the consequences of what actors do, intentional or unintentional, are events which would not have happened if the actor had behaved differently, but which are not within the scope of the agent's power to have brought about (regardless of what the agent's intentions were)". Relating back to the individual and power, it can be restated that the actions, intentional or not, are determined by the capability of the individual to carry out the act in the first place. Therein lays power, motivation, and intention. This can best be expressed through example.

In an article on practical and prestige technologies, Brian Hayden explores power and its interferences with material culture in a society. According to Hayden (1995), some societies, regardless of economic strategy employed, will contain a small number of individuals identified as "aggrandizers" – individuals who are more aggressive and acquisitive than other individuals in the society. Actions characteristic of aggrandizers include the construction of monumental architecture, the development of new technologies, and the establishment of extensive trade networks. There are particular structures, both social and economic, that need to be present in order for an individual to be an aggrandizer. For example, the society, must be large enough – 200 to 300 individuals. With a social structure of this size we also see the emergence of stratification. Resources must also be abundant; thus, there must be opportunity for surplus resources.

Giddens (1984:16) discusses the concept of power, stratification and the ability to act within this framework and observes that power within a social system has continuity over time and space and "presumes regularized relations of autonomy and dependence" between actors in the context of social interaction. However, he also calls attention to dependence and suggests that "all forms of dependence offer some resources whereby those who are subordinate can influence the activities of their superiors," such as aggrandizers (Giddens 1984:16).

Eclecticism and Redlining

In the introduction to the edited volume *Social Theory in Archaeology* (2000), Michael Schiffer discusses what he terms "the strategy and ideology of eclecticism". This ideology is based on two beliefs (1) that human phenomena cannot be sufficiently understood by just one theoretical paradigm; and (2) obligation to one theoretical paradigm is seen as unwise – as it may quickly fall out of fashion. Schiffer (2000:3) argues that the strategy of eclecticism is desirable for those researchers with no real interest in social theory *per se*. This gives the impression that the researcher need not clearly understand the literature involved in any particular social theory. According to Robb (2001), this is demonstrated in the misunderstanding of 'the individual' in social agency. Schiffer further argues that two factors must be considered in deciding what social theory is appropriate for investigations: (i) relation to paradigmatic affiliation and (ii) level of social complexity of the people being studied. He calls this decision-making process, "redlining." According to Schiffer (2000:3), redlining "gives the archaeologist justification for not engaging themselves with other theoretical paradigms because they *feel* that it does not pertain to their culture or population of interest."

Schiffer believes the Strategy of eclecticism and redlining, divides archaeology in more ways than theoretically and must be addressed. Schiffer suggests the building of bridges. This means establishing connections between different theoretical perspectives – conjoining, or creating a *theoretical toolkit*. This is different from eclecticism in that the strengths and weaknesses of various theoretical perspectives are known and drawn upon to reach the common goal. Schiffer (2000:6) suggests, for example, that there is a unifying quality for both selectionists (such as perhaps populational theory of culture), and post-processualists (agency theory) in that they emphasize historical contingency and focus on individual agents. Likewise, processual and selectionist perspectives using evolutionary formulations have practical application with small-scale hunter-gatherer systems yet there are few applications of post-processualism to these small-scale systems. Through the building of bridges between the two perspectives, the common goal can be attained.

Neo-Darwinian Uses of Agency

Associated with eclecticism, but with a unique set of issues is the recent trend to incorporate agency into neo-Darwinian interpretations of past populations. Timothy Pauketat (2000:114-115; 2001:75-77) takes aim at those who apply a neo-Darwinian approach to agency. There are three groups of neo-Darwinists: selectionists, individualists, and transmissionists. Selectionists, in Pauketat's opinion, are the most problematic of the three. According to Pauketat (2001:75), selectionists advocate "a rather strict adherence to Darwin's concepts of variation and selection as applied to human technologies", and "it seems largely irrelevant to selectionists whether or not selection was intentional or contingent on human agency or whether or not technological 'know-how' was affected by social change outside the technological dimension."

On the other hand, Pauketat (2001:77) criticizes individualists in that they "are not concerned with the agency of *all* people, nor are they free of the behavioral essentialism that characterizes their selectionist counterparts." Individualists theorize that those few charismatic or aggrandizing individuals who competed for prestige were, by themselves, responsible for changing societies." This is essentially the same issue Robb expresses in relating intention and action to social reproduction.

The transmissionists appear to be the least of the neo-Darwinian offenders in that, although they explain the transmission of ideas through concepts such as 'fitness' and 'heritability', they acknowledge symbols as the "media of people's experiences and interpretations" (Pauketat 2001:77).

Summary

This chapter examined the concept of agency. The origins of agency come from French philosopher, Pierre Bourdieu, and British sociologist, Anthony Giddens. Boudieu's concept of habitus is understood in terms of as a system of thinking. Habitus, in turn, structures human action. Giddens' concepts of agency and structure can be understood in terms of the action of human beings structuring social relations. Pauketat (2001:79) aptly states that "the gist of both Bourdieu's (1977) practice theory and Gidden's (1979) agency theory is that all people enact, embody, or re-present traditions in ways that continuously alter those traditions."
Archaeology has continuously struggled to understand past human behavior. Agency, in all its dimensions, has provided a template or *thinking toolkit* for shedding light on who did what, why, and how. Five approaches to agency in archaeological research were discussed. The collective-agency perspective focuses on the objective – the structure. Individual intentionality, on the other hand, places focus back on the subjective – the individual. The rational-actor approach is similar to collective-agency in that it focuses on shared human ideas and activity. However, the rational actor approach also relates to individual intentionality in that it concentrates on the subjective – there is an interest in the acts of *certain individuals*. Historical Processualism approach advocates the notions of practice and habitus. Historical processualists also advocate large-scale approaches to understanding how meanings or traditions were constructed and transmitted. Finally, the practical rationality approach focuses on negotiation and practical rationality, assuming that practically skilled and knowledgeable actors perform goal-orientated actions (Dornan 2002:314).

This research takes an agency approach similar to historical processualism, as advocated by Pauketat, and practical rationality, as advocated by Joyce. Both approaches are similar in that they consider agency as an analytical tool, in essence, part of the *thinking toolkit*. Both approaches also advocate the importance of structures in individual and group decision-making and knowledge. I particularly agree with Pauketat (2001:86) in his appeal for an agency approach that focuses on proximate rather than ultimate causes of social reproduction and change. Where I disagree with Pauketat, as do others (Dornan 2002:313), is in his reliance on Bourdieu's notion of unconscious disposition (unconscious knowledge).

In contrast, I agree with Joyce in his concentration on behavioral strategies, with people viewed as dynamic actors in a social process as people develop behavioral strategies, these strategies, as well as their material and ideological correlates, become part of the environment. This follows Giddens' view of agency through structuration. However, I depart from Joyce's research objectives in that I am not attempting to interpret ideological power. Rather, I am attempting to understand how behavioral strategies are manifest as material correlates.

Where I also depart from the previous approaches is that I include a framework in which to apply an agency perspective. Here, I side with Gamble (1999:42) in the view that agency, or structuration theory, provides a means for conceptualizing the problem but does not focus on material culture as a means to investigate social life or its contribution to the structuring of social life. For Gamble, the spatial arrangement of social interaction is best described through network analysis, where it is understood that (1) individuals create ties through interaction; (2) that resources that generate both social and ecological structure can be characterized as emotional, material, or symbolic and; (3) that the spatial arrangement of interaction can occur at several demographic extents. This framework enables Gamble to use agency as an analytic tool that stresses the importance of structures in individual and group decision-making and knowledge. The use of a network analysis also enables Gamble to focus on proximate rather than ultimate causes of social reproduction, thus concentrating on behavioral strategies and people as dynamic actors in a social process.

While I agree with some of the ideas of historical processualism and practical rationality, I believe that all approaches, including the two just mentioned, fail to acknowledge that space and time are two major aspects of structuration, that space and time are central aspects to social life and that they are actors in the construction of social life rather than merely the stage or backdrop for social life. To fully understand and use structuration as a thinking toolkit, space and time must be incorporated. This is where my approach to understanding social interaction and relationships in past human populations departs from other approaches. I follow the structuration approach that recognizes the significance of temporal and spatial elements in social analysis. I demonstrate through the modeling of interactive agents.

Time is a problematic issue in archaeology. Radiocarbon dating is not always possible for each individual site discovered and recorded. For example, radiocarbon dates are available for less than half of the Natufian sites available for this research. Given the type of materials recovered from archaeological sites, it is possible to place sites in a general temporal and cultural context, such as Early or Late Natufian, but it is not possible, at this point, to demonstrate continuous temporal framework.

The spatial aspects of everyday life can be observed from the individual, local level to the group, regional level. Reiterating Giddens' observation, social sciences tend to treat space as a characteristic of the physical world, as an environment where social activity occurs. Part of using structuration theory as a construct for this research is to understand space as an integral role in the occurrence of social activity, including all forms of human interaction. Examining a cultural region, a large area of space, is a difficult task. However, through the use of other tools, such as geographical information systems, it is now possible to examine the occurrence of social interaction and the relationships formed through this interaction, from a structuration construct. This is the premise of this research.

This chapter provides the foundation for this research. Its focus is on the role of agency and structure in understanding Natufian interaction and the subsequent social relations. Agency framed by spatial analysis is part of the *thinking toolkit* or *temporary construct* for this research. The following chapter provides a second part to this toolkit – information on the history of research on the Natufian and its relevance to agency.

CHAPTER 3
TIME, SPACE, AGENCY AND THE NATUFIAN

The space in which we live, which draws us out of ourselves, in which the erosion of our lives, our time and our history occurs, the space that claws and knaws at us, is also, in itself, a heterogeneous one.
–Foucault 1986:23

The Natufian in Context

In the previous chapter, I discussed the concept of agency from its inception, with the notion of habitus from Bourdieu's practice theory, to Giddens and structuration theory, and its application to past cultures. Archaeology, like most social sciences, has vigorously adopted the concept, as well as its associated terms. While there are some misrepresentations of the concept of agency in archaeological research, there is continuous improvement in the application of an 'agency approach' to past individuals.

This chapter continues with the discussion of agency in archaeology but it takes on a reflexive tone. The objectives of this chapter are two-fold. The first objective is to discuss past interpretations of the Natufian culture. This is not a comprehensive discussion of past interpretations of the Natufian. Rather, key themes are distinguished. These themes have a temporal context but are not exclusive to particular periods of archaeological research. As I will demonstrate, some themes are introduced early in Natufian research and persist to the present date. The second is to re-examine these interpretations from an agency position and to construct a series of hypotheses based on the past interpretations as well as the agency position. I contend that, although an agency perspective in archaeological interpretation is a relatively recent phenomenon, it is possible to identify elements of agency in past interpretations and to produce a testable hypothesis of Natufian interaction.

The Natufian is critical to our understanding of the transition from mobile hunter-gatherers to sedentary hunter-gatherer-farmers. The period in which the Natufian population lived, based on radiocarbon dates from numerous archaeological sites, is approximately 13,000 or 12,800 BP to 10,500 or 10,300 BP (Bar-Yosef and Belfer-Cohen 1999:403). The Natufian occupied the Levant, which now encompasses Israel, Jordan, Lebanon and much of Syria (see fig.1.1).

The Early and Late Natufian are primarily characterized by their material culture, especially their lithic technology. The lithic technology is a distinctive microlith technology characterized by lunates, short and wide bladelets, and multiplatform cores (Bar-Yosef 1998; Bar-Yosef & Belfer-Cohen 1991; Sellars 1998). However, the Natufian is easily distinguishable from other cultures on the basis of its diversity of material culture beyond the chipped lithic artifacts (Bar-Yosef 1998; Bar-Yosef and Belfer-Cohen 1991, 1999; Bar-Yosef & Vandermeesch 1989; Belfer-Cohen 1991a; Campana 1991; Henry 1989). The Natufian had a ground-stone technology that included mortars, pestles, mullers, plates, shaft-straighteners, and whetstones. These ground-stone artifacts were made from limestone, basalt, or sandstone. It is during this culture that we also see a proliferation of tools manufactured from bone. These include points and barbed points, pierced points, awls, borers, and sickle hafts. Of particular social importance are artifacts classified as art or ornamentation, also very abundant in the Natufian. Art and ornamentation recovered include necklaces, bracelets, belts, earrings and pendants made of bone, stone, or most commonly, marine shell. There are also engraved ostrich-shell fragments and human and animal figurines made of stone and bone (Bar-Yosef and Belfer-Cohen 1999; Belfer-Cohen 1991a, 1991b; Boyd 1995; Goring-Morris 1998; Noy 1991).

Final distinguishing characteristics of the Natufian culture are the features recorded at various sites. Architectural remains are identified during the Early Natufian period and include semi-subterranean, circular and curvilinear structures made of modified stone (Bar-Yosef 1999; Belfer-Cohen 1991a; Henry 1989). Aside from Ohalo (Nadel 2002), these are the earliest structures recorded in the Levant. Other features include bedrock mortars and burials.

This chapter has four main sections. The first three are defined by the time period in which excavations took place as well as research goals of these excavations. The research goals coincide with theoretical perspectives. The final section will develop a series of hypotheses that will be examined with particular consideration to the agency position.

Chronology – Time and the Agent

The first reports on the Natufian appeared in the early 1930's and were based on excavations at Shukba, el-Wad and Wadi en-Natuf. Dorothy Garrod was the first to pay particular attention to the Natufian, which appeared to differ from earlier and later cultures. Initially known as a Mesolithic or microlithic culture with agriculture, the Natufian was later renamed after the first archaeological site where the characteristics of this culture were discovered, Wadi en-Natuf. So different was the Natufian that, in an early publication, Garrod states that "the Natufian makes its first appearance apparently full-grown with no traceable roots in the past" (1957:212).

The goal of these early excavations was to establish a chronology of human occupation in the Near East based on stages of human development, and particularly on the lithic industry. Three stages or phases are associated with the Natufian: Early, Middle and Late. These divisions are chronological and based on the presence of microburins (emerging in the Middle Natufian but also occurring early in the Qalkhan and Nebekian) and the presence of arrowheads (a characteristic of the Late Natufian). In considering the Natufian stage of human history, Garrod discusses how these stages relate to the stages of advancement developed in American archaeological research – Archaic, Pre-Formative and Formative – and argues that these stages are not satisfactory for the Near East. When talking of cultural evolution, Garrod's position is that there is a need for a "system which expresses various stages of development without the chronological implications of the old terms" (1957:226). Garrod was also concerned with the distribution of the Natufian. She argued that all Natufian sites lie in a narrow belt that included southwest Syria, Lebanon, and Palestine, with no site farther than 40 miles (64 km) from the Mediterranean Sea (Garrod 1957:212). Furthermore, Garrod states that it is probable that the Natufian was an "indigenous Palestine-culture" [sic] that extended only slightly to the north and south. Garrod also remarks that the Jordan valley is not an absolute boundary but that there is little evidence of the microlithic industry east of the Jordan.

Garrod states that, when attempting to make comparisons over a larger area, "we are at once struck by the general lack of affinity between the Stone Age of Palestine and that of Egypt and Little Africa" (1937:118). She (1937:118) further postulates:

> In theory, one might expect Palestine to be merely an extension of the North African province, or a corridor in which *influences* from the south and from the north alternately held sway; in fact, one may say that the Northern border of Egypt in Paleolithic times lay very much where it does today, and that from the cultural point of view Palestine was neither an African dependency nor a debatable ground, but essentially a part of Eurasia.

Steven Rosen (1991) demonstrates how preconceptions governed by modern political situations affect perceptions in the prehistoric record. The above statement from Garrod possibly reflects a strong European presence in the Levant that was a result of the British Mandate in Palestine. As Rosen (1991:311) suggests, "in a physical sense, the imposition of a European framework was a result of European political control."

In discussing the distribution of Natufian sites, Garrod does draw attention to some marked similarities that suggest that there was movement of humans in the cultural region. For example, she (1957:219) points out that dentalium shells are found, not only in sites close to the sea, but also in sites in the Judean desert and even as far north as the eastern slopes of the Anti-Lebanon. For Garrod, this signified "movement and intercourse between the coastal and inland settlements" (1957:219). She also notes remarkable similarity in the Natufian toolkit regardless of the site location. She (1957:213-214) interprets this as evidence for a shared "way of life."

Based on the information stemming from the early excavations, two observations stand out. First, it is apparent that the primary concern of earlier Natufian research was to develop chronological stages of development. Second, the concern of these early researchers was to determine the extent of settlement of this enigmatic culture. However, any comparison between sites was mainly for the purpose of chronological ordering. For example, Turville-Petre (1932:276) writes in his report on Kebarah:

> If we try to correlate the Mughara el-Kebarah culture with that of the two other known Natufian sites, namely, Shukbah and the Mughara el-Wad, it will be found that it most closely resembles that of the lower Natufian or B2 level at the Mughara el-Wad and therefore represents the earliest Natufian phase at present known.

Similarly, Garrod (1932:267-268) discusses at length where the Natufian *fits* into Near Eastern prehistory and states that the exact dating of the Natufian is a difficult problem in that it is not comparable to any earlier or later culture in the "narrow belt" of habitation. In attempting to find chronological correlates outside of the Natufian, Garrod turns to Egyptian prehistory. Garrod notes that the site of Helwan has an identical lithic industry but, because it is the only known site of its kind in Egypt, it is not possible to give it a relative date. Fayum has a similar bone tool assemblage but the lithic industry differs considerably from that of the Natufian. The Badarian appears to have nothing in common with the Natufian with the exception that they both lack pottery. Based on that fact alone, Garrod believes that they are similar in age but she is not confident in this correlation. It is now recognized that Fayum and Badarian are Neolithic and Helwan is Pre-Dynastic.

It is of interest to note that Garrod is eager to treat the Natufian as a descriptive level of organization - a cultural-historical framework. However, she offers no speculation on the social, political, or ideological organization of the Natufian other than the statement that "village life, even in its simplest form, had apparently not yet begun" (Garrod 1957:214). Furthermore, aside from the observation that the presence of dentalium shell is evidence for interaction, no real correlation between sites took place other than for chronological purposes. In this instance, early research does not see the Natufian as consisting of agents. Rather, it is more realistic to propose that early research focused on chronological and spatial ordering with the future goal of establishing a cultural-historical formation. Time and space are treated as an environment, rather than integral to social activity.

Cultural Ecology and Evolution – Structure and the Agent

The 1970's marks a flourish of theoretical thought and methods in archaeology. During this time, there is consideration for new approaches to understanding the nature of cultural change. Inspired by the materialist approach of Julian Stewart, some archaeologists showed increased awareness of the role of ecological factors in shaping prehistoric socio-cultural systems. At this point, the focus shifted from stylistic analysis of artifacts to the study of changes in economies, population size, and settlement patterns (Trigger 1993:279).

An area where the role of ecological factors are thought to shape socio-cultural systems involves the application of geographical location models to understand settlement and movement of past hunter-gatherer populations. One model, site-catchment, is first applied to Natufian site in the Mount Carmel area in 1970. Vita-Finzi and Higgs (1970:5) define the site-catchment model as "the study of the relationships between technology and those natural resources lying within economic range of individual sites." Site-catchment analysis examines both the economic catchment area and the site-exploitation territory as a means of interpreting the relationship between resources that were potentially available for use by hunter-gatherers and resources that they actually used. The exploitation territory is defined as the area surrounding the archaeological site that the hunter-gatherer population habitually exploited (Vita-Finzi and Higgs 1970:7). The size of the exploitation territory depends on the terrain. Vita-Finzi and Higgs (1970:7) estimate that the exploitation territory of a hunter-gatherer site extends over two hours' walk from the site. On relatively flat ground, the exploitation territory can be quite immense while, in a mountainous region, the exploitation territory is typically limited. The site-catchment model facilitates interpreting the economy of prehistoric populations.

The site-catchment model initially characterized the Natufian culture as having a mobile-cum-sedentary economy where the population is primarily sedentary with a mobile component (Higgs and Vita-Finzi 1972:29). In this type of economy, there are two types of sites: base camps and transitory camps (Vita-Finzi and Higgs 1970, 1972). Base camps are large camps located in the lowlands while transitory camps are smaller in size, and lie in the adjacent uplands. The location of transitory camps makes it possible to exploit resources from two different ecological environments, the uplands provide animal protein and the lowlands provide staple plant foods for collecting (Higgs and Vita-Finzi 1972:29). The development of this site catchment models for Natufian sites is limited to the Mount Carmel area in the Mediterranean forest biome.

The 1970's also marks increasing survey and excavation in the south, particularly east of the Jordan Valley, the Sinai, and Negev. The initial goals of activities in these area included increasing the number of known prehistoric sites in the Levant, further understanding the cultural chronology, and imposing a framework for classifying Epipaleolithic sites. This leads to the discovery of Early and Late Natufian sites in both the steppe and desert vegetation zone. This discovery led Donald Henry to investigate alternative explanations for Natufian settlement. These alternative explanations draw on the culture-ecology paradigm.

D.O. Henry first entered the "Natufian arena" through his 1973 dissertation, *The Natufian of Palestine: Its Material Culture and Ecology*. In this work, Henry sets out to demonstrate a significant correlation between Natufian lithic assemblages and temporal, environmental, and activity factors (Henry 1973: iv). This marks a shift in Natufian research in that he sees the Natufian as an adaptive strategy and a homogenous behavioral system (Henry 1973: v).

Henry sought to understand prehistoric adaptation strategies at the regional and local levels (Henry 1981, 1982, 1995, 1998). Dissatisfied with explanations of Natufian settlement behavior that were based on the climatic and vegetation conditions at the macro-scale (the Mediterranean, Irano-Turanian and Arabian-Saharan Desert vegetation zones), Henry argues that "cultural-ecological explanations dominate our attempts to understand prehistoric behaviors at various scales (regional, local, and diachronic)" (Henry 1998:10).

Advocates of the cultural-ecological approach maintain that the Early Natufians were a permanently settled population that preferred the Mediterranean woodland environment. The evidence for settlement outside the Mediterranean is justified through the conditions of *micro-scale* environments in the non-Mediterranean areas. For example, the upper elevation of the Piedmont, where Wadi Judayid, an Early Natufian site, is located in the southeastern region, resembles the Mediterranean woodlands. Variability among Early Natufian sites in the Near East could then be related to the location of each site with respect to its micro-environment (Henry 1982). Elevation and associated climatic conditions principally determined this micro-environment, which in turn would inevitably influence human behavior and adaptation strategies.

The culture-ecology paradigm gained widespread acceptance, especially in Natufian research in Jordan (Byrd 1989; Garrard 1985, 1987; Schuldenrein & Clark 2001). Byrd (1989), concurring with Henry, suggests further emphasis on ecological variables, including flora and fauna, in his model for Natufian settlement. Olszewski (1988) suggests that site type (whether open-air or rock shelter) be included as a factor in understanding Natufian settlement from a cultural-ecology perspective.

It is understandable why this approach is widely accepted. It stems from the fact that the Near East is a region with great ecological diversity and recognition that the history of human habitation in the region cannot be explained by one simple model. The culture-ecology model is also instrumental in sparking interest in research outside the Mediterranean setting of the Levant.

François Valla (1998) approaches Natufian settlement and adaptation from a different angle – seasonality. Through the development of one of the first regional models, he attempts to show a system of aggregation followed by short periods of dispersal. Valla identifies factors such as seasonality, geographical location, and length of dispersal as the causes for differing forms of aggregation and dispersal. Regardless of these differing forms, cultural characteristics are identified as shared in all regions. Valla discovered that when he included chronology in the model (Early versus Late Natufian), the transition to the Late Natufian signifies the end of the Natufian culture in the Mediterranean core. The proliferation of aggregation and dispersal patterns, characteristic in the core during the Early Natufian, is now replicated in the peripheral areas. In other words, the Natufian no longer existed in the core but was thriving in the peripheral areas. In his conclusions, Valla states that "a kind of equilibrium seems to have been achieved" (1998:103) between the core and peripheral areas. Valla (1998:104) further concludes that the settlement system that prevailed in the core "was considered an attractive model by groups in the neighbouring areas."

Although it concentrates on settlement, subsistence and adaptation to a particular environment, the culture-ecology approach to the Natufian, does contemplate social interaction. According to Henry (1994:337), "interfingering site distributions and synchronous radiometric dates suggests opportunities for contact and social interaction between neighboring populations, but artifactual clues confirm the exchange of ideas between living groups." Henry (1994:337) further states that evidence for social interaction is found principally in the lithic industry. This coincides with an agency perspective in its recognition that material culture represents the world within which the Natufian, as well as the people themselves, acted.

This approach to understanding Natufian behavior represents a departure in that: (a) the Natufian is expressed as spatially diverse; (b) the Natufian is viewed as adaptive to ecological environments through its culture; and (c) the Natufian is not viewed as isolated but, rather, as a entity that interacts with others. These ideas changed the way we think about the Natufian. In the context of agency, the cultural-ecology approach can also be seen as the initial recognition of past humans making decisions. These decisions are related to spatial and chronological experience. Rather than limiting settlement at the local synchronous level, Natufian settlement can be seen at the regional synchronic level. At this regional level, the Natufian is viewed as a population that engages with ecological structures and makes decisions on the basis of preference for one ecological setting over another. In the absence of preferred settlement location, Natufian social groups will seek out similar settings.

The cultural ecological approach recognizes that the Natufian did not live in a vacuum, that there was social interaction among neighboring populations and that the Natufian was a homogeneous cultural entity in that its members sought out specific settlement settings. Support for this interaction is evident in the similarity of the lithic industry throughout the region. The issue with this statement, from an agency perspective, is that it does not address the duality of social structures that facilitates social interaction. In the cultural-ecology approach, dualism, rather than duality, takes precedence. Dualism is the separation of macro from micro, while duality recognizes that both macro and micro are interwoven. Therefore, structures are not external to individuals.

Structural constraints believed to limit preferences for settlement locale (e.g., elevation, climate) do not necessarily limit movement. Similarly, enabling structures, including socio-cultural ones, are mutually interdependent with the system, how humans organize themselves. Further more, the dualism characteristic of the cultural-ecology approach tends to create spatial and temporal boundaries that do nothing for the understanding of the creation and *maintenance* of social relations. Cultural ecology does not consider that at the spatial and temporal level; the macro and micro are interwoven through human interaction.

The *Bricoleur* Agent

This final theme, characteristic of research on the Natufian, refers to the use of multiple sources, or thinking toolkits, to construct a descriptive system for the Natufian. The key player, Ofer Bar-Yosef, is what Claude Levi-Strauss refers to as a *bricoleur*. A bricoleur is "adept at performing a large amount of tasks…but does not subordinate each of them to the availability of raw materials and tools conceived and procured for the purpose of the project" (Levi-Strauss 1966:17). In other words, Bar-Yosef does not subscribe to a particular theoretical paradigm or limit himself to a particular model to achieve his goal of constructing a descriptive system for Near Eastern archaeology. Furthermore, he constructs this system through examination of "shifting boundaries between prehistoric populations who inhabited the Mediterranean Levant during the Late Pleistocene and Early Holocene" (Bar-Yosef 1987:219).

According to Bar-Yosef (1981; 1983), the Natufian are characterized as having two types of sites: base camps and transitory camps. Base camps are large (> 1000 m^2), exhibit architecture and burials, and are richer in material culture. Transitory camps are smaller, were used for a short period of time, do not have architecture or burials, and have limited material remains. Base camps are located exclusively in the Mediterranean vegetation zone, regardless of their elevation. Transitory camps are located primarily in the Irano-Turanian and Saharo-Arabian Desert vegetation zones, but could also occur in the Mediterranean (usually within 50 km of a base camp in the Mediterranean vegetation zone).

In this sense, Bar-Yosef (1970) applies the site-catchment model to the Natufian; however, he further speculates that there is a general core and peripheral area of habitation for all Natufian populations. The core area is located within the Mediterranean vegetation zone. Within this core area, base camps are Early Natufian while transitory camps, located up to 50 km from the base camps, are Geometric Kebaran B. An important point to make here is that Bar-Yosef considers only base camps as Natufian in the core area.

The peripheral area is located in the Irano-Turanian vegetation zone. Only Late Natufian sites are located in the periphery. No sites identified as Natufian are located in the Desert vegetation zone, suggesting that only the

Mediterranean vegetation zone could provide adequate resources for the Natufian economy and that these resources were within one day's walk (Bar-Yosef 1987:224, 232). The Late Natufian relocated from the Mediterranean to the Irano-Turanian because of climate changes leading to the deterioration in size of the Mediterranean core area. This reduction in area led to a deterioration in resources - mainly vegetational resources - and a need to expand the resource base (Bar-Yosef 1998; Goring-Morris and Belfer-Cohen 1998; Henry 1981, 1995).

This stage of Natufian research marks the point when the Natufian was no longer defined purely by its lithic industry. This brought re-evaluation of the definition of the Natufian. Belfer-Cohen (1989:300-302) observes that, although the Natufian lithic industry is seen both in and out of the core area, other characteristics common to Natufian sites, such as bone and ground-stone tools and burials, are uncommon outside the core area. As she asserts (Belfer-Cohen 1991b:175), "similarities in lithics between two entities do not necessarily indicate a close resemblance in social structure." This affirms Bar-Yosef's classification of transitory camps in the core area (above) as Geometric Kebaran B rather than Natufian, regardless of characteristics of the lithic industry (Bar-Yosef 1970:175). Belfer-Cohen (1989:303) argues that non-lithic artifacts have cultural meaning; therefore, their absence or presence at sites "should overrule the lithic similarities in stating that we are dealing with separate entities." She acknowledges that this definition will result in numerous "nameless archaeological occurrences," but argues that it will provide more insight into the cultural history of the region (Belfer-Cohen 1989:303).

Bar-Yosef terms the use of a descriptive system, rather than a chronological or spatial approach, to defining the Natufian as a "historical narrative explanation." This explanation takes into account geographical conditions, archaeological history, reconstructed social structures and subsistence strategies and environmental changes (Bar-Yosef 1998:173). This explanation also adds weight to the argument that a dense spatial distribution of combined resources, such as we might expect to have existed in the Mediterranean zone, enabled foragers, such as the Natufian, to survive in biologically viable populations in small territories. Through this historical narrative "environmental impacts are screened through a cultural filter" (Bar-Yosef 1998:173). This cultural filter is constructed through particular group histories.

Given this approach to defining the Natufian, what can be said of agency? Clearly, there is a move towards seeing the Natufian as a cultural entity rather than a chronological entity but how does this incorporate the Natufian agent?

In considering agency and the research discussed in this section, two themes are prominent: over-reliance on ecological environmental structures and lack of explicit attention to the technological skill and knowledge needed to produce material culture. It is understood, using this approach, that the Natufian inhabit the core area, which is defined by its ecological condition. Believing that a site-catchment area is the territory that can support a population and that its size depends on the terrain, Bar-Yosef (1987:232) makes the argument that the Mediterranean is the only area that could adequately support the Natufian. Furthermore, he argues that Early Natufian boundaries were ecologically determined (Bar-Yosef 1987:233).

From an agency perspective, it is agreed that ecological surroundings do play an important role in individual decision-making. However, they alone cannot account for the decisions that the Natufian made. Socio-cultural surroundings play an equally important role. One of the main principles of agency is that the structures, be they ecological or socio-cultural, are dualistic in nature: they are both the medium and outcome. Thus both serve as enabling or constraining factors in individual decision-making. This interpretation of the Natufian, based primarily on ecology, is also based heavily on the constraining nature of the ecological structures.

The core area is primarily identified by its ecological structure and secondarily by material culture. According to social agency, the technological skill and knowledge that is required to produce and reproduce artifacts is part of decision-making and social action. Using this logic, artifacts can be viewed as inactive traces, residues, or correlates of particular kinds of human activity and agency. In essence, artifacts represent people in that they signify the communication of technological skill and knowledge. This leads to the question of why non-lithic materials are considered to have cultural meaning and should overrule lithic materials. It is argued that similarity in material culture (using lithics as an example) does not necessarily imply similar social structure. Although there could be variation in social structure, similarity in material culture strongly suggests similarity in technological knowledge and skill. In order to have this similarity, certain actions, such as communication and sharing of knowledge, must occur. It can be further argued that, in order for this social action to occur, a social structure must have been in place to enable this action.

The Natufian Agent

The previous sections focus on chronological, cultural-ecological, and historical narrative approaches to understand Natufian behavior. These approaches are further discussed in a social-agency context. All three approaches do make reference to social interaction and organization but these references are brief and suggest no interest in further understanding how interaction took place or how social interaction might be visible in archaeological data over a varied space region. Rather, they pay attention to chronological order, adaptation, and cultural definition to particular environments.

In 1990, at a conference on the Natufian, the discussants, C. Perlès and J.L. Phillips, proposed four models based on information presented. The first model is known as "year-round sedentism in the core area." This model coincides with the historical narrative model that Bar-Yosef proposes. Figure 3.1 illustrates this model. According to Perlès and Phillips (1991:639), this model represents those populations occupying sites in the Irano-Turanian and Saharan areas as different populations than the groups occupying sites in the Mediterranean zone. Alternatively, a second model, titled the "progressive group-splitting and displacement model," is also linked to the core-and-periphery model. Figure 3.2 represents this model. According to Perlès and Phillips (1991:640), this model illustrates that common traits are "a mere reflection of common origins between groups which will progressively interact less and less." Furthermore, "small groups that split from the core-area and progressively settle in marginal zones free themselves from the strongly conservative attitude characteristic of the central sites of long duration" (Perlès & Phillips 1991:640). The third model Perlès and Phillips propose (1991:640) coincides with the interpretations of Natufian adaptation and settlement proposed by Vita-Finzi & Higgs, Henry, and Valla. This model is titled "semi-sedentary and nomadic groups." According to this model, semi-sedentary groups occupy the larger sites (core-area base camps) in the winter and move to smaller, short-term specialized sites in the hill areas (higher elevation) during the summer. Sites populated in the desert areas represent a different population. Figure 3.3 illustrates this model.

In my research I recognize the chronological position of the Natufian and accept the bipartite subdivision of Natufian history into two phases, Early and Late. I also recognize that the Natufian is a culture that can be characterized by its material culture. However, I question the exclusivity of material culture as the basis for defining Natufian. It is the position of this research that the sharing of *knowledge* required to produce material culture through space and time defines a culture.

Finally, I recognize that the physical region that surrounds the archaeological region of the Natufian is diverse. According to Bar-Yosef (2001:2), "what distinguishes the Levant, as a sub-region of western Asia, is that within a short transect (e.g. 80 to 150 kms) one finds an almost globally unmatched topographic and vegetational heterogeneity." Given this heterogeneity, at the macro scale (Mediterranean, Irano-Turanian, and Desert) and the micro scale (diversity within these areas), the assertion that the Natufian entity is limited to a particular ecological area within the region is questionable.

The combination of material and ecological limits, supported by cultural historical and ecological approaches, is interpreted, from an agency perspective, as over-indulgence in the constraints of structures, with little consideration to the enabling qualities of structures. We are left with little information on how people transmitted culture (belief, values, knowledge and skill) over space and time. For example, it is apparent that natural rhythms influenced Natufian settlement, but social needs were the ultimate influence (Valla 1998:95). It is also apparent that the Natufian in their distinct areas did not live in a void; there was exchange of ideas as seen through the influences on material culture. Regrettably, because of the restrictive notion of the core and its periphery, social influences on cultural material are ignored.

What remains to be explained is the fact that, although there is variability at both inter- and intra-site levels, there is general homogeneity of Natufian material culture throughout the region. This research addresses this concern. Rather than following the lead of previous research that was driven by the desire to identify variability, this research approaches the Natufian from an opposite stance – to identify similarity. This approach will broaden our understanding of social interaction, relations and communication among the Natufian.

This approach is not unique. In a 1999 article on the Natufian, Valla acknowledges that, despite diversity in the ecological environment of the region, there is cultural homogeneity among Natufian assemblages over the entire region. He makes a clear attempt to "identify unity rather than diversity" (Valla 1999:226) among Natufian assemblages throughout the region. However, Valla (1999:226) also points out that "cultural unity and diversity in ways of life" are two things that we must keep in mind when observing Natufian culture. Given these statements, a "territory" approach is used, one that continues to highlight spatial diversity rather cultural unity. Valla (1999:233) suggests that we examine objects brought to the site and further suggests that there are three ranges for these objects: (1) nearby environment, (2) Natufian zone of influence, and (3) the world outside the Natufian cultural area. However, Valla (1999:233-234) further states that, "unfortunately, this avenue does not lead to any means of accessing the collective representations of these increasingly removed ranges."

What is needed to investigate how past populations interacted with one another is a model that addresses the duality of structures. We must also understand that structures are not external to individuals. I propose that we need a model guided by social agency to conduct research on Natufian interactions. This model, built upon the principles of social agency, as discussed in the previous chapter, incorporates socio-cultural structures (material culture) as well as ecological structures (vegetation, elevation, natural resources). However, this model abandons the concepts of core and periphery, and territory. All sites that exhibit Natufian traits are included, regardless of their location in space.

This model stems from a fourth model Perlès and Phillips (1991:640) propose, the "semi-sedentary occupation of the larger settlements and logistical organization." According to this model, large sites in the Mediterranean are only occupied part of the year. In other seasons the populations disperse to the hills of the Irano-Turanian zone with specialized trips to the desert. Figure 3.4 illustrates this proposed model. This model follows Conkey's (1980) notion of aggregation/dispersion settlement strategy, whereby hunter-gatherers follow an annual cycle of concentration and dispersion. This settlement strategy also has implications for human interaction where aggregation settlements signify periods of intense social interaction. During these periods of intense interaction, there is sharing of individual ideas and actions within a larger population. As well, there is construction, validation, and maintenance of social structures. This aggregation/dispersion settlement strategy also takes place within the ecological structure of the population in that large aggregation sites occur in particular ecological zones, such as the Mediterranean.

Perlès and Phillips report that this model fits well with certain existing observations and that each of the four models proposed can be tested on an archaeological basis. Given the past research on the Natufian and Perlès and Phillips corresponding models, a series of hypotheses can be formulated. A summary of these hypotheses appears in table 3.1.

Included in this series of hypotheses is an additional hypothesis based on the model I propose for this research. My model departs from the four models outlined in that I hypothesize that social interaction in the Natufian, and hence social definition of the Natufian, was based on a model of aggregation and dispersion throughout the entire region. Groups gathered seasonally at large sites. When these groups dispersed, they took with them shared knowledge and material culture. This shared knowledge and material culture is demonstrated through its continuous presence throughout spatial and time. Aggregation, while influenced by ecological structure, does not depend on biome. Rather, time-space edges and time-space distanciation are considered integral to aggregation and dispersal of Natufian social groups. Given this consideration, the substantiation of aggregation and dispersal in all three biomes becomes a viable possibility. Once information, knowledge, material culture, and action was shared, the groups dispersed to the various areas in the region (see **H** in table 3.1).

The following chapters focus on the data and the methods used to test these hypotheses. I will use the resulting information to develop further the model of social interaction I propose for this research.

Figure 3.1 Year-round sedentism model (Perlès and Phillips 1991).

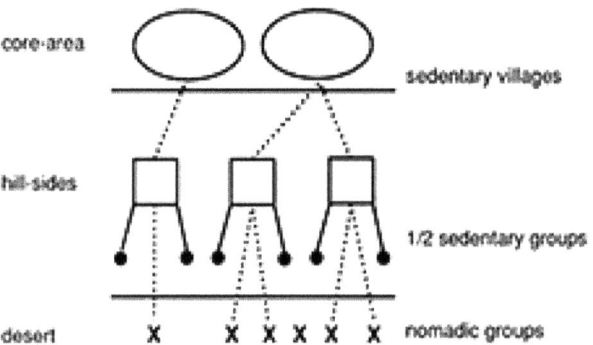

Figure 3.2 Progressive group fission and displacement model (Perlès and Phillips 1991).

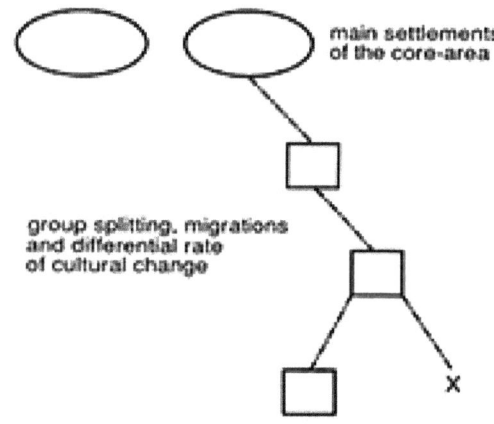

Figure 3.3 Semi-sedentary groups and nomadic groups model (Perlès and Phillips 1991).

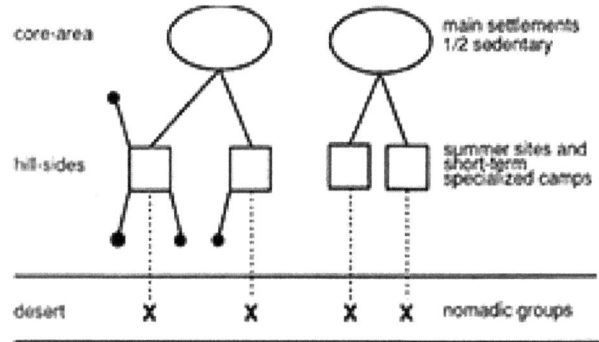

Figure 3.4 Semi-sedentary occupations of the large settlements and logistical organization model (Perlès and Phillips 1991).

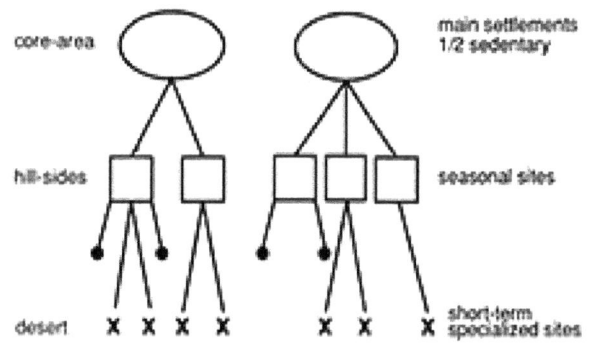

Table 3.1 Hypotheses tested in this research and potential alternatives.

H	**Semi-sedentary occupation of the large settlements and logistical organization.** Social interaction based on a model of aggregation and dispersal of Natufian social groups. Aggregation and dispersal occurs to fulfill a purpose that is supported by the enabling and constraining features of social and ecological structures. Aggregation and dispersal are evident in all biomes. All sites are defined as Natufian on the basis of their intensive social interaction.
H_{A1}	**Semi-sedentary occupation of the large settlements and logistical organization.** Social interaction based on a model of aggregation and dispersal of Natufian social groups. Aggregation occurs in the Mediterranean forest and dispersion occurs in the Irano-Turanian hills and Saharo-Arabian desert. All sites are defined as Natufian on the basis of their intensive social interaction.
H_{A2}	**Semi-sedentary groups and nomadic groups.** Social interaction based on a model of aggregation and dispersal of Natufian social groups. Aggregation occurs in the Mediterranean forest and dispersion occurs in the Irano-Turanian hills. Saharo-Arabian desert sites host a different population, as indicated by absence of interaction.
H_{A3}	**Year-round sedentism in the Mediterranean forest.** Social interaction is limited. Large sites in the Mediterranean are occupied permanently and are Natufian. Sites in the Irano-Turanian hills and Saharo-Arabian desert represent different populations as indicated by absence of interaction. There may or may not be interaction between Irano-Turanian hills and Saharo-Arabian desert sites.
H_{A4}	**Progressive group fission and displacement.** Common traits for sites in all ecological zones reflect the common origin of groups but, as groups split from the Mediterranean core area to settle in peripheral areas, they progressively interact less and less. Sites outside the Mediterranean forest are no longer considered to be Natufian because of absence of interaction.

CHAPTER 4
DATA PART I: ARCHAEOLOGICAL SITES AND MATERIAL CULTURE

Introduction

Chapters two and three lay out the theoretical and historical setting for this research. These two chapters result in the construction of a model based on a testable hypothesis – that the Natufian displays semi-sedentary occupation of the large settlements and logistical organization. I further hypothesize that structures, both ecological and social, space and time play major roles in model of human settlement. To develop the model further and test the hypothesis requires archaeological sites and their material culture.

In this chapter, I describe the archaeological data used to test the hypothesis for this research. Organization of data is by level, from large data sources (sites), to variables (artifact classes), and finally to attributes of the variables. Figure 4.1 conceptualizes these levels of data. The structure of the chapter is as follows: (a) discussion of site selection, followed by a brief description of the sites; (b) discussion of variable selection, followed by a brief description of the variables used; and (c) discussion of the attributes selected for the variables, and a brief description of these variables. The outcome of this chapter will be a clear understanding of how the data were selected, why certain data were selected, and a description of the actual data available for this research. This data facilitates the first of two methods – cluster analysis. This chapter satisfies the first two steps in the clustering process: deciding the objects to cluster and the variables to use.

Figure 4.1 Conceptualization of data at the site, variable and attribute level.

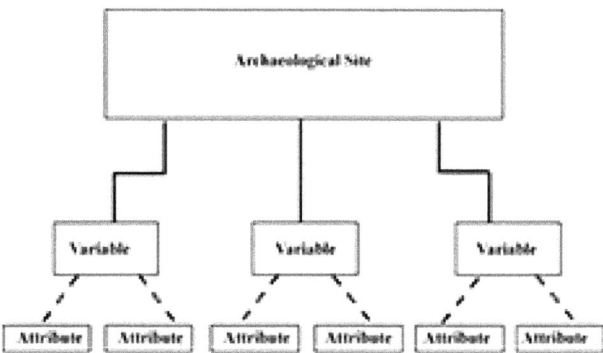

Archaeological Sites

The ideal research strategy would be to include all known Natufian sites in the archaeological region. Early on, it became apparent that this would not be possible because, although many sites have been recorded, not all are excavated. In this case, the selection of Natufian sites for this research was based primarily on publication of excavation record and materials. In other words, those sites with significant publications are included. The published material needs to be complete in that there is sufficient discussion of the history of the site, excavation procedures, and the recovered material culture (artifacts). Published material included various forms: monographs, site reports, journal articles, as well as yearly excavation reports. After initial collection of published material on Natufian sites, I realized that the database would contain very few Natufian sites. Therefore, I expanded my search and included unpublished material, such as dissertation research and personal communications.

The published material conventionally groups Natufian sites into three temporal phases: Early, Late and Final. I chose to focus on Early and Late Natufian sites and categorized Final Natufian sites as Late. Final sites are grouped with Late sites because: (a) there is no clear definition of the Final Natufian other than different microburin indices, *slightly* smaller structures and burials similar to those of Early Natufian; (b) there are relatively few sites identified as Final Natufian, and (c) as there is no clear transition from Late/Final Natufian to Early PPN (pre-pottery Neolithic) sites, one could argue that Final sites are either Late Natufian or Early PPN.

My goal was to collect the maximum amount of information for each site. I then organize this information by dividing it into two categories – site information and artifact information. Site information includes:
- Site name,
- Geographical coordinates, including a physical description of the area
- History of excavation of the site
- Site phase (Early or Late),
- Site size,
- Area excavated and volume excavated,
- Radiocarbon dates, and
- Screen (mesh) size, if material was sieved.

Collection of site information is for the purpose of understanding how to compare and contrast the sites. Clearly, there are problems with treating all sites as equivalent. These problems occur at several levels. For example, excavations at some sites occurred for only one season while other sites underwent several seasons of excavation. Some sites, although only excavated for a short time, were excavated over an extensive area. In addition, Natufian cultural deposits are comparatively thick at some sites (> 50 cm) while, at other sites, particularly where deflation has occurred, the deposits are quite thin (<15 cm). The area excavated and depths of cultural deposits are reflected in the volume of material recorded. Finally, there are some sites, particularly those excavated prior to the 1970s, where the practice of excavation did not include sieving of excavated material. This affects the recovery of small cultural material. Some of these issues are addressed in previous regional analysis (Belfer-Cohen 1991a:174-175), but they did not take into consideration past excavation practices, most notably scale of excavation and sieving.

I use information from a total of 26 Natufian sites for this research. The following pages describe these sites to the extent of the information available for the sites. I also acknowledge that there are several sites that cannot be included due to the lack of published information. The Natufian sites described here are arranged according to their location in present day terrestrial vegetation zones (Mediterranean forest, Irano-Turanian hills and Saharo-Arabian desert). Figure 4.2 illustrates the location of Natufian sites in their terrestrial vegetation zone. A summary of the Natufian sites and their general information is located in appendix A.

Natufian Sites in the Mediterranean Forest

a) **Mallaha:** Located north of Lake Kinneret (Galilee/Tiberias), near the perennial spring Áin Mallaha (72 m asl); the Natufian site of Mallaha is the subject of a long history of excavation programs. First excavated in 1954 by J. Perrot, with renewed excavations in the 1980s through F. Valla, Mallaha is thought to be the most thoroughly excavated Natufian site. At the end of the 1999 season of excavation, an estimated 120 m^2 of the Late Natufian component of the site was excavated in a four-year period. For the Early Natufian, 250 m^2 were excavated to a total volume of 150 m^3 (Byrd 1987:301). Although early excavations were not subject to sieving, it is understood that recent excavations sieve all material through a mesh (no record of size). The area if the site is estimated at 2000 m^2. Radiocarbon determinations from charcoal samples range from 11,740 ± 500 to 11,310 ± 880 BP (12,500 to 10,000 cal BC)[1].

b) **el Wad:** Located on the southern escarpment of Nahal Me'arot (Valley of the Caves)/Mount Carmel Caves in the northern coast (Weinstein-Evron 1998:19), el-Wad contains both an Early and Late Natufian component. This multi-chambered cave site lies at an elevation of 45 m asl and is approximately 840 m^2 in size. Five soundings were tested (three in the cave, two in the terrace) during C. Lambert's original 1928 excavation. Dorothy Garrod continued excavations in the cave and on the terrace until 1933. In the early 1980s, Valla continued limited excavations on the northeastern area of the terrace. Mina Wienstein-Evron renewed excavations in the late 1980s with a focus on chamber III, the terrace, and the back-dirt piles of previous excavations (Wienstein-Evron 1998). These excavations covered an area of 33 m^2 to a depth of 5-10 cm. All material was sieved through a 2 mm mesh. Although there is evidence of both Early and Late Natufian occupations, Garrod reports that Late material is almost indistinguishable from Early Natufian material and is restricted to the terrace (Garrod & Bate 1937). Radiocarbon determinations on bone and charcoal samples range from 12,950 ± 200 to 10,680 ± 190 BP (13,750 to 10,420 cal BC).

c) **Kebara:** Located on the western escarpment of Mount Carmel (60-64 m asl), Kebara is a multiple-period site with historical, Natufian, Kebaran, Aurignacian, Upper Paleolithic and Mousterian occupations. Level B's lithic assemblage is classified as Early Natufian. 1927 marks Stekelis' first test sounding near the cave entrance. In 1930, Garrod dug a small trench, 2.5 m by 2.5 m, and Turville-Petre, along with Baynes, further excavated in 1931. The total excavation area is approximately 300 m^2 to a depth of 3 m (Bar-Yosef et al. 1992:500). The result of these limited excavations is a rich Early Natufian assemblage. However, no radiocarbon dates are available and the 900 m^3 of deposit did not undergo sieving.

d) **Nahal 'En Gev II:** This Late Natufian site is located on a large flat terrace on the left bank of the nahal (wadi) on the eastern side of Lake Kinneret (Galilee/Tiberias). The open-air-site is approximately 1700 m^2 in area. Although Bar-Yosef initiated excavation in 1973, information in the form of publication did not appear until 2000 (Bar-Yosef and Belfer-Cohen 2000). A surface collection and two 50 cm by 50 cm units were excavated to a depth of 1.3 m. Natufian material extends to a depth of 13 cm with a total volume of material recovered 0.07 m^3. All material was sieved using a 2 mm screen. No radiocarbon dates are available.

e) **Hayonim Cave:** This site is located on the right bank of Nahal Meged (a small tributary of Nahal Yassaf) on the geographical boundary between western and lower Galilee (Bar-Yosef 1991). The initial series of excavations, under the direction of Arensburg, Bar-Yosef, and Tchernov, lasted from 1965 to 1970. The most recent series of excavations, under the direction of Bar-Yosef, began in 1992 and continue to the present. Hayonim has a long history of occupation from Mousterian to modern times. Layer B is identified as Natufian and, although radiocarbon dates indicate an Early Natufian occupation (12,360 ± 160 BP and 12,010 ± 180 BP; 12,320 to 11,140 cal BC, based on determinations on seeds), there is also evidence for a Late Natufian presence (Bar-Yosef 1991). The estimated size of the cave chamber, where there is evidence of Natufian remains, is approximately 230 m^2 but the extent of excavation of Natufian deposits is approximately 50 m^2. Published documents do not indicate the depth of the Natufian deposits but the volume excavated is estimated to be 20 m^3. Although all material was sieved, the mesh size of the screens is unknown.

f) **Hayonim Terrace:** This open-air site is located beneath Hayonim Cave (35 m below the mouth of the cave) on the highest of four terraces that fall to the bed of the Nahal Yassaf tributary. The area of the site, based on surface artifact concentration, extends

---

[1] A list of available radiocarbon and calibrated dates for Natufian sites are available in Appendix B. The confidence interval on calibrated dates is 68% using the CalPal 2005 calibration curve.

over approximately 600 m². On the basis of seven radiocarbon dates from charred bone, 11,920 - 10,000 BP (12,110 to 11,790 cal BC) (Byrd 1994), the site was occupied during the Late Natufian. Two series of excavation occurred at Hayonim Terrace. The first, under the direction of Henry, was from 1974 to 1975. He tested an 8 m by 1 m trench to a depth of 1.5 m in 1974 and a subsequent 6 m by 7 m block the following year (Henry 1976). All material was sieved through a 3 mm screen. The second series of excavations, under the direction of Valla, occurred from 1980 to 1987. The goal of these excavations was to expose further the architecture on the terrace and to excavate burials (Valla 1989). The total volume excavated on the terrace is unknown but, according to reports (Valla 1988), the thickness of the Natufian layer ranged from 0.15 m to 0.4 m throughout the site.

g) **Faza'el IV:** The site is situated in the lower Jordan valley on the slope of the Fazael stream, in close proximity to Salibiya. Although Bar-Yosef excavated the site in 1971, detailed publication of the material culture of the site did not appear until 1999 (Grosman et al. 1999). The size of this open-air site is approximately 300 m² but the extent of surface material is more than 1,000 m² (Goring-Morris 1980; Bar-Yosef et al. 1974). A total of 3 m² was excavated to a depth of 50 - 55 cm, with a total excavated volume of 1.55 m³. There is no information on whether the material was sieved. Although no radiocarbon dates are available, Faza'el IV is accepted as a Late Natufian occupation on the basis of its cultural material.

h) **Hilazon Tachtit:** This cave site is located on the right bank of Nahal Hilazon, western Galilee, 12 m above the stream channel (Grosman 2003). Although Bar-Yosef and Valla discovered Hilazon Tachtit in the 1960s, Berger and Khalaily did not carry out a surface collection until 1994. Subsequently, Leore Grossman conducted four seasons of excavation (1995, 1997, 2000-1) and continues to excavate. These four seasons have revealed a large chamber excavation of 44 m² with a total area of 30 m² containing Natufian remains. The total volume of the Natufian area excavated is approximately 18 m³. Although it is certain that all material was sieved, there are no published accounts of the size of the screen. The Natufian layer is 0.6 m in thickness. One radiocarbon date for the site from a charcoal sample (10,750 ± 50 BP; 10,771 cal BC) indicates a Late Natufian occupation.

i) **Hatoula:** On the south bank of Nahal Nahshon, on the western margins of the Judean Shefela (215 - 19 m asl), lies the site of Hatoula. The site is approximately 2000 m² in size. During eight seasons of fieldwork at the site (Ronen and Lechevallier 1991), a total of 30 m² of the sight was unearthed. Published reports on the site indicate that the cultural deposits of the site reach depths of 80 cm. The total volume of the Natufian material excavated reaches 6.6 m³. Sieving of material culture and mesh size, if the material was sieved, are not reported. One radiocarbon date from a bone sample (11,020 ± 180 BP; 11,017 cal BC) places occupation during the Late phase.

j) **Nahal Oren:** On a steep terrace, between Nahal Oren cave and the stream bed of Nahal Oren (50 m asl), in the vicinity of the western escarpment of Mount Carmel, lies the site of Nahal Oren. Stekelis first excavated this site in 1941, with subsequent excavations from 1954 to 1959. According to published reports, excavation encompassed three 2.5 m by 2.5 m units, with further extensions to two of the three units totaling 1.06 m³ of deposits excavated. The material was sieved but the screen size is unknown. One radiocarbon date from a bone collagen sample from the Natufian layer (10,046 ± 318 BP; 9769 ± 518 cal BC) indicates a Late occupation but the material culture indicates both Early and Late occupation. Other issues concerning the human occupation of Nahal Oren include the possible admixture of PPN material at the site as well as alleged stratigraphic confusion.

k) **Wadi al-Hammeh 27:** This site is situated on the northern end of the mouth of Wadi al-Hammeh (79 m below sea level), a westward-flowing remnant tributary of the Jordan River, stratified above a travertine cap (Edwards 1988, 1992). Wadi al-Hammeh is an Early Natufian, open-air site, approximately 2,000 m² in size. Radiocarbon dates from charred seeds range from 12,200 ± 160 to 11,920 ± 150 BP (12,280 to11,740 cal BC). Survey and excavation in Wadi al-Hammeh started in 1975 (Ibrahim et al. 1976) with a total of seven seasons of excavation carried out between 1983 and 1989. The area of excavation encompasses approximately 350 m² or17.5 % of the site (Edwards 1991). All material was sieved through a 2 mm screen.

l) **'Ain Rahub:** This Late Natufian site is approximately 13 km northeast of the city of Irbid, northern Jordan. 'Ain Rahub is situated on the lower terrace of the west bank of Wadi ar-Rahub (420 m asl). Z. Kafafi and S. Mittmann discovered the site in 1981, with excavation carried out in 1985. Although road construction has now destroyed the site, estimates of its size reach upwards of 1,600 m². Excavation of 'Ain Rahub over 20 m² of the site removed a volume of 7.2 m³ or 1.25 % of the site area. All material was sieved through a 5 mm screen. This is the first open-air Late Natufian site recorded in the present "semi-arid mild-warm and arid-mild regions of northern Jordan" (Muheisen et al. 1988:472).

m) **Wadi Mataha:** This multiple-occupation site, located in the Petra basin of southern Jordan, lies on a steep talus slope at the southern edge of Mughur al-Mataha (950 m asl), a large sandstone monolith

(Janetski & Chazan 2002). The site was discovered in 1997 with two subsequent field seasons in 1999 and 2000. Based on the lithic scatter, the site area is at least 1100 m². The total volume of extraction in 1999 was 28 m², but there are no reports of the volume excavated in 2000. Two radiocarbon dates from humic acid from bone, 14,140 ± 130 BP and 11,200 ± 50 BP (15,576 to 11,153 cal BC), have placed the site in the period corresponding to the Geometric Kebaran and Late Natufian. The overwhelming presence of Early Natufian diagnostics, such as Helwan retouch and ground stone tools, however, indicates an Early Natufian occupation.

Natufian Sites in the Saharo-Arabian desert

a) **Upper Besor 6:** This site is situated in the central Negev, close to the watershed that separates the westward-flowing Nahal Besor and Zipporim and the eastward-flowing tributary of Nahal Zin. Upper Besor 6 is located on the westward flanks, on the Haluqim anticline (500 m asl). This site was recognized during the TAHAL prehistoric survey of the 1980s (Goring-Morris and Rosen 1987). Although deflated, it is likely that the site extends over an area as much as 1000 m². Systematic collection and excavation of some 80 m² is recorded but the depths of the Natufian cultural deposit, as well as the total volume excavated, remain unpublished. It is also not reported whether the material excavated was sieved and, if so, what size mesh was used. No radiocarbon dates are available for Upper Besor 6 but, based on the material culture, both Early and Late Natufian occupations are evident.

b) **Givat Hayil I:** This site lies at the southern edge of the western Negev dune fields. Givat Hayil I is located between low dune crests Givat Hayil and Nahal Pakuah (300 m asl) at the southern edge of the Shunera dunes (Goring-Morris 1997). The site was reported during a series of surveys in the area in the 1960s but excavation and initial publication of the site did not appear until the 1980s and 1990s (Goring-Morris 1987; 1997). Although the site suffers from slope wash and deflation, Givat Hayil I is approximately 150 m² in size. A total of 34 m² of the site has been excavated to date. The Natufian deposit reaches a maximum depth of 15 cm below the surface. This corresponds with an excavated volume of Natufian material of 5.1 m³. Sieving of material culture and mesh size, if the material was sieved, is not reported. There are no radiocarbon dates for Givat Hayil I but material remains suggest a Late Natufian occupation.

c) **Rosh Horesha:** This open-air site is located northeast of Har Harif (Negev) in a broad, shallow valley on the bank of the Horesha tributary (730 m asl) (Goring-Morris 1987). Marks and Larson (1977) initially discovered and tested the site in the early 1970s, with a second expedition led by Goring-Morris and Gopher in the early 1980s. The site is approximately 5000 m² in size, but it was partly eroded upon discovery and excavation. Test excavations took place in four different areas of the site and Natufian deposits reach depths of up to 40 cm. The total volume of Natufian material excavated is 7.8 m³. All material was sieved through a 6 mm screen. Two radiocarbon dates are available from charcoal samples, 10,880 ± 280 and 10,490 ± 430 BP (10,799 ± 331 and 10,190 ± 590 cal BC), indicating a Late Natufian occupation.

d) **Rosh Zin:** This open-air site, also situated in the Negev, occupies a triangular plateau bounded by the north-south Zin tributary and the east-west Havarim tributary (520 m asl) (Goring-Morris 1987). The Southern Methodist University (SMU) expedition discovered and excavated the site in the early 1970s (Henry 1976). Although the site suffers from deflation, it extends over an area of 900 m². Testing of Rosh Zin consisted of seven randomly placed 1 m² units. The Natufian deposits extend to a depth of 30 cm. The total volume of Natufian material excavated totals 21.3 m³. All material was sieved through a 2 mm screen. No radiocarbon dates are available for Rosh Zin but, on the basis of its material culture, the site is a Late Natufian occupation.

e) **Nahal Sekher VI:** This site, originally discovered in the 1950s through road construction, has been the focus of amateur collections for many years (Goring-Morris 1987). Nahal Sekher VI lies midway between Beersheva and Revivim in the Negev. The size of the site is approximately 60 m². A total of 12 m² was excavated in 25 cm by 25 cm quadrants during an emergency salvage excavation in the 1980s. The Natufian occupation lies at a depth of 5 - 10 cm. All material culture during this excavation was sieved through a 3 mm screen. A charcoal sample from the site has yielded a radiocarbon date of 9,460 ± 130 BP (8,845 ± 227 cal BC). Although this is younger than expected, Nahal Sekher VI is a Late Natufian site.

f) **Salibiya I:** This site is located on the west side of the lower Jordan River valley, where it is surrounded by highly dissected badlands topography (Crabtree et al. 1991). Salibiya I is an open-air Late Natufian site occupying an area of approximately 1200 m². Although Bar-Yosef and Goldberg originally discovered Salibiya I in 1980, Crabtree, Campana and Belfer-Cohen did not initiate excavation until 1987. One 2 m by 2 m and another 1 m by 1 m trench revealed Natufian deposits to a depth of 95 cm. All material was sieved through a 1 mm screen. A radiocarbon date from a charcoal sample of 11,530 ± 1550 BP (11848 ± 2258 cal BC) places Salibiya I in the Late Natufian.

g) **Saflulim:** This open-air site was discovered near Rosh Horesha in 1981 as part of the Emergency Archaeological Survey of the Negev (Goring-Morris et al 1999). It is located on the south, left bank of a small but deep gully. An initial 6 m² surface collection of material was conducted and Goring-Morris et al. (1999) estimate that the site may extend to upwards of 1000 m². In 1988, a total of 9 m² was excavated, encompassing the area of the surface collection. All material was sieved through a 3 mm screen. Two radiocarbon dates from charcoal samples are available for the site (11,150 ± 100 BP and 10,930 ± 130 BP; 11,097 ± 147 and 10,943 ± 123 cal BC) indicating a Late Natufian occupation.

(h) **Beidha:** Located near Petra, southern Jordan, the site of Beidha is situated in an alluvial valley (1040 m asl) that is seasonally drained by Wadi al-Ghurub (Byrd 1991). This Early Natufian site is 2,400 m² in size but, because of erosion, only a portion of the site remains. It is possible that this open-air site could originally have been up to 4,000 m² in size. Excavations at Beidha originally occurred from 1958 to 1959 and 1964 to 1967 under the supervision of Diane Kirkbride. A renewed season of excavation occurred in 1983, also under her supervision. Excavation totals 80 m² or 3.3 % of the site as preserved. Sieving of material was carried out using a 3 mm screen. Radiocarbon dates from charcoal samples indicate a Late Natufian occupation, ranging from 12,910 ± 250 to 10,910 ± 520 BP (13,750 to 10,100 cal BC).

(i) **'Ain as-Saratan (Azraq 18):** This Early Natufian site, in north-central Jordan, is situated in the central Azraq basin, beside 'Ain as-Saratan, a minor spring. 'Ain-as-Saratan has a history of only one season of excavation, 1985 (Garrard 1991). During this season, excavation of 6 m², less than 0.5 % of the approximately 1,400 m² area of this open-air site took place. Sieving of material culture and mesh size, if the material was sieved, is not reported. The site is deflated and no radiocarbon dates are available.

(j) **Wadi Humeima (J406a):** This open-air site, near Wadi Judayid, rests at the lower edge of the piedmont and covers the upper portions of a slope that extends from the base of Jebel Humeima (1000 m asl) (Henry 1995). Investigation of this site occured in the late 1970s, along with Wadi Judayid. Two 1 m² units are excavated with cultural deposits 20 to 30 cm in depth for a total excavated volume of 0.5 m³. All material was sieved through a 3 mm screen. The site is 400 m² in size. No radiocarbon dates are available for the site but, on the basis of its material remains; it is a Late Natufian site.

Natufian Sites in the Irano-Turanian hills

(a) **Tabaqa (Wadi al-Hasa 895):** This Early Natufian site occupies a remnant terrace of Wadi Ahmar (710 m asl), a major tributary of Wadi el-Hasa in southern Jordan (Byrd and Colledge 1991). Burton MacDonald's survey team originally discovered this site in 1982. A surface collection and a small sounding were conducted in 1986 under Byrd's direction. All material was sieved through a 3 mm screen. Renewed excavations, under the direction of Olszewski, took place in 1997 (Olszewski 1998). The actual volume, or percentage, of the site excavated is unknown as the dimensions of the soundings are not published. However, it is known that one sounding was excavated in 1986 with an additional four soundings excavated in 1997 (probably 1m by 1m). The site approaches 1,200 m² in area but is partially destroyed by erosion. No radiocarbon dates are available.

(b) **Khallat Anaza (Black Desert Survey 14/7):** This open-air site lies on a small outcrop of jagged basalt slabs, overlooking a bend in Wadi Rajil (878 m asl), a few kilometers downstream from the site of Jawa in northeastern Jordan (Betts: 1986; 1988; 1998). Although much of the area is deflated, the site covers an area upwards of 2,000 m². No radiocarbon dates are available for the site but, based on the near absence of lunates with Helwan retouch; Khallat Anaza is a Late Natufian site. Crews of the Black Desert survey, initiated in 1981, carried out a total of three field seasons at Khallat Anaza with a total excavation of 12 m² or 0.6 % of the site (Betts 1986). All material was sieved through a 3 mm screen.

(c) **Wadi Judayid (J2):** This open-air site lies at the foot of an alluvial terrace on a plateau near the eastern margin of the Juyayid basin (1100 m asl) (Henry 1995). In 1979, a 1 m by 5 m trench was tested. The following year, four 1 m by 1 m units were excavated. The Natufian deposit is 50 to 60 cm deep. All material was sieved through a 3 mm screen. Judging by surface scatter, the site is approximately 400 m² in size. Three radiocarbon dates (12,090 ± 800; 12,750 ± 1000; 12,780 ± 660 or 14,500 to 11,200 cal BC) indicate an Early Natufian occupation.

Sites not included in the study

Israel

The majority of sites included in this research are from Israel but a substantial number of sites remain excluded. As indicated earlier, the reason for this exclusion was lack of excavation or excavation reports. Numerous sites in the Negev could potentially be included in this research. Problems of site classification (whether Terminal Ramonian, Natufian or Harifian) and site disturbance through erosion have made inclusion impossible. Gorring-Morris (1987:257-284) provides a comprehensive list of sites surveyed and recorded in the Negev.

Jordan

Coverage of Natufian sites in Jordan is high for this research, but a few sites that could not be included are worth mentioning.

One of these is 'Ala Safat, discovered in the 1940s (Waechter 1948). It is located on the eastern slopes of the Jordan River valley. This was the first Natufian site discovered in Transjordan but publication does not indicate its exact geographical coordinates, only indicating that it is a few kilometers east of Jisr Damiya (Damiya Bridge). The chipped-stone industry is the only artifact class discussed in the publication.

Other sites not included in this research could be considered *sibling sites* in that they occur in the same wadi, or very near, sites that are included in the research. These sites deserve a closer inspection but activity has been limited to surface collections or small soundings because of time and resource constraints of other ongoing projects. These sites include WHS 1065 (a possible Natufian component) and Yutil Hasa, both located in Wadi Hasa, near Tabaqa, and Jebel ash-Shubi, located in the Black Desert in the vicinity of Khallat Anaza.

Lebanon

Several Natufian *occurrences* are reported in Lebanon but the publications of these sites are not well known. Aside from Saiide II, other sites that deserve further investigation include 'Ain Sha'ib, Ji'ita III, Ji'ita II East, Burj Barajne, Antelias, and Nashsharini Cave. Schroeder (1976) indicates that Nashsharini Cave, located in the Anti-Lebanon Mountains, has an *in situ* Natufian occupation. Copeland (1991) questions the validity of an *in* situ Natufian occupation because there are several occupational phases, many disturbed, at the site. Continued survey of the Nashsharini area is under the direction of Andrew Garrard as well, survey or the Qadisha Valley in Lebanon is also turning up Natufian material (Garrard et al. 2003, Garrard and Yazbeck 2003).

Syria

Abu Hureya 1 is an open-air Late Natufian site on the lower terrace of a flood plain in the valley of the Euphrates River, 130 km east of Aleppo (Moore 1991). The entire site, including Abu Hureyra 2, a Neolithic village, consists of a mound approximately 11.5 ha in extent. Although there are no published Figures, the Late Natufian component extends over 112 m^2. Abu Hureyra was discovered during a salvage campaign that took place prior to the construction of the Assad Dam across the Euphrates and now lays underwater. Excavation took place in 1972 and 1973 with 49 m^2 of the Natufian level uncovered. A total of 17 radiocarbon dates for Abu Hureyra 1 indicate a continuous occupation from ca. 11,500 - 10,000 BP (Moore et al. 2000).

Aside from Abu Hureyra, other Natufian sites in Syria deserve closer examination but are not be included in this research. One of these, the Ba'az Rockshelter, excavated in 1999, is located 35 km northeast of Damascus. To date, only one publication is available (Conard 2002). Radiocarbon dates from this site (10,942 ± 65, 10,667 ± 97. and 10,470 ± 121 BP; 10,933 to 10,416 cal BC) indicate a Late Natufian occupation. Further published information on Ba'az Rockshelter is anticipated. Four sites, Jayroud 1, 2, 3, and 9, investigated in the early 1980s, are defined as Natufian (Cauvin 1991). While their existence is known and cited in publications that compare Natufian assemblages and site locations, there is very little published data on these sites. One other significant site, Mureybet, is identified as a Final Natufian site. It is 86 km southeast of Aleppo, near the Euphrates River and northwest of Abu Hureyra.

Figure 4.2 Location of Natufian sites used in this research. 1 'Ain as-Saratan; 2 'Ain Rahub; 3 Beidha; 4 el Wad; 5 Kebarah; 6 Faza'el IV; 7 Givat Hayil I; 8 Hatoula; 9 Hayonim Cave and Terrace; 10 Hilazon Tachtit; 11 Khallat Anaza; 12 Mallaha; 13 Nahal Ein Gev II; 14 Nahal Oren; 15 Nahal Sekher VI; 16 Rosh Horesha; 17 Rosh Zin; 18 Saflulim; 19 Salibiya I; 20 Tabaqa; 21 Upper Besor 6; 22 Wadi Hammeh 27; 23 Wadi Humeima; 24 Wadi Judayid; 25 Wadi Mataha.

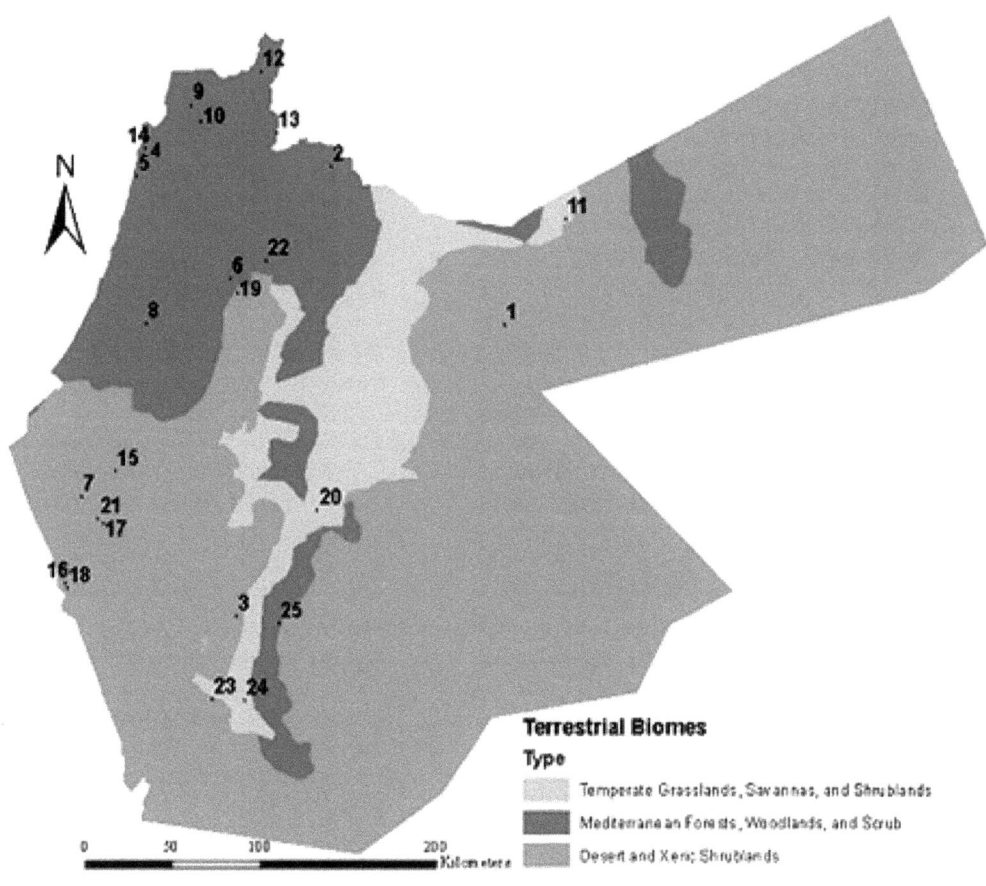

Material Culture

The previous section discusses the physical and historical characteristics of Natufian sites used in this research. Aside from the grouping of sites based on terrestrial biome (Mediterranean forests, Irano-Turanian hills, and Saharo-Arabian desert), phase (Early or Late Natufian), and site type (open-air, rock-shelter or cave), no other similarities or groupings are of sites are identified at this stage of research. This information is general in scope because it does not reveal any information on the past human populations inhabiting these archaeological sites. The next stage in the description of Natufian data is to move from this general data level, the site, to the more specific data level, the assemblage within the site. The goal here is to describe the material culture through the creation of typologies. Banning (2000:53) defines typology as "a classification or grouping that has explanatory (or meaningful) relationships with attributes that are not intrinsic to the classification or grouping itself." Adams and Adams (1991: xvi-xvii) state that the creation of typologies is not an automatic or objective process. Rather, typologies are created to serve human purposes. While this section does not address typologies in the Natufian assemblage *per se*, the statement made by Adams and Adams has meaning in that how humans organize material objects, whether in the present by the archaeologists or in the past, serves a purpose. As already demonstrated, in examining the concept of Natufian and the idea of *agency* in a historical context, typology has served a purpose, albeit one concerned primarily with the creation of a culture in a historical, spatial, and ecological context.

Classification – Dunnell

According to Dunnell (1971:200), systematics involves "the procedures for the creation of sets of units derived from a logical system for a specific purpose." Essentially, systematics involves the *arrangement* of objects. Dunnell (1971:43) further defines arrangement as encompassing "any activity which has as its product an order or orders, any procedure which [sic] leads to *unitizing*." There are two types of arrangement: classification and grouping. Classification is the creation of units of meaning by stipulating redundancies (classes), while grouping, on the other hand, creates units of things (groups) (Dunnell 1971:44). To explain further the differences between classification and grouping, it is proposed that classification belongs in the ideational realm while grouping is part of the phenomenological realm. The ideational realm includes those things that have no objective existence, such as ideas, while the phenomenological realm consists of those things that we can observe, such as physical objects and events (Dunnell 1971:26). Given these definitions, Dunnell (1971:44) also states that classification and grouping are connected by means of identification – the process of using classes to assign phenomena to groups.

Strictly focusing on classification, for the moment, there are two major types of classification: paradigmatic and taxonomic. In paradigmatic classification, "the classes are defined by means of unordered, un-weighted, dimensional features", that are formed by intersection of dimensions (Dunnell 1971:84). Taxonomic classification refers to the definition of classes through serial ordering, weighting and non-dimensional features; classes are defined by means of distinction or subdivision (Dunnell 1971:84). Regardless of whether classification is paradigmatic or taxonomic, creating these units of meaning or redundancy must follow a set of "axioms" or statements (Dunnell 1971:46-59):

1. *Classification is arbitrary*: classification can produce an infinite number of levels and the term arbitrary means that discriminations made are not limited to the phenomenological world.
2. *Classification is a matter of qualifications*: classification is a process involving units that are qualities (not quantities) that serve both as input and output.
3. *Classification states relations only within and between units in the same system*: classifications are systems of classes and these classes are closed.
4. *Classificatory units have primacy over labels applied to such units*: a label can never bear a necessary relationship to the class; a label is simply a device to identify the class for purpose of discussion.
5. *Classification, classifications, and classificatory units have primacy over structures, structuring, models, and mode-building*: models and structures are devices for illustrating relationships between classes which [sic] are not part of the same classification.

This brief description of Dunnell's principles of classification serves the purpose of helping to organize or arrange the material culture of the Natufian archaeological sites previously discussed.

While one appreciates that Dunnell is one of the first to attempt to build a theory for classification in archaeology (Read 1982:62), there are also those who do not agree with his proposals. One of the main problems with Dunnell's *Systematics in Prehistory* (1971) is that, although he acknowledges that classification is a cognitive action that depends on *a priori* knowledge at an individual and group level, he then attempts to place the action of classification into a formal, empiricist realm. Salmon (1982:151) states that Dunnell admits that choice of particular classificatory scheme depends on which problems the classification is designed to solve but he then advocates a single, general model of classification. Watson (1986:446), in her critique of Dunnell's empirical approach, also questions his emphasis on "the hard phenomena of the archaeological record." In a more recent publication (Adams and Adams 1991:273), criticism is not only directed at Dunnell's empirical approach but also at his obscure theoretical position that only has limited reference to the real world. Adams and

Adams (1991:273) also argue that the dialectical factor – "the continual feedback between objects and our conceptions of them" – is not recognized.

Types of Classification

One can understand, through the introduction of Dunnell and the concept of systematics, that the meaningful arrangement of material culture or artifacts from archaeological sites is possible. Given the critiques of Dunnell's proposed empirical classification scheme, it is clear that there is more to classification of artifacts than empirical reduction. Table 4.1 (adapted from Adams and Adams 1991:216-217) illustrates that several classification schemes are available. Although each scheme suits a general and specific purpose, they are not mutually exclusive. This research is inclusive in that no one archaeological classification is employed exclusively. This will become evident in the following section, in defining the classes.

For this research, the terminology that Dunnell introduces is used because the goal here is to arrange the material culture into purposive, meaningful units. In addition to Dunnell's terminology, two other words need to be introduced: variable and attribute. In Whallon and Brown's 1982 edited publication, *Essays in Archaeological Typology*, the terms variable and attribute are discussed in detail in the first three chapters (Spaulding 1982; Hodson 1982; and Cowgill 1982). To summarize the arguments, there are two traditions of use for these terms, the mathematical/statistics tradition and social science tradition. The first point of view makes no distinction between variable and attribute. Both are a trait or characteristic of an object that can vary from observation to observation (Dunnell 1971:200; Hodson 1982:22; Walsh and Ollenburger 2001:301). The latter draws a distinction between the two terms in that the term, variable, applies to a kind of observation on an object and is taken into account in the definition or description of types (e.g., length, color, sex), while the term attribute refers to the state or score of a variable (e.g., 5 cm, red, female). For the purposes of this research, I will use the latter definitions for variable and attribute.

Table 4.1: Kinds of archaeological classification and their purposes (after Adams & Adams 1991:216-216).

Kinds of Classification	Kinds of Purpose	Specific Purpose
Phenetic	Descriptive	Economically describe material from one site
	Comparative	Describe and compare material from different sites
	Analytical-intrinsic	Learn about nature and variability of material classified
	Incidental	Convenience of filing and storage
Stylistic	Analytical-intrinsic	Learn about stylistic evolution
	Ancillary	Ethnic and cultural identification
		Chronological ordering of associated materials Reconstruction of social and economic patterns
		Learn spatial distribution of material classified
Chronological/ Spatial	Analytical-historical	Learn historical development of material classified
	Ancillary	Dating of associated materials and sites
		Use as basis for defining "cultures"
		Chronological seriation of sites and "cultures"
Functional	Analytical-interpretive	Reconstruct activities of makers and users
	Ancillary	Identify different activity areas or sites
Emic	Analytical-interpretive	Understand mind-set of makers and users
"Cultural"	Descriptive	Define and differentiate prehistoric "culture" units
	Analytical-historical	Seriate "cultures" units in successive stages
	Ancillary	Construct basic time/space grid for ordering artifacts and sites

Variables and Attributes in Relation to Classification

Table 4.2 illustrates the variables, attributes and the related kind of classification used for the Natufian archaeological data. An issue to address is the selection of variables and their corresponding attributes. It is observed that the variables, for the most part, are characterized by raw material (shell, ground stone, basalt, bone, etc.). The decision to select variables based on raw material was due to (a) the publication record and (b) the resource location of the raw material. All publications classify artifacts on the basis of their raw material rather than the function or form of the artifact. In other words, bone points and chipped stone points are never classified together. In addition, basalt mortars and ground-stone mortars are also classified differently, regardless of the similar (or even identical) technology used to produce these artifacts and similar (or even identical) function.

The geographical locations of raw materials also play an important role in that not all materials are available throughout the archaeological region. The occurrences of some species of marine shell are restricted to either the Red Sea (e.g., *Dentalium elephantinum*, *Nerita* species and *Cypreae moneta*), the Mediterranean Sea (e.g., *Collumbella* species, *Nassa* species, and *Glycymeris* species), or fresh-water sources (e.g., *Theodoxus jordani*). Conversely, basalt outcrops occur throughout the region, but in specific locations.

Table 4.2: Variables and attributes defined for research.

Variable	Attributes	Kind of Classification
Shell	Various species in three classes: Gastropoda, Bivalves and Scaphopoda	Phenetic (morphological), Chronological/Spatial
Ground-stone	Mortar, pestle, quern, etc.	Phenetic (morphological), Chronological/Spatial, Stylistic
Basalt	Mortar; pestle, quern, etc.	Phenetic (morphological), Chronological/Spatial, Stylistic
Bone	Needle awl, point, etc.	Phenetic (morphological), Chronological/Spatial, Stylistic
Chipped Stone	Scraper, perforator, notched, retouched, geometric microlith, etc.	Phenetic (morphological), Chronological/Spatial, Stylistic
Features	Wall, bedrock mortar, pit, hearth, burial	Phenetic Chronological/Spatial, Stylistic
Exotics	Ochre, greenstone, ostrich shell, raptor claw, etc.	Chronological/Spatial

The attributes are related to the state of the variables. In examining the attributes for each variable, it becomes apparent that the kind of classification plays a role in the attributes. For example, mollusc class and species are used for the variable, shell. These attributes are both phenetic (morphological) and chronological/spatial. The classification is phenetic in that it serves the purpose of (a) describing the material from one site (descriptive); (b) comparing material from different sites (comparative), and (c) informing about the nature and variability of the material classified (analytical-intrinsic). Shell classification is also chronological/spatial in that it serves the purpose of helping us to understand the spatial distribution of material classified (analytical-historical).

Classification of several variables (ground stone, basalt, bone, chipped stone, and features) is through stylistic classification. Stylistic classification has an ancillary purpose in that it can say something about ethnic or cultural identification. This identification can extend to individual and group identification. This ancillary purpose also applies to the reconstruction of social patterns, the primary objective of this research. The objective of this research is not to understand the mindset of the makers and users (i.e., *chaînes opératoire*), but decisions by individuals or groups and the sharing of information, part of social patterning and identification, are interconnected to mindset through analytical-interpretive purpose.

Encoding the Data

A final concern regarding the material culture, aside from classification, purpose of classification, and variables and their associated attributes, is the method for recording the data. Attribute data is measured through four scales, or systems of measurement: nominal, ordinal, interval and ratio. The nominal scale consists of categories that are mutually exclusive, unordered and of equal weight. One form of nominal-scale data is known as binary or dichotomous data. This kind of nominal data consists of only two categories, such as present/absent, or female/male. Ordinal data consist of categories that are ordered or ranked, such as "Early", "Late", and "Final" Natufian. Interval data is ordered and there is also a precisely defined interval (or distance) between the data. The ordering and equal distance of intervals is best illustrated by stating that the distance between 3 and 5 is the same as the distance between 6 and 8 or 7 and 9 (Banning 2000:9). Ratio data are essentially the same as interval data with the exception that zero points are non-arbitrary and express "an absolute absence of some quantity" (Banning 2000:9). A good example of ratio data would be volume excavated in cubic meters, or area of excavation in square meters.

These four scales or measurements are further categorized into either discrete or continuous data. Discrete data is made up of indivisible or non-fractional units and the data is classified according to their characteristics. Nominal and ordinal data are always discrete. Interval and ratio data, on the other hand, although frequently continuous, can also be discrete. Continuous data can theoretically take on any value between two points on a scale and be classified according to their characteristics.

The first step in assigning a scale or measurement to the attribute data is to decide whether it should be continuous or discrete. In the case of the attribute data used in this research, the data could be either discrete or continuous. Possible scales of measurement that can be used to characterize the material culture in this research include dichotomous (such as present/absent), ordinal (such as Early/Late or low/medium/high), or ratio (for example, representing a percentage of either the total assemblage or variable or an actual count of the attribute in the assemblage). The method of data measurement will affect the kind of research questions asked and analysis that can be conducted.

For this research, I decided to use nominal measurements in dichotomous format for the attribute data. As indicated in the previous section on the history of research at Natufian sites, there is diversity in the period of excavation (in terms of number of seasons) as well as the extent of excavation (in terms of volume excavated). This affects the quantity of information recovered, as represented by artifact count that can potentially lead to bias in analysis. A second issue concerns the level of reporting for each archaeological site. If all material culture is quantified for each site, other forms of measurement are possible. This, however, is not the case for the Natufian data. Some site reports record only the presence and quality of material culture, but not the quantity. The absence of empirical data for some variables makes it difficult to encode using an ordinal or ratio scale.

To demonstrate the difficulties outlined, I decided to examine the probability of an object being present given the size, or area, of an archaeological site as well as the volume excavated. For this example, I use Red Sea Dentalium as the variable of interest. Of the 26 Natufian sites, 15 report the number of Red Sea Dentalium recovered. The scatterplot illustrated in Figure 4.3 shows the association between the number of Red Sea Dentalium recovered from each site and its corresponding size (area). A local linear regression (LLR) curve is added to the plot to demonstrate that, although there is a general trend where site size is correlated to number of Dentalium recovered, there are also data fluctuations. Using site size to predict the presence and quantity of an object is not a good measure because there are several factors that can affect (a) the size of the site, and (b) the chance of artifact recovery. These factors include site type (open air versus cave or rock shelter), thickness of deposit (indication of multiple periods of occupation), volume excavated, and deflation.

Given the decision to use a dichotomous measurement for the data, there is one exception, the chipped-stone data. This variable, and its corresponding attributes, are in a continuous data format using a ratio scale (percentage of total chipped stone tool in each assemblage). The rationale for this decision is twofold: (1) all published reports record the lithics in percentage of total tool type and, (2) all sites contain the tool classes (attributes) used, so all sites would show a measurement of "present." This presents two scales of data that introduces a set of issues that are addressed in the following chapter on methodology.

Figure 4.3 Scatter plots correlating the area of Natufian sites with the number of Red Sea Dentalium. A local linear regression (LLR) curve is added to the plot to demonstrate data fluctuations.

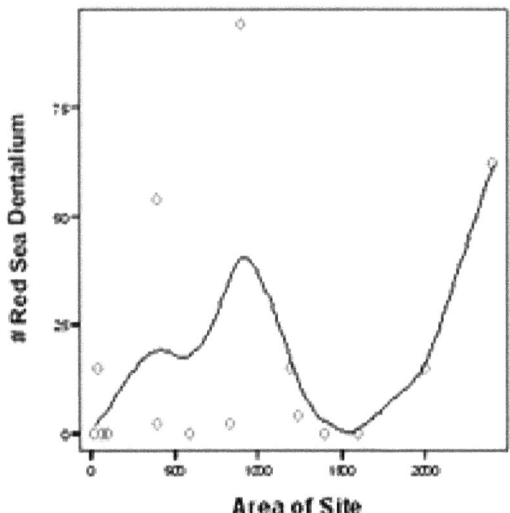

Summary

This research consists of more than one type of data. This chapter concentrates on archaeological data at a variety of levels. The first level is that of the archaeological sites. Each site used in this research is briefly described and given a historical account of research conducted. From this section, it can be concluded that each Natufian site is unique in its location, dimensions, consideration, and time period. Sites not included in this research are acknowledged to illustrate the potential size of the data. However, inclusions of these sites are not possible for this research because of lack of sufficient publication.

The next level is that of the assemblage (material culture) of the Natufian sites used in this research. There are several concerns to address regarding the material culture. The notion of classification of material culture and the theory and methods used to support kinds of classification have a long history. This history needs to be acknowledged prior to describing the classification design used in this research. It is concluded that, while the terminology that Dunnell provides in his 1971 book, *Systematics in Prehistory*, constitutes an adequate starting point, there are other views that are more applicable to the design of the material culture for this research. While I acknowledge that classification is the arrangement of objects into units of meaning, this arrangement serves a purpose and this purpose may vary from object to object. The decision on terminology regarding the objects (artifacts) and the state or value of the object is also addressed. The terms variable and attribute sufficiently meet the needs for this research.

Once the issue of classification is addressed, the measurement scale of the attribute data needs to be examined. After reviewing the different ways of measuring or scaling the data, I decided that, with exception of the chipped-stone variables, the data would be encoded as dichotomous, in that a binary unit of present or absent is used. The following chapter discusses methods for analyzing this dichotomous data.

CHAPTER 5
METHODS PART I – CLUSTER ANALYSIS

Introduction to Clustering

This chapter outlines the first method in the process of grouping Natufian sites. The previous chapter illustrated that material culture can be classified in various ways (phenetic, stylistic, chronological/spatial). Previous research on Natufian material culture has focused on the "cultural" classification, whose goal is to define and differentiate prehistoric culture units; to organize these units in successive stages, and to construct basic time/space grids for the ordering of artifacts (Pirie 2005). This research has different goals. Here, classification is concerned with cultural identification, reconstruction of social patterns and to learn about the nature and variability of the material classified. In this sense, the kind of classification with which this research is concerned can be considered phenetic and stylistic for analytical-intrinsic and ancillary purposes.

Cluster analysis is a multivariate statistical technique used to group similar data using multiple attributes (Aldenderfer & Blashfield 1984:7; Everitt 1993:4; Romesburg 1990:2). This technique, first implemented in the fields of biology and zoology, is also used in other sciences and social sciences under the names numerical taxonomy, Q-analysis, unsupervised pattern recognition, and grouping. Cluster analysis can be used to achieve five main goals: (1) developing a general - or specific - purpose typology; (2) investigation of useful conceptual schemes for grouping identities; (3) data exploration; (4) hypothesis testing and; (5) facilitating planning and management (Aldenderfer & Blashfield 1984:9; Romesburg 1990:262-274). For the purpose of this research, cluster analysis is used as an exploratory tool to generate a scheme for Natufian group identity and to test the hypotheses concerning Natufian interaction within the archaeological region generated in chapter three. To reiterate, I hypothesize that Natufian interactions are related to semi-sedentary occupation of the large settlements and logistical organization where social interaction is based on a model of aggregation and dispersion of Natufian groups. This aggregation occurs in the Mediterranean forest with dispersion occuring in the Irano-Turanian hills and Sahara desert.

Prior to clustering the data, several steps should be considered (Milligan 1996).

1. *Objects to cluster*: Objects should be representative of the cluster structure believed to be present.
2. *Variables to be used*: Variables should only be included if there is reason to think they will define the clusters. Redundant (masking) variables should be excluded. A solution to this problem is to employ the data matrix to suggest variable weights.
3. *Variable standardization*: Not necessarily always indicated and can sometimes be misleading. A solution to the problem of choosing an appropriate unit of measurement is to employ a cluster method that is invariant under scaling.
4. *Similarity measurement*: There are a few general guidelines for this but knowledge of the context and type of data may suggest suitable choices.
5. *Cluster Method*: Methods should be designed to recover the types of clusters suspected; effective at recovering them; insensitive to error; and available in software. It is also advisable to consider data-generating processes, and this might suggest the application of a model-based method.
6. *Number of Clusters*: Where different stopping rules suggest different numbers, the highest should be taken to be conservative. An alternative would be to consider the possibility that there are no clusters present.
7. *Replication, testing and interpretation*: Can include cross-validation techniques to investigate how far clusters identified in the sub-sample are still identifiable among the sub sample of objects not used in the clustering.

Chapter four covers the first two steps. A total of 29 Natufian sites are sampled. Among the 29 Natufian sites, eight variables used in the cluster analysis are identified: shell, chipped-stone tools, bone, basalt, ground stone, features, exotics, and burials. A total of 100 attributes are included in the variables. The choice to convey the attributes as discrete dichotomous data was also addressed in the previous chapter. Each attribute is given a numerical value – 1 for present, 0 for absent. The lithic variables are presented as continuous interval data – represented by percentage of entire lithic tools for each site. Appendix A gives a detailed list of the sites along with the attributes and variables used in this study.

The third step concerns the standardization, or creation of uniformity, of the data. According to Romesburg (1990:78), there are two reasons for standardizing data: (1) the data type (nominal, ordinal, interval, ratio) selected for measuring attributes can arbitrarily affect similarity among objects (sites), and (2) standardization makes attributes contribute more equally to the similarities among objects (sites). Many texts on cluster analysis (see Aldenderfer and Blashfield 1984:20-21 for a good review) question the need for standardization of the data prior to clustering of the data. Standardization of the data can reduce differences between groups based on the variables that may be the best discriminators. In addition, standardizing each variable could obscure possible correlations between variables (Everitt 1993:38-39). If the data are in different formats, the following alternatives to standardization can be considered: (a) convertion to binary variables; (b) separate analysis of each variable and synthesis of the results; and (c) employing mixture models (Everitt 1993:39). Because all the attributes for the variables, with the exception of chipped-stone tools, have been recorded in binary (dichotomous) format, standardization is not necessary. Individual analysis will be carried out for each variable and synthesized. This allows observation of the individual variables and addresses the different data format used for the chipped-stone data.

This chapter focuses on steps four through seven. I begin with a detailed examination of the techniques used in step four through the creation of the proximity matrix. It becomes clear that step three is very important because it sets the stage for the resulting clusters in step five. Methods and techniques for clustering and validation of the clusters are reviewed. It also becomes clear that clustering the data can be a simple, yet powerful, technique used to explore and generate models for Natufian interaction within the archaeological region.

Proximity Matrix - Similarity measures for binary data

There are four similarity measures or coefficients identified: correlation coefficients, distance measures, association coefficients, and probabilistic similarity measures. I will discuss all four similarity measures but, association coefficients receive more attention because they are the most frequently used similarity measures for binary data.

Correlation coefficients are also termed angular measures because of their geometric interpretations of the data (Aldenderfer & Blashfield 1984:22). One of the most popular correlation coefficients is the Pearson's product moment coefficient, which measures the linear association between two variables. This coefficient is commonly used for interval data, while a product moment coefficient, known as the Phi 4-Point Correlation, is commonly used for binary data. While this coefficient is popular among social scientists, there are problems. The major problem is its sensitivity to shape at the expense of the extent of difference between the variables or attributes (Aldenderfer & Blashfield 1984:23). In other words, two sets of cases can have an identical correlation measure, or shape, yet not be identical.

Dissimilarity coefficients, also known as distance measures, evaluate the distinction between a pair of cases (sites) based on their variables and attributes. Several techniques to calculate dissimilarity are identified. The common feature of most distance measures is that they have a metric property where $d_{ij} + d_{ik} \geq d_{jk}$ (Everitt 1993:46). The most well-known of the distance measures is Euclidian distance but it is believed to be unsatisfactory in that its value depends on the scale of the variables chosen. This makes it an unsuitable distance measure for binary data. Three other popular distance measures include the squared Euclidean, Manhattan, Minkowski and Mahalanobis. These distance measures are also subject to data type and are not suitable for binary data. Distance-measure analogues for binary data include pattern difference and variance.

For **probabilistic similarity measures**, the distance is not actually calculated. When clusters are formed, the information *gain* of the combination of two cases (sites) is evaluated while the combination of cases that provides the least amount of *gain* is fused or grouped (Aldenderfer & Blashfield 1984:33). Use of this similarity measure is unique in that it can only be applied to binary data.

Association Coefficients

Association coefficients measure the strength of the relationship between a pair of cases (sites) based on the variables and their attributes (Aldenderfer & Blashfield 1984:17; Cheetham & Hazel 1969; Everitt 1993:40; Romesburg 1990:12). The most frequently used association coefficients are for binary variables, with greater than twenty measures developed. For a comprehensive discussion of the available association coefficients see Romesburg 1990; Sokal and Sneath 1973 and Gower 1985.

Essentially, the association coefficient works with the number of 1-1, 1-0, 0-1, and 0-0 matches in a two-by-two table. Below is an example to illustrate, on the basis of the number of matches in the two-by-two table, a number of similarity coefficient formulas that can be applied. For comparative purposes, I will only illustrate nine of the more popular association coefficients.

Table 5.1. Section of the data matrix coded with qualitative data - 1 for present, 0 for absent

	Site	
Attribute	Rosh Horesha	Rosh Zin
theodoxus jordani	1	0
dentaluim-med	1	1
dentaluim-red	1	1
nerita-red	0	0
cowrie-red	0	1
conus-red	0	0
nassa-med	1	1
columbella-med	1	1
conus-med	0	0

Table 5.2. A two-by-two table giving the number of 1-1, 1-0, 0-1, and 0-0 matches from the data matrix shown in Table 5.1

		Rosh Zin	
		1	0
Rosh Horesha	1	$a=4$	$b=1$
	0	$c=1$	$d=3$

(a) **Jaccard Coefficient**: indicates maximum similarity when the two cases have identical positive (1-1) values. A value of 1.0 represents perfect similarity and a value of 0.0 represents perfect dissimilarity. This coefficient does not take into account 0-0 matches. The coefficient is written as:

$$C_{RH, RZ} = \frac{a}{a+b+c} \quad 0.0 \leq C_{RH, RZ} \leq 1.0$$

Using the example data of Table 5.2,

$$C_{RH, RZ} = \frac{4}{4+1+1} = 0.7$$

(b) **Simple Matching Coefficient**: similar to Jaccard coefficient with the exception that both 1-1 and 0-0 matches are given equal weight. This gives the coefficient intuitive meaning. Again, a value of 1.0 represents perfect similarity and a value of 0.0 represents perfect dissimilarity. The coefficient is written as:

$$C_{RH, RZ} = \frac{a+d}{a+b+c+d} \quad 0.0 \leq C_{RH, RZ} \leq 1.0$$

Using the example data of Table 5.2,

$$C_{RH, RZ} = \frac{4+3}{4+1+1+3} = 0.8$$

(c) **Yule Coefficient**: similar to the simple matching coefficient, in that both 1-1 and 0-0 matches are given equal weight, with the exception that the range goes from 1.0 to -1.0 where a value of 1.0 represents perfect similarity and a value of -1.0 represents perfect dissimilarity. A 0 value represents the midway point between the two extremes. The coefficient is written as:

$$C_{RH, RZ} = \frac{ad - bc}{ad + bc} \quad -1.0 \leq C_{RH, RZ} \leq 1.0$$

Using the example data of Table 5.2,

$$C_{RH, RZ} = \frac{(4)(3) - (1)(1)}{(4)(3) + (1)(1)} = 0.85$$

(d) **Hamann Coefficient**: similar to the Yule coefficient except the Hamann coefficient relates variables by addition rather than multiplication. Again, a value of 1.0 represents perfect similarity and a value of -1.0 represents perfect dissimilarity with a 0 value representing the midway point between the two extremes The coefficient is written as:

$$C_{RH, RZ} = \frac{(a+d) - (b+c)}{(a+d) + (b+c)} \quad -1.0 \leq C_{RH, RZ} \leq 1.0$$

Using the example data of Table 5.2,

$$C_{RH, RZ} = \frac{(4+3) - (1+1)}{(4+3) + (1+1)} = 0.6$$

(e) **Sørenson Coefficient**: this coefficient, like the Jaccard coefficient, does not include 0-0 matches but, it gives 1-1 matches double weight. This coefficient is also known as the Dice coefficient. The coefficient is written as:

$$C_{RH, RZ} = \frac{2a}{2a+b+c} \quad 0.0 \leq C_{RH, RZ} \leq 1.0$$

Using the example data of Table 5.2,

$$C_{RH, RZ} = \frac{8}{8+1+1} = 0.8$$

(f) **Rogers and Tanimoto Coefficient**: similar to simple matching in that both 1-1 and 0-0 matches are included but, 0-1 and 1-0 matches are given double weight. With this coefficient, perfect similarity is achieved if $b = c = 0$. The coefficient is written as:

$$C_{RH, RZ} = \frac{a+d}{a+2(b+c)+d} \quad 0.0 \leq C_{RH, RZ} \leq 1.0$$

Using the example data of Table 5.2,

$$C_{RH, RZ} = \frac{4+3}{4+2(1+1)+3} = 0.64$$

(g) **Sokal and Sneath Coefficient**: again, this coefficient is similar to simple matching in that both 1-1 and 0-0 matches are included but, 0-1 and 1-0 matches are given half weight. Like Rogers and Tanimoto, perfect similarity is achieved if $b = c = 0$. The coefficient is written as:

$$C_{RH, RZ} = \frac{2(a+d)}{2(a+d)+b+c} \quad 0.0 \leq C_{RH, RZ} \leq 1.0$$

Using the example data of Table 5.2,

$$C_{RH, RZ} = \frac{2(4+3)}{2(4+3)+1+1} = 0.88$$

(h) **Russell and Rao Coefficient**: this coefficient measures the proportion of 1-1 matches in the total number n cases. This coefficient resembles the Jaccard coefficient in that 0-0 matches are not included, therefore it stresses perfect similarity. The coefficient is written as:

$$C_{RH, RZ} = \frac{a}{a+b+c+d} \quad 0.0 \leq C_{RH, RZ} \leq 1.0$$

Using the example data of Table 5.2,

$$C_{RH, RZ} = \frac{4}{4 + 1 + 1 + 3} = 0.44$$

(i) **Ochiai Coefficient**: this is known as a cosine coefficient for binary data where the cases are viewed as "two points in their attribute space and each point is connected by a line from their origin" where $C_{RH, RZ}$ is the cosine of the angle between the two lines (Romesburg 1990:100). 0-0 matches are not included in the coefficient and the values range from 1.0, perfect similarity, to 0.0, perfect dissimilarity. The coefficient is written as:

$$C_{RH, RZ} = \frac{a}{[(a+b)(a+c)]^{1/2}} \qquad 0.0 \leq C_{RH, RZ} \leq 1.0$$

Using the example data of Table 5.2,

$$C_{RH, RZ} = \frac{4}{[(4+1)(4+1)]^{1/2}} = 0.8$$

Choice of Similarity Coefficient

The previous section focused on association coefficients because they have the most wide-spread use when data is in binary format. It is observed from these examples that there are some common resemblances among several of the coefficients. These resemblances include the inclusion of 0-0 matches in measuring similarity, and the scale ranging from either 0.0 to 1.0 or -1.0 to 1.0. The resemblances between the coefficients can be further illustrated. Romesburg (1990:151) points out that the sharing of common variables also plays a part in the correlation of the coefficients. For example, if there were no 0-0 matches in a data matrix, the Jaccard and Simple Matching coefficient would be identical. A second issue is known as a monotonic relationship. The principle of a monotonic relationship is that "because of their mathematical properties, in some cases the coefficients are perfectly correlated irrespective of the data used with them" (Romesburg 1990:151). These relationships will produce identical cluster trees (dendrograms). There are monotonic relations between the Jaccard and Sørenson (Dice) coefficient and between Simple Matching, Sokal and Sneath, Roger and Tanimoto, and Hamann coefficients.

In considering which similarity coefficient to use, the resemblances and monotonic relations must be taken into account. For example, in comparing similarity coefficients for the purpose of research, one may compare the results of several coefficients. There would be no point in comparing coefficients that have a monotonic relation because their outcome would be identical. This could be misconstrued as an effect of the data when, in fact, it is an effect of the coefficients compared.

There has been much written on the role of 0-0 matches and whether it is beneficial to include these matches in the similarity coefficient. Romesburg (1990:154), makes three points regarding the inclusion of 0-0 matches: (1) more often than not, 0-0 matches are used (2) similarity coefficients that leave the 0-0 matches out actually tend to correlate to those that include the matches, thus they produce identical cluster trees, and (3) logically, 0-0 matches contribute to similarity. Aldenderfer and Blashfield agree with Romesburg in stating that the decision to include 0-0 matches is not critical, but, they do call attention to how this issue can affect archaeological data. According to Aldenderfer and Blashfield (1984:29):

> The problem of whether to include negative matches has not apparently been an issue in most social sciences, but the problem has arisen in archaeology. If an object is not found with a burial, its absence may be due to either cultural prescriptions or natural processes of disintegration and attrition. It would be inappropriate to base the estimation of similarity between two burials upon the joint absence of an artifact if it is impossible to know which of the two possible explanations is responsible for the absence.

Outside of archaeology, the debate on whether or not to use 0-0 matches is not as clear. Boyce & Ellison (2001) compare similarity indices for ecological (botanical) in binary format. After testing nine indices, they conclude that the top four indices that consistently rank higher are also those that do not include 0-0 matches. In a discussion on the use of 0-0 matches, Boyce and Ellison (2001:717-718) remark that plant-community ecologists normally do not include 0-0 matches. Other plant community ecologists (Gower 1985; Legendre & Legendre 1998) suggest that indices that include 0-0 matches should not be used because of the lack of information for 0-0 matches and the unimodal distribution of the data in question (i.e., plants). This lack of information and unimodal distribution can be applied to archaeological data in the sense that a 0-0 match can have more than one meaning. For example, a 0-0 match can be affected by the sample size of material culture for a particular site, the excavation methods used for a site (sieving of material, surface collection versus test trench versus large scale excavation) and reporting style for publication.

Given this information, we know that (a) similarity coefficients that share a monotonic relationship would not make a good comparison and (b) the decision to use 0-0 matches does not seem to be critical, especially in the sciences, but there are certain instances where this may be misleading. The question now becomes – what similarity coefficient would be most beneficial to this research? Logic plays an important role in this decision. Referring to the similarity coefficients that were discussed previously, Table 5.3 summarizes the similarity measure for the nine coefficient equations applied to the data matrix in Table 5.2.

As this small data set illustrates, the distances calculated using the various equations differ. In comparing equations that include 0-0 matches with those that do not include the matches, we can see that there is not a critical difference. In fact, there is greater difference in distance when comparing techniques that include the 0-0 matches. For this research, I will use two similarity indices: one that includes 0-0 matches and one that does not.

The most common equations used in social science research using binary variables are Jaccard, Simple Matching and Sørenson (Dice) (Aldenderfer and Blashfield 1984:29; Romesburg 1990:151). Jaccard and Sørenson measures do not include 0-0 matches while the Simple Matching measure does. Additionally, the Jaccard and Sørenson measures have a monotonic relation. To further investigate the three similarity coefficients, a similarity matrix is prepared for all three measures using limited marine shell attributes for all 28 Natufian sites (see Appendix B). Examining the matrices for these three similarity coefficients it becomes evident that Jaccard and Sørenson do, in fact, have a very similar outcome compared to Simple Matching. What is interesting to note is that, when 0-0 matches are not included, extreme measures of similarity and dissimilarity occur, while inclusion of 0-0 matches results in fewer extreme measures. In fact, there are no two sites that are perfectly dissimilar. The similarity indices that I will use are Simple Matching, which includes 0-0 matches, and Sørenson, which does not. The decision to use these two indices is based on their measurement of similarity, rather than distance, and the fact that they do not have a monotonic relationship.

Table 5.3. Summary of similarity coefficient equations as well as the calculated similarity distance for the data matrix in Table 5.2

Similarity Coefficient	Includes 0-0 matches	Range	Similarity Distance
Jaccard	N	0 - 1	0.7
Simple Matching	Y	0 - 1	0.8
Yule	Y	-1 - 1	0.85
Hamann	Y	-1 - 1	0.6
Sørenson	N	0 - 1	0.8
Roger and Tanimoto	Y	0 - 1	0.64
Sokal and Sneath	Y	0 - 1	0.88
Russell and Rao	N	0 - 1	0.44
Ochiai	N	0 - 1	0.8

Clustering Methods

A cluster is a set of one or more objects that are similar to each other and is visually represented in a two-dimensional diagram known as a dendrogram or tree diagram (Everitt 1993:55; Romesburg 1990: 15). According to Sneath and Sokal (1973:202-213), there are eight aspects to clustering methods.

1. Agglomerative versus divisive methods: moving from several clusters to one cluster (agglomerative) or moving from one large cluster to several clusters (divisive).
2. Hierarchical versus nonhierarchical methods: clusters that exhibit rank (hierarchical) or those that do not exhibit rank (nonhierarchical).
3. Non-overlapping versus overlapping methods: whether the ranks are mutually exclusive (non-overlapping) or inclusive (overlapping).
4. Sequential versus simultaneous methods: whether a recursive sequence of operations is applied in clustering the cases through disjoint partition – agglomerative or conjoint partition – divisive (sequential) or not (simultaneous).
5. Local versus global criteria: relates to the degree of tight clustering at different hierarchical levels.
6. Direct versus iterative solutions: when a cluster method proceeds to the construction of a classification in a straight-forward manner and the solution arrived at is seen as optimal (direct) versus cluster procedures that are subject to self correction (iterative).
7. Weighted versus un-weighted clustering: to weigh certain types of variables and their attributes as more important (closer, tighter) than others through transformation.
8. Non-adaptive versus adaptive clustering: whether the cluster method proceed either directly or iteratively toward a solution in which the clustering method is fixed (non-adaptive), or *learns* through initial exploration of data types and modifies its methods (adaptive).

Taking into consideration these aspects of clustering, there are seven families of clustering methods (Aldenderfer & Blashfield 1984:35):

1. hierarchical agglomerative
2. hierarchical divisive
3. iterative partitioning
4. density search
5. factor analysis
6. clumping, and
7. graph theoretic

Of the seven families of clustering methods, the three most used in social sciences are hierarchical agglomerative, iterative partitioning and factor analysis (Aldenderfer & Blashfield 1984:35). Both iterative partitioning and factor analysis work primarily with quantitative data (interval or ratio) and will not be discussed. Binary analogues for iterative partitioning and factor analysis have been created, but their application is not common in archaeology. I intensively discuss hierarchical agglomerative clustering in this section for two reasons: (1) hierarchical procedures allow more flexibility in the use of a number of similarity measures; and (2) you do not need to specify the number of clusters *a priori*. For these reasons, several of the methods (density search, clumping and graph theoretic) are rarely discussed in publications on cluster analysis.

Hierarchical Clustering Methods

Hierarchical clustering is used when sets of objects are compared on the basis of a large number of weighted attributes and those objects that are most similar are grouped together and compared by means of a coefficient of similarity or dissimilarity (Banning 2000). These groupings are then presented in a dendrogram or a tree diagram. The data are not partitioned into a particular number of clusters in a single step; rather the clustering consists of a series of partitions (Everitt 1993:55). The more common procedures for hierarchical grouping include single-linkage, complete-linkage, average-linkage, centroid, median and Ward's method (Aldenderfer & Blashfield 1984; Everett 1993; Romesburg 1990). Table 5.4 summarizes these methods.

(a) **Single Linking:** This method, also known as nearest neighbor, is one of the simplest agglomerative hierarchical methods. In this clustering method, "cases are joined to existing clusters if at least one of the members of the existing cluster is of the same level of similarity as the case under consideration" (Aldenderfer & Blashfield 1984:38). Single linkage operates directly on the similarity matrix. This method is good for large data sets.

(b) **Complete Linking:** This method, also known as farthest neighbor, is the opposite of single linking. Rather than calculating the distance of the closest pair of cases, the distance between groups is now defined as that of the most distant pair of individuals. Complete linkage also operates directly on the similarity matrix.

(c) **Average Linking:** This method was developed as an alternative to the extremes of single and complete linking. Average linking calculates the average distance (similarity) of all pairs of cases. This method also operates directly on the similarity matrix.

(d) **Centroid:** With this method, clusters formed are represented by their mean value for each variable (Everitt 1993:62). Thus, the resemblance between two clusters is equal to the resemblance between their centroids – the centre (Romesburg 1990:136). Rather than operating directly on the similarity measure matrix, this method operates directly on the raw data.

(e) **Median:** This method is identical to the Centroid method with the exception that the variables/attributes are weighted. This method weighs the variables/attributes most recently admitted to a cluster equally with all previous members (Sneath & Sokal 1973:234). Again, this method operates on raw data.

(f) **Ward's:** this method forms partitions in a manner that minimizes the loss associated with grouping. According to Everitt (1993:65), "at each step in the analysis, union of every possible pair of clusters is considered and the two clusters whose fusion results in the minimum increase in information loss are combined." Ward's method also operates directly on the similarity matrix.

Table 5.4. Summary of hierarchical agglomerative clustering methods considered.

Method	Used With:	Distance between clusters:	Remarks
Single Linking (Nearest Neighbor)	Association or Distance	Minimum distance between pair of objects, one in one cluster, one in the other	Tends to produce unbalanced and straggly clusters (chaining), especially in large data sets. Does not take account of cluster structure
Complete Linking (Farthest Neighbor)	Association or Distance	Maximum distance between pair of objects, one in one cluster, one in the other	Tends to find compact clusters with equal diameters (max. distance between objects). Does not take account of cluster structure
Average Linking	Association or Distance	Average distance between pair of objects, one in one cluster, one in the other	Tends to join clusters with small variances. Intermediate between single and complete linkage. Takes account of cluster structure. Relatively robust.
Centroid	Distance	Squared Euclidean distance between mean vectors (centroids)	Assumes points can be represented in Euclidean space. The more numerous of two groups dominates the merged cluster, subject to reversals
Median	Distance	Squared Euclidean distance between weighted centroids	Assumes points can be represented in Euclidean space for geometric interpretation. New group intermediate in position between merged groups, subject to reversals
Ward's	Distance	Increase in sum of squares within clusters, after fusion, summed over all variables	Assumes points can be represented in Euclidean space for geometric interpretation. Tends to find same-sized, spherical clusters; sensitive to outliers

Given the description of the agglomerative clustering methods available, the decision to choose one method over another is based on both logic and the similarity measure used. Both single and median linking tend to cluster cases together at low levels of similarity, thus forming long, elongated clusters (Everitt 1993:68). This is known as chaining. However, Jardine and Sibson (1971) point out that chaining merely describes what a method does. A second issue pertaining to single linking is that it does not suggest how many clusters are formed; in other words, there are no clear groupings (Aldenderfer & Blashfield 1984:40). The centroid and Ward's methods tend to form circular clusters even when the data contains clusters of other shapes (Everitt 1993:69). This means that, regardless of the distance between variable or attribute values, these techniques will attempt to conform the distances to a circular shape. Finally, with regards to the similarity coefficient, only single, complete and average linking can use either similarity or distance coefficients.

Several comparative studies on clustering methods have been published. Cunningham and Ogilvie (1972:212) conclude that average linking performs best, closely followed by complete linking, when goodness-of-fit and stress tests are performed. In another study, Hands and Everitt (1987) use a Monte Carlo approach to investigate the performance of five hierarchical agglomerative techniques on binary data. This study reveals that single linking has a very poor response to binary data, regardless of the number of cases, while Ward's method performs very well, as long as the data sets have approximately equal proportions. However, for data sets in which proportions of observations from each group (sites) differ, the centroid method excels. Group average performs quite well when the number of variables in the case is moderate to large (≥ 100 variables/attributes). An interesting note on this study is that the simple matching coefficient is used for all five clustering methods (single, complete, average, centroid and Ward's) but, as we know from earlier discussions, both centroid and Ward's methods use distance measures. Table 5.5 illustrates the results of their findings.

Table 5.5. Results of Hands and Everitt's (1987) study on hierarchical clustering methods using binary data.

Method	Number of 'good' fits
Ward's	25
Single linking	1
Complete linking	17
Average linking	27
Centroid	30

With this information, deciding what clustering method to use in this research becomes clearer. Given the choice to use the simple matching coefficient, and given the poor response of single linking on binary data, the choice is limited to complete or average linking. However, if it is possible to use the simple matching coefficient, regardless of the cluster method, then clearly Ward's or centroid methods are superior for binary data.

For this research, average linking will be used as the clustering method. The decision to use this method was based on (a) its compatibility with the simple matching association coefficient; (b) the fact that it takes account of cluster structure; and (c) the fact that it is a relatively robust method.

Number of Clusters

Aldenderfer and Blashfield (1984:53) state that this fundamental step is also one of the least understood steps in cluster analysis because of a lack of a suitable null hypothesis and the complex nature of multivariate sampling distributions. They further state that those techniques that have established a null hypothesis, such as the random graph hypothesis and the random position hypothesis, are extremely limited in scope and have not been applied to practical data analysis (Aldenderfer & Blashfield 1984:53-54). Several approaches have been suggested to determine the number of clusters created in a cluster analysis. Heuristic procedures are common. One approach essentially 'cuts' or 'prunes' branches of the resulting dendrogram based on subjective, visual inspection (Romesburg 1990:213). A second approach is to graph the number of clusters against the fusion or amalgamation coefficient – the numerical value where various cases merge to form a cluster (Aldenderfer & Blashfield 1984:54). Fusion coefficients provide an index of the relative distance of variables joined at each stage of the clustering. The greater the distance, the less similarity between variables being clustered. A large jump in the degree of fusion coefficients (a knee in the curve) indicates an optimal number of clusters. Figure 5.1 illustrates how the number of clusters is derived from the fusion coefficient. A third heuristic approach is to identify a significant jump in the amalgamation coefficient - Stopping Rule #1 - and base the number of clusters on this jump.

In the end, assessing the number of clusters in a given analysis is a subjective matter based on insight. For this research, the initial decision on the number of clusters formed in the analysis will be based on pruning; however, the resulting amalgamation coefficient will also be graphed against the number of clusters.

Figure 5.1 Graph of the number of clusters against the fusion or amalgamation coefficient. As the fusion coefficient (distance) increases, number of clusters decreases. The red line indicates the optimal number of clusters.

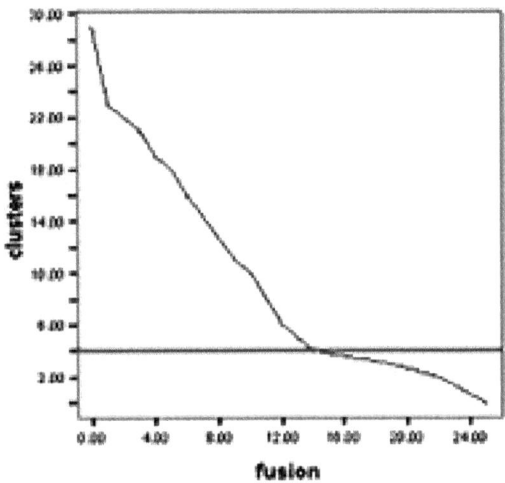

Validation Techniques

There are five techniques for validating the resulting clusters from the analysis: cophenetic correlation; significance tests on variables used to create clusters; replication; significance tests on independent variables; and Monte Carlo procedures. The following is a brief description of each as well as some concerns about employing these validation techniques.

(a) **Cophenetic correlation:** The cophenetic correlation examines the relationship between the values in the original similarity matrix and the values in an implied similarity matrix (Aldenderfer & Blashfield 1984:63). The implied similarity matrix is based on similarities between all pairs of cases in the dendrogram. Numerical taxonomists favor this validation technique but it is not without its problems (Aldenderfer & Blashfield 1984:63). The main problem is that the cophenetic correlation assumes normal distribution and, therefore, is not an optimal estimator. A second problem is that the data in each matrix is quite different. The similarity matrix created from the information in the dendrogram contains a limited number of unique values, thus the implied matrix is much smaller than the similarity matrix, which has a greater amount of unique values.

(b) **Significance tests on variables used to create clusters:** This validation technique performs a multivariate analysis of variance (MANOVA) on the variables used in the analysis (Aldenderfer & Blashfield 1984:64). There is not much information on using MANOVA as a validation technique but Aldenderfer and Blashfield (1984:65) state that cluster analysis separates entities into clusters that have no overlap on the variables being used. Thus, a significance test looking for difference among clusters will always be positive. The performances of these tests are consequently misleading.

(c) **Replication:** This technique essentially checks for stability of a clustering solution through replication of the results across a split sample of data (Aldenderfer & Blashfield 1984:65; Romesburg 1990:258). Alternatively, replication techniques can be defined as reproduction of the cluster analysis through various multivariate techniques. Finally, replication validity through a demonstration of stability and robustness involves the removal of a case, variable, or attribute if such removals do not affect the cluster solution when the method is repeated, the results are considered replicated (Romesburg 1990:258). Although these validation techniques are both simple to perform and relatively self-explanatory, their use requires caution because successful replication does not necessarily validate a clustering solution.

(d) **Significance test on independent variables:** Aldenderfer and Blashfield (1984:66) believe that these significance tests are probably one of the better forms of validation techniques and have also been among the least used. Simply explained, this validation technique performs significance tests that compare the clusters on variables not used to generate the cluster solution (ibid. 66). This technique can be performed through F-statistics using a one-way analysis of variance (ANOVA).

(e) **Monte Carlo procedures:** This final validation technique is one of the more complicated yet also among the better validation techniques. This technique employs a random number generator to create a data set with general characteristics that match the overall characteristics of the original data used. Once the data is generated, it undergoes the same cluster analysis as the original data and then the cluster solutions are compared with the original solutions (Aldenderfer & Blashfield 1984:67). In general, Monte Carlo simulations compare clusters generated from those generated from a random model (Manly 1991).

Although five validation techniques are available, given the information on these techniques, only two – the significance test on independent variables and the Monte Carlo procedure are considered creditable. However, given that validation is just as important a step as the clustering itself, a selection of validation techniques is critical. For this research, I will use the Monte Carlo procedure because of its creditability as a validation technique. Once considered time-intensive, Monte Carlo is now a relatively quick procedure because of advances computer programming and greater processing capabilities.

Summary

Previous research on Natufian material culture using clustering methods (Byrd 1987; Henry 1982; Olszewski 1988) has met with strong objection. Belfer-Cohen (1991:174-175) critiques previous cluster analysis because (a) the data used was fragmentary; (b) all clustering analysis was based on percentages from only a sample of the data; and (c) chipped stone tools were used to perform the initial clustering of sites, with non-lithic materials being added as a sub-class.

This chapter examines the first of a two-part methodology for this research. This first part concentrates on analysis of the material culture from Natufian sites. The purpose of the cluster analysis is to identify similarity among Natufian sites. The goal is to complement the developing hypothesis that the Natufian population, although cognizant of variability in and limitations of their ecological environment, was also affected by a strong sense of social structure, which I equate with interaction.

Central to cluster analysis are the steps involved in executing the analysis. In the introduction, seven steps are illustrated. The first two steps are covered in the previous chapter. The final five steps are covered in this chapter. I decided that standardization of the attributes is not necessary because the data is in categorical, binary format. Given that the data is in this format, the similarity coefficient measures are limited to the association coefficient. There is a variety of association coefficients available for binary data, each based on the scale, ranging from -1.0 to 1.0, whether 0-0 matches are included, and whether certain values in the two-by-two table are weighted. I decided to use the simple matching coefficient because it ranges in scale from 0.0 to 1.0 and, does not display extreme measures.

Several clustering methods were also described but, given the nature of the data and the similarity coefficient, it is evident that hierarchical agglomerative methods are the practical choice. Of the various agglomerative methods available, I selected average linking. I based this selection on its compatibility with the simple matching association coefficient, the fact that it takes account of cluster structure, and that it is a robust method. Equally important steps discussed here were the various methods that can be used to decide the number of clusters in the dendrogram, and the numerous validation techniques.

The next chapter will take into consideration the decisions made in this chapter and demonstrate the results of these decisions by applying the steps to the Natufian material culture data. The results will be incorporated into a model of Natufian social interaction that is based on the hypothesis that Natufian social interaction and organization is based on a model of aggregation and dispersion of Natufian groups.

CHAPTER 6
RESULTS PART I – ARCHAEOLOGICAL SITES AND MATERIAL CULTURE

Introduction

This chapter presents the results of the first part of analysis for this research. These results are the product of grouping Natufian sites through clustering of their material culture. In chapter five, I introduced the methods applied to the data discussed in chapter four. These methods are examined in a series of four stages: proximity measure, clustering methods, number of clusters and validation techniques. This chapter follows the same format. Remarks on trends in the data or issues I encountered are presented in this chapter but no interpretation will occur at this point.

What becomes evident in this first application of the methods is that archaeological data in dichotomous (binary) format can be analyzed and validated to form clusters based on similarity. It is also evident that, through clustering, a pattern can be formed for Natufian sites. This pattern, based on similarity of material culture, supports the position of this research. This position is also influence by the theoretical paradigm of agency – the structuring of social relations and the ongoing production, maintenance, and transformation of societal institutions across time and space. This is demonstrated through the reoccurrences of various materials and their attributes.

Calculating the Proximity Measure and Applying the Clustering Method

As I indicate in chapter five, both Simple Matching and Sørenson's similarity measures are calculated for the Natufian data recorded in binary format. Once these measures are calculated, the Average linkage clustering method is applied. At this point, solutions ranging from two to five clusters are presented for each similarity measure (Table 6.1 a and b). The factors determining these cluster memberships - the proximity matrix and the dendrogram - are presented in appendix c. These results enable me to make several observations on the resulting cluster memberships of both similarity measures.

The Simple Matching similarity measure produced clusters of Natufian sites where (a) one site – Hatoula– always occurs in its own cluster when cluster membership is based on four or five clusters and; (b) two sites – el-Wad and 'Ain Mallaha (Late) – always occur clustered together. Several sites – 21 in total – always remain in the same cluster, regardless of the number of clusters produced.

The Sørenson's similarity measure produced clusters of Natufian sites where (a) one site – Wadi Humeima – always occurs in its own cluster and; (b) three sites – 'Ain Rahub, Khallat Anaza, and Upper Besor 6 – always occur clustered together. Several sites – 19 in total – always remain in the same cluster, regardless of the number of clusters produced.

When comparing the two similarity measures and their potential cluster memberships, it becomes obvious that the two similarity measures produce completely different results. This brings into question whether or not to include 0 – 0 matches in calculating similarity. As I discuss in chapter five, there are differing opinions on the validity of these 0 – 0 matches in the clustering of binary data. Depending on the data, there are no right or wrong answers. However, there are also no suggestions on how to solve this dilemma.

Table 6.1. Possible cluster membership solutions for (a) Simple Matching and (b) Sørenson's similarity measures.

(a) Simple Matching similarity cluster solutions

Case	5 Clusters	4 Clusters	3 Clusters	2 Clusters
1:'Ain el-Saratan	1	1	1	1
2:'Ain Rahub	1	1	1	1
3:Beidha	1	1	1	1
4:El Wad	2	2	2	2
5:Kebarah	1	1	1	1
6:Faza'el	1	1	1	1
7:Givat Hayil	1	1	1	1
8:Hatoula	3	3	1	1
9:Hayonim Cave (e)	4	4	3	1
10:Hayonim Cave (l)	4	4	3	1
11:Hayonim Terrace	1	1	1	1
12:Hilazon	1	1	1	1
13:Khallat Anaza	1	1	1	1
14:Mallaha (e)	4	4	3	1
15:Mallaha (l)	2	2	2	2
16:Nahal 'en Gev	1	1	1	1
17:Nahal Oren	1	1	1	1
18:Nahal Sekher	1	1	1	1
19:Rosh Horesha	1	1	1	1
20:Rosh Zin	1	1	1	1
21:Saflulim	1	1	1	1
22:Salibiya	1	1	1	1
23:Tabaqa	1	1	1	1
24:Upper Besor	1	1	1	1
25:Wadi Hammeh	5	4	3	1
26:Wadi Humeima	1	1	1	1
27:Wadi Judayid	1	1	1	1
28:Wadi Mataha	1	1	1	1

(b) Sørenson's similarity measure cluster solutions

Case	5 Clusters	4 Clusters	3 Clusters	2 Clusters
1:'Ain el-Saratan	1	1	1	1
2:'Ain Rahub	2	2	2	1
3:Beidha	3	1	1	1
4:El Wad	1	1	1	1
5:Kebarah	1	1	1	1
6:Faza'el	1	1	1	1
7:Givat Hayil	4	3	2	1
8:Hatoula	1	1	1	1
9:Hayonim Cave (e)	1	1	1	1
10:Hayonim Cave (l)	1	1	1	1
11:Hayonim Terrace	1	1	1	1
12:Hilazon	1	1	1	1
13:Khallat Anaza	2	2	2	1
14:Mallaha (e)	1	1	1	1
15:Mallaha (l)	1	1	1	1
16:Nahal 'en Gev	1	1	1	1
17:Nahal Oren	1	1	1	1
18:Nahal Sekher	4	3	2	1
19:Rosh Horesha	1	1	1	1
20:Rosh Zin	1	1	1	1
21:Saflulim	1	1	1	1
22:Salibiya	1	1	1	1
23:Tabaqa	3	1	1	1
24:Upper Besor	2	2	2	1
25:Wadi Hammeh	1	1	1	1
26:Wadi Humeima	5	4	3	2
27:Wadi Judayid	3	1	1	1
28:Wadi Mataha	1	1	1	1

For this research, I decided to test these two similarity measures against other measures. In the interest of avoiding redundancy through monotonic relationships, I decided to use measures that are not under the umbrella of association coefficient similarity measures. Instead, I use similarity measures that fall under the categories of correlation coefficient, distance measure, and probabilistic similarity measures. I will not define these similarity measures as there are descriptions of them in chapter five. Table 6.2 details the similarity measures used to test the validity of the Simple Matching and Sørenson's measure, including their formula and whether or not they include 0 – 0 matches. The goal is to incorporate measures that both include and exclude 0 – 0 matches for each similarity measure type. It must be noted that there is only one correlation coefficient measure available for binary data – Phi 4-Point similarity measure – and it includes 0 – 0 matches.

A proximity matrix and the resulting dendrogram are produced for each measure. Appendix c illustrates the results of these methods. To test the two association coefficients with these five similarity measures, I use Pearson's r correlation coefficient using the results for five cluster membership. Table 6.3 and 6.4 illustrate the cluster membership for all similarity measure as well as the Pearson's r correlation coefficient values.

The outcome of Pearson's coefficient demonstrates that there are correlations between each association coefficient (Simple Matching and Sørenson's) and the five test similarity measures. Variance has a perfect positive correlation (1.000) with Simple Matching whereas Bray-Curtis has perfect positive correlation with Sørenson's. There is also a significant correlation between Sørenson's and the Kulczynski 2 measurement (.696). Alternatively, Kulczynski 2 has a significant *negative* correlation with Simple Matching (-.453). However, this correlation is not as strong as the correlation between Sørenson's and Kulczynski 2. In general, Sørenson's is correlated most strongly with other similarity measures. Therefore it is the similarity measure used for this research.

A second significant reason for using Sørenson's similarity measure is that it not only excludes 0 – 0 matches, but it also gives double weight for 1 – 1 matches. This means that 1 – 1 matches are "driving" cluster membership, rather than 0 – 1 or 1 – 0 pairs. The Bray-Curtis similarity measure also excludes 0 – 0 matches and gives double weight for 1 – 1 matches. The Kulczynski 2 is based on the "conditional probability that the characteristic is present in one item, given that it is present in the other."

A proximity matrix and the resulting dendrogram are produced for each measure. Appendix c illustrates the results of these methods. To test the two association coefficients with these five similarity measures, I use Pearson's r correlation coefficient using the results for five cluster membership. Table 6.3 and 6.4 illustrate the cluster membership for all similarity measure as well as the Pearson's r correlation coefficient values.

Table 6.2. Proximity measures used to test accuracy of Simple Matching and Sörenson's Measure.

Proximity Measure	Type	Formula	Includes 0 – 0 Matches
Phi 4-Point	Correlation coefficient	$\dfrac{ad-bc}{\sqrt{(a+b)(a+c)(b+d)(c+d)}}$	Yes
Variance	Distance Measure (dissimilarity)	$\dfrac{b+c}{4(a+b+c+d)}$	Yes
Bray-Curtis	Distance Measure (dissimilarity)	$\dfrac{b+c}{2a+b+c}$	No
Kulszynski 2	Probabilistic Similarity Measure	$\dfrac{a/(a+b)+a/a+c}{2}$	Yes
Sokal and Sneath 4	Probabilistic Similarity Measure	$\dfrac{a/(a+b)+a/(a+c)+d/(b+d)+d/(c+d)}{4}$	No

Table 6.3. Cluster membership for all similarity measures based on five clusters.

Natufian Site	Simple	Sorenson	Phi	Variance	Bray-Curtis	Kulczynski 2	Sokal-Sneath 4
1:'ain el-Saratan	1	1	1	1	1	1	1
2:'ain Rahub	1	2	2	1	2	2	2
3:Beidha	1	3	3	1	3	3	3
4:el Wad	2	1	4	2	1	1	4
9:Hayonim Cave (e)	4	1	1	4	1	1	1
10:Hayonim Cave (l)	4	1	1	4	1	1	1
11:Hayonim Terrace	1	1	1	1	1	1	1
12:Hilazon	1	1	1	1	1	1	1
13:Khallat Anaza	1	2	4	1	2	2	4
14:Mallaha (e)	4	1	1	4	1	1	1
15:Mallaha (l)	2	1	4	2	1	1	4
16:Nahal 'en Gev	1	1	1	1	1	1	1
17:Nahal Oren	1	1	1	1	1	1	1
18:Nahal Sekher	1	4	2	1	4	4	2
19:Rosh Horesha	1	1	2	1	1	4	2
20:Rosh Zin	1	1	2	1	1	2	2
21:Saflulim	1	1	2	1	1	2	2
22:Salibiya	1	1	2	1	1	4	2
23:Tabaqa	1	3	3	1	3	3	3
24:Upper Besor	1	2	2	1	2	2	2
25:Wadi Hammeh	5	1	1	5	1	1	1
26:Wadi Humeima	1	5	3	1	5	5	3
27:Wadi Judayid	1	3	3	1	3	3	3
28:Wadi Mataha	1	1	2	1	1	2	2

Table 6.4. Outcome of Pearson's *r* correlation coefficient.

		Simple Matching	Sorenson's	Phi 4-Point	Variance	Bray-Curtis	Kulczynski 2	Sokal & Sneath 4
Simple Matching	Pearson Correlation	1	-.309	-.132	1.000(**)	-.309	-.453(**)	-.132
	Sig. (1-tailed)		.055	.252	.000	.055	.008	.252
Sorenson's	Pearson Correlation	-.309	1	.282	-.309	1.000(**)	.696(**)	.282
	Sig. (1-tailed)	.055		.073	.055	.000	.000	.0732
Phi 4-Point	Pearson Correlation	-.132	.282	1	-.132	.282	.220	1.000(**)
	Sig. (1-tailed)	.252	.073		.252	.073	.130	.000
Variance	Pearson Correlation	1.000(**)	-.309	-.132	1	-.309	-.453(**)	-.132
	Sig. (1-tailed)	.000	.055	.252		.055	.008	.252
Bray-Curtis	Pearson Correlation	-.309	1.000(**)	.282	-.309	1	.696(**)	.282
	Sig. (1-tailed)	.055	.000	.073	.055		.000	.073
Kulczynski 2	Pearson Correlation	-.453(**)	.696(**)	.220	-.453(**)	.696(**)	1	.220
	Sig. (1-tailed)	.008	.000	.130	.008	.000		.130
Sokal & Sneath 4	Pearson Correlation	-.132	.282	1.000(**)	-.132	.282	.220	1
	Sig. (1-tailed)	.252	.073	.000	.252	.073	.130	

** Correlation is significant at the 0.01 level (1-tailed).

The outcome of Pearson's coefficient demonstrates that there are correlations between each association coefficient (Simple Matching and Sørenson's) and the five test similarity measures. Variance has a perfect positive correlation (1.000) with Simple Matching whereas Bray-Curtis has perfect positive correlation with Sørenson's. There is also a significant correlation between Sørenson's and the Kulczynski 2 measurement (.696). Alternatively, Kulczynski 2 has a significant *negative* correlation with Simple Matching (-.453). However, this correlation is not as strong as the correlation between Sørenson's and Kulczynski 2. In general, Sørenson's is correlated most strongly with other similarity measures. Therefore it is the similarity measure used for this research.

A second significant reason for using Sørenson's similarity measure is that it not only excludes 0 – 0 matches, but it also gives double weight for 1 – 1 matches. This means that 1 – 1 matches are "driving" cluster membership, rather than 0 – 1 or 1 – 0 pairs. The Bray-Curtis similarity measure also excludes 0 – 0 matches and gives double weight for 1 – 1 matches. The Kulczynski 2 is based on the "conditional probability that the characteristic is present in one item, given that it is present in the other."[2]

Number of Clusters

The total number of clusters created using Sørenson's similarity measure and the average linkage solution is plotted against the fusion coefficient to identify the optimal number of clusters for Natufian sites. Recalling from chapter five, the fusion coefficient, or amalgamation coefficient, is the numerical value at which various cases merge to form a cluster in the dendrogram. Figure 6.1 exemplifies this graphically. This optimal number of clusters is recognized at the *knee* of the line. This *knee* or boundary in the line determines that the ideal number of clusters based on Natufian sites and their material culture is five.

Validation of Clusters

Cluster validation occurs early in this analysis with the section investigating the decision to include or exclude 0 – 0 matches. Comparing several proximity measurements through correlation is a method of replication validation. In re-examining table 6.3, one can see that Sørenson's proximity measure correlates significantly with the Bray & Curtis and the Kulczynski 2 proximity measures. Furthermore, there is a positive, albeit not necessarily significant, correlation between Sørenson's measure and the Phi 4-point and Sokal and Sneath 4 measures. This replication of proximity measures indicates that Sørenson's is indeed a applicable technique and that the resulting clusters are reasonably reliable.

Figure 6.1. Plot of number of clusters versus Fusion Coefficient, Sørenson's Similarity Measure and Average Linkage solution.

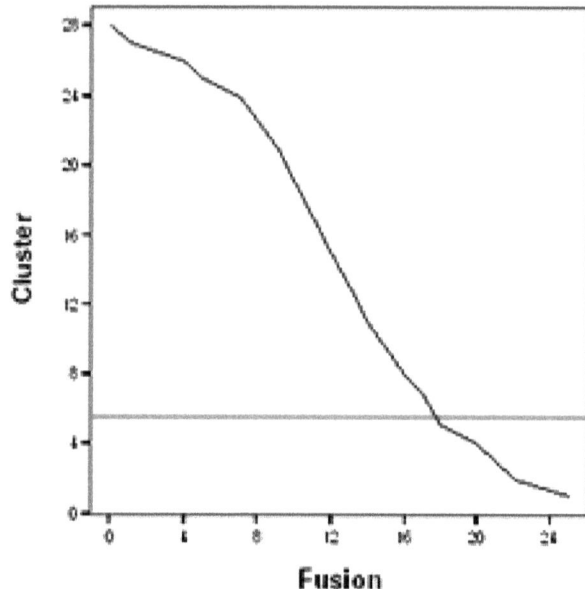

To investigate validation of the resulting clusters further, I also undertake cophenetic correlation. To reiterate, the cophenentic correlation is defined as the Pearson's *r* correlation between the theoretical (dendrogram) values and the empirical (Sørenson's) similarity matrix. Table 6.3 illustrates the results of the cophenetic correlation. There is a strong negative correlation – as the dendrogram distance measure increases, the Sørenson's measure decreases.

Table 6.5. Cophenetic correlations between values in the original (Sørenson's) similarity matrix and the implied matrix (dendrogram measures).

		Dendrogram	Sørenson's
Dendro-gram	Pearson Correlation	1	-.706
	Sig. (2-tailed)		.000
Sørenson's	Pearson Correlation	-.706	1
	Sig. (2-tailed)	.000	

At times, it is preferable to apply a nonparametric correlation measure if interest lies in the geometric structure of the dendrogram rather than the length of its branches. In this instance, nonparametric correlation coefficients, such as Kendall's *tau* or Spearman's *rho*, are used. Nonparametric correlation coefficients are also preferable if normal distribution is not assumed. Table 6.4 illustrates the results of nonparametric cophenetic correlation measures for the original (Sørenson's) and implied (dendrogram) matrices.

---

[2] SPSS (2000) help files.

Table 6.6. Nonparametric cophenetic correlations between values in the original (Sørenson's) similarity matrix and the implied matrix (dendrogram measures).

			Dendrogram	Sørenson's
Kendall's tau_b	Dendrogram meas.	Correlation Coefficient	1.000	-.489**
		Sig. (2-tailed)	.	.001
	Sørenson's	Correlation Coefficient	-.489**	1.000
		Sig. (2-tailed)	.001	.
Spearman's rho	Dendrogram meas.	Correlation Coefficient	1.000	-.629**
		Sig. (2-tailed)	.	.000
	Sørenson's	Correlation Coefficient	-.629**	1.000
		Sig. (2-tailed)	.000	.

** Correlation is significant at the 0.01 level (2-tailed).

The nonparametric correlation coefficient measures also show a significant negative correlation, particularly with Spearman's *rho*. Once again, there is a strong negative correlation – as the dendrogram distance measure increases, the Sørenson's measure decreases.

The results of the replication and the cophenetic coefficient validation confirm that Sørenson's proximity matrix, along with average linkage clustering, is reliable for the data used in this research.

Chipped-Stone Data

At this point, I have only discussed those variables and attributes that are in dichotomous (binary) format. The chipped-stone attributes are, in essence, tool types. Each tool type is recorded as a percentage of the total tools recorded for the assemblage of a particular site. This makes their scale ratio, rather than dichotomous. Hierarchical cluster analysis is performed on this data but the measures used are particular to the data format – continuous and ratio. The measures used for ratio data are also different from those used for dichotomous data in that they look for dissimilarity. The most common measure of dissimilarity is the Squared Euclidean Distance measure. Using this measure, Natufian sites are grouped into five clusters, as indicated by the material culture coded into binary format. The results of this grouping show that the majority of Natufian site fall within one of two clusters (see Table 6.7). Out of interest, two additional measures of dissimilarity – Minkowski and City block – are calculated to see what groupings of Natufian sites occur. Both measures produce the same results as the Squared Euclidean up to the four-cluster level but, at the five-cluster level, Squared Euclidean differs from Minkowski and City Block. To test if the optimal number of clusters is actually four, I created a fusion graph for the Squared Euclidean (Figure 6.2). The results show that the optimal number of clusters is in fact four.

Table 6.7. Comparison of proximity measures tested for chipped-stone data.

Site	Squared Euclidean Distance	Minkowski	City Block
'Ain el-Saratan	1	1	1
'Ain Rahub	2	2	2
Beidha	2	2	2
el-Wad	3	3	3
Kebarah	4	4	4
Faza'el	3	3	3
Givat Hayil	2	2	2
Hatoula	2	2	2
Hayonim Cave (E)	3	3	3
Hayonim Cave (L)	3	3	3
Hayonim Terrace	3	3	3
Khallat Anaza	3	2	3
Mallaha (E)	3	3	3
Mallaha (L)	3	3	3
Nahal Ein Gev	3	3	3
Nahal Oren	3	3	3
Nahal Sekher	1	1	1
Rosh Horesha	2	2	2
Rosh Zin	2	2	2
Saflulim	1	1	1
Salibiya	3	3	3
Tabaqa	2	2	2
Wadi Hammeh	3	3	3
Wadi Humeima	2	2	2
Wadi Judayid	1	1	1
Wadi Mataha	2	2	2

Figure 6.2. Plot of number of clusters versus Fusion Coefficient, Squared Euclidean Distance Measure and Average Linkage solution for chipped-stone data.

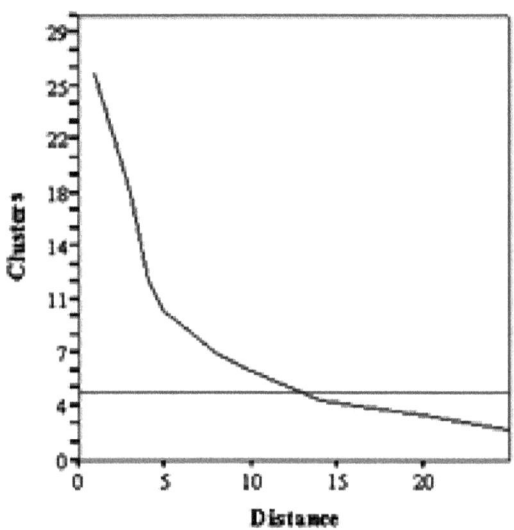

Summary of Results

The resulting clusters for non-chipped-stone material culture show that there are five clusters. Cluster one consists of 19 sites, while clusters two and three consist of three sites each. Cluster four is comprised of two sites, while cluster five includes only one site. Clusters one and two contains both Early and Late sites, cluster three is limited to Early Natufian sites, and clusters four and five are limited to Late Natufian sites.

In chapter two, I discuss the biotic communities in which these sites are currently located and how these biotic communities have played a part in the classification of Natufian sites. In examining the resulting clusters with reference to the biotic communities, there is no immediate correlation between the two. However, this will be further investigated in the subsequent analysis.

Clustering based on chipped-stone data shows that there are four main groups of sites. Cluster one includes four sites ('Ain as-Saratan, Nahal Sekher, Saflulim, and Wadi Judayid). Clusters two and three consist of 9 and 12 sites, respectively. Cluster four includes only one site – Kebarah. Examining these clusters on the basis of site phase shows that both Early and Late Natufian sites are represented in all clusters with the exception of cluster four, which contains only Kebarah – an Early Natufian site. Once again, the results show that these clusters are not correlated with the biotic communities in the study region.

Two issues arise from the results of this initial analysis. The first relates to the fact that material culture of the Natufian sites is split into two categories – non-chipped-stone and chipped-stone. The first reason for this split is simply that the data is in two formats – dichotomous and ratio. The second reason for this split relates to past studies on Natufian sites. Previous publications that have clustered Natufian sites focus exclusively on the chipped-stone assemblages and their relationship to biotic community (Byrd 1987; Henry 1994), with the exception of Olszewski (1988), who also uses site type as a variable. In these publications, the methods used to cluster the sites are not specified. The results of all three of these publications demonstrate a correlation between the chipped-stone assemblage and biotic community. In the interests of this research, I decided to re-examine the chipped-stone variables on their own to test my results against the results previously published as well as to test the results against the results of the non chipped-stone variables. The number of known Natufian sites has increased since these initial publications so I have a larger sample size.

As I indicate, there is no immediate correlation between clusters based on chipped-stone tools and biotic community. When comparing the chipped-stone to the non-chipped-stone clusters, the most apparent observation is the optimal number of clusters (5 versus 4). The second observation is the cluster membership. There appears to be no consistency in cluster membership. There is no clear explanation for this inconsistency. It can be speculated that the inconsistency lies in the difference in number of variables and attributes used. A second explanation to consider is the format of the data as well as their ensuing values. While the non-chipped-stone variables only have a value of present or absent, all attributes for the chipped-stone tools are present to varying degrees. This inconsistency is further examined in the second stage of analysis.

The second issue, again relating to the chipped-stone variables, relates to the sample size. Two sites, Upper Besor 6 and Hilazon, do not have any publications communicating the complete analysis of chipped-stone tools. If these two sites were to be included in the analysis, they would appear as outliers and the results would be artificial. I considered running the cluster analysis for the chipped-stone variables using only two attributes – the percentage of geometric microliths and non-geometric microliths, but I believe that this is not an effective means for clustering sites.

The second stage of this research will now be discussed. This stage incorporates the results conveyed in this chapter. These results are placed in a spatial context.

CHAPTER 7
DATA PART II – SPATIAL DATA

Introduction

The previous three chapters concentrate on archaeological data and methods used to analyze this data. The objective of this first part of data analysis is to group Natufian sites based on similarities in material culture. While this first stage of analysis demonstrates that there is a material relationship between the Natufian sites, it does not confirm the hypothesis constructed for this research – that Natufian sites are *spatially* interrelated and that this interaction is facilitated through structures and the system.

In this chapter, I introduce the spatial data required to execute the second stage of analysis. Here I discuss the conception of spatial data and define it in terms of spatial data types. I also address the precision, accuracy, scale, and resolution of spatial data. Finally, I will present the spatial data for this research.

Prior to discussion of spatial data, it is necessary to understand the science and systems used to view, process, create, and analyze spatial data. This science is known as the geographical information sciences (herein termed GIScience) and its primary tool is collectively known as geographical information systems (herein termed GIS). The use of GIS in archaeology has a short history. This chapter includes a brief discussion of this history because it is crucial to understand the history of archaeological analysis through GIScience prior to understanding the data and methods used for this research.

What is a Geographical Information System?

GIS are systems of computer hardware, software, and procedures designed to support the capture, management, mathematical manipulation, analysis, modeling, and display of spatially referenced data for solving complex planning and management problems (Aldenderfer & Maschner 1996:4; Green 1990:3; Heywood 1990:849; Korte 1997:401; Kvamme 1989:139; Lock & Harris 1992:90; Martin 1996:30; Stine & Lanter 1990:80). GIS are also defined as "spatially referenced databases that allow one to control for the distribution of form over space and through time" (Green 1990:3). Essentially, GIS are the integration of computer-aided mapping, computerized databases, and statistical packages. As such, they have the potential to be very useful for archaeological research studying regional processes.

GIS consist of two parts: a standard relational database that allows for cross-tabular searching; and a graphic or mapping database, that allows for an examination of space, time, and form (or shape) simultaneously (Green 1990:5). The computerized database component of GIS allows the storage and retrieval of information found on maps and attaches features on the maps. GIS store two forms of data: spatial data and attribute data. Spatial data are "data pertaining to the location of geographic entities together with their spatial dimensions (longitude and latitude)" (Korte 1997:406). Attribute data are the descriptive characteristics of spatial data (Korte 1997:596). For example, the location of an archaeological site - the latitude and longitude coordinates - are spatial data, while the data pertaining to an archaeological site - the site type, and the cultural materials recovered, and any other information on an archaeological site - are the attribute data.

In a large number of GIS applications, the data encoded into a system relates to both physical and human aspects of the geographical world (Martin 1996:51). In this case, some social scientists, such as Martin (1996:68), view GIS as "merely a toolbox for the answering of questions with spatial dimensions." Martin also states, that although the study and practice of GIS are neither a science, nor an academic discipline, GIS do permeate the boundaries of many "conventionally defined disciplines" (Martin 1996:68). Others view the application of GIS quite differently. Openshaw (1996:676) states that "the absorption of GIS into geography offers the basis for a long overdue reconciliation between the soft pseudo-science of the social sciences and the hard spatial science of which GIS are a part."

In a survey of the tool-versus-science debate on a GIS-L Listserve, Wright, Goodchild, and Proctor (1997) realize that there are not two, but three positions in this debate. According to the authors (1997:351-357), GIS are viewed as either (1) tools; (2) toolmakers, or; (3) a science. Those who take the position that GIS are tools claim that GIS describes processes related to the handling of spatial data. Those who see GIS as toolmakers are concerned with the creation of methods to handle and analyze spatial data. In this sense, GIS are methodologies. Finally, those whose position is that GIS are a science emphasize that the science of GIS involves theory and assume that the development of processes and methods to handle spatial data *is* a science. Others who take this position compare GIScience to other sciences in that it has applications in a broader context, as do geology, geography, and computer science. Finally, others see GIS as a scientific discipline of information science. My position in this research is that GIS are tools and toolmakers in the broad context of GISciences.

GIS in Archaeology

According to Lock and Harris (1992:89), understanding the potential of GIS for archaeological research in North America began in the early 1980s. By 1985, both the Commission IV of the Union International des Sciences Pre- et Proto-historiques (UISPP) and the Annual meeting of the Society for American Archaeology (SAA) included sessions on the uses of GIS in archaeology. Papers in these sessions cover methods, principles, and specific regional applications of GIS. By 1986, Kenneth Kvamme developed an archaeologically focused GIS - TERRAINPAC. In 1989, Stanton Green organized a GIS symposium at the World Archaeological Congress (Green 1990). In the same year, NASA sponsored a conference with the goal of encouraging anthropologists and archaeologists to engage in some of the new technologies available, particularly GIS, GPS (Global Positioning Systems), and GPR (Ground Penetrating Radar). The result of this conference was "substantive research that could not have been done without these methodological tools" (Maschner 1996:762). The definitive characteristic of the initial archaeological research involving GIS is that it was used primarily as a tool for the inventory, simple contextual analysis, site-location analysis and predictive modeling, and publication (Fisher 1999:8).

At the beginning of the 1990s, a critical turn of events occured in archaeological research using GIS. Criticism over increasingly positivistic archaeological research driven by GIS led to the *socio-theoretical critique* of GIS (Lock & Harris 2000: xvi). This critique is a direct reaction to the New Archaeology tradition and its position on the relationship between data and theory as well as the "inherent bias in technology" (Lock & Harris 2000: xvi). Criticisms are characterized under the sub-headings of context, determinism, and cognition and perception (Fisher 1999:9-10).

Critiquing context, one can conclude that e*ither* methods are developed in one context, using one dataset to solve one problem; *or* methods are developed without any real data, only the totally data-free context of a statistician's mind. Determinism relates to the debate as to whether GIS is an environmentally deterministic tool. This criticism is linked to the positivistic critique of New Archaeology. Finally, it is argued that some GIS functions allow archaeologists to address issues of cognition and perception. However, some methods, such as site-location models that suggest one can measure landscape perception through site catchments and cost surfaces, do not actually contribute to the understanding of human cognition or perception (Fisher 1999:10). One can further argue that these site-location models are embedded in purely functional models. Along this line, others have argued that GIS in archaeology is spatially deterministic in that "qualitative or alternative forms of knowledge representation that are crucial to understanding nature and place are largely excluded from GIS" (Lock & Harris 2000:xvii).

Given this critique, the focus of archaeological research in a geographical information system context has dramatically expanded. Emerging fields of inquiry in the mid-1990s are directed at spatial analysis through visualization (Fisher 1999:20-23). Spatial analysis is a movement from producing pretty pictures for publication to theoretically driven archaeological research involving the GISciences. Uncertainty handling addresses the data and methods used in archaeological analysis involving GIS. According to Fisher (1999:7), "geographic phenomena are commonly very difficult to define" and these definitions are "context, observer, purpose and topic dependent." Visualization includes line-of-sight analysis as well as visual models.

Spatial Data

Spatial data are "information that describes the distribution of things upon the surface of the earth…any information concerning the location, shape of, and relationships among geographical features" (Gillings & Wise 1998:10). Spatial data, conceptualized in a GIS environment, can be in two forms: vector and raster (Burrough & McDonnell 1998; Gillings & Wise 1998; Wheatley & Gillings 2002). Vector data represent spatial locations and objects (features) as discrete, defined point, line or polygon units. Vector data are sometimes referred to as 'primitives' in that they are static representations of locations and objects in terms of x and y coordinates and do not contain any information about temporal or spatial variability (Burrough & McDonnell 1998:22; Wheatley & Gillings 2002:33). Figure 7.1 illustrates the three forms of vector data.

Raster data, on the other hand, are represented by sets of regular (square) units known as grid cells, cells, or pixels. Values representing each grid cell occur at the center and are recorded as the value for that cell. These grid cells continuously cover an entire area resembling a mesh or grid so a set of grid cells representing a surface is known as a raster grid. The raster grid is geo-referenced, meaning that it is *fixed* to a relative spatial position through assigned planar coordinates. The cell size in the grid is known as the resolution. The finer the resolution, the more detailed and possibly more true the raster grid is likely to represent the intended surface. Figure 7.2 illustrates raster data.

Both vector and raster data can be acquired from reputable sources however, this does not mean that it is in the format needed to immediately conduct analysis. Van Leusen (1993:108) reports that about one-third of the total amount of time available for his research is spent on the process of checking and converting maps into a format-readable file in a GIS. Wheatley and Gillings (2002:59) state that, in their experience, Van Leusen's time estimate is rather low. I concur with these reported experiences. However, I would include acquiring data in this laborious, time-intensive process. Depending on the geographical area of research, the expenditure, in terms of time and economic resources, can range from a relatively small to enormous cost. In some instances, both a large amount of time and financial resources are required. As well, there may be situations where a particular expenditure must be emphasized over the other. This is the case for this research. After an extensive search, I was able to locate geographical data for the research area, but the quality of the data is questionable. High-quality data could be produced, but the costs were out of the range of my available resources. In the end, I chose mid-range data that that takes into consideration time and resource expenditure. However, this choice brings into question issues of accuracy and precision as well as scale and resolution.

Figure 7.1 Three vector data formats: (a) point; (b) line; (c) polygon.

Figure 7.2 A simple raster (a) and corresponding data file (b).

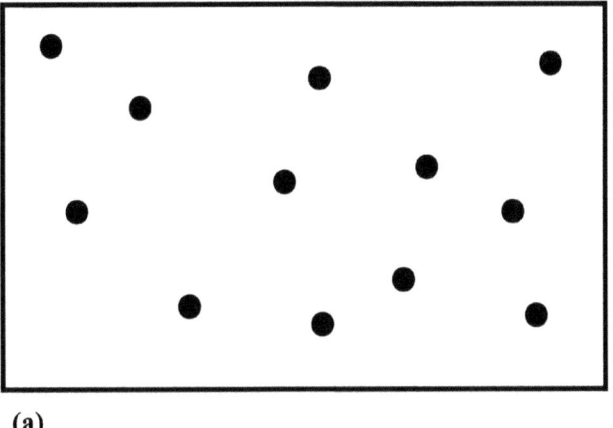

(a)

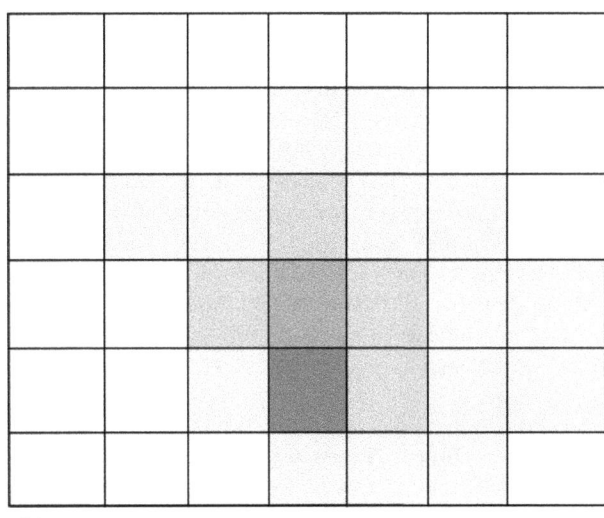

(a)

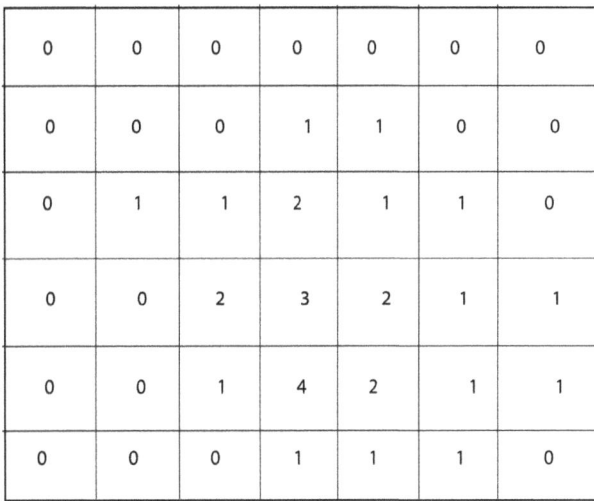

(b)

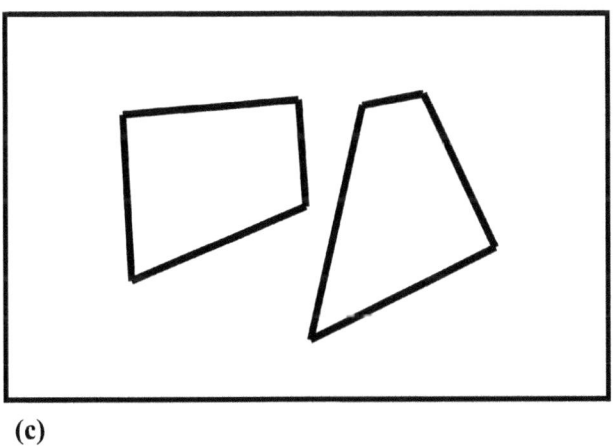

(b)

(c)

Most publications on spatial data address accuracy and precision (Burrough & McDonnell 1998; Gillings & Wise 1998; Wheatley & Gillings 2002). Accuracy refers to how close the value of spatial data, such as a point that has x (longitude), y (latitude), and z (elevation), is to the true value in the real world. Precision refers to the measure of dispersion – the methods used to represent this spatial data. In other words, "the finer the unit of measurement that can be resolved by the instrument, or stored by the computer, the more precise the data is said to be" (Wheatley and Gillings 2002:83). In statistical terminology, accuracy refers to "the degree with which an estimated mean differs from the true mean" whereas precision refers to "the degree of variation about the mean" (Burrough & McDonnell 1998:298,304).

The outcome of spatial data in terms of precision and accuracy is primarily set when the data is initially recorded. If spatial data is obtained from an outside source, it is important to know something about the precision and accuracy of the data. The data, once created or acquired, cannot necessarily be 'altered' so that it becomes more precise or accurate. According to Wheatley and Gillings (2002:84), good data quality "is partly a matter of ensuring that the data we use is appropriately precise and appropriately accurate for the job we have in hand, which itself is predicated on knowing what the accuracy and precision of our data are."

Scale refers to the ratio of the distance on a map to that measured on the ground. For example, a paper map may give a scale of 1:100,000. This translates to 1 cm on the map being equal to 100,000 cm, or 1,000 m. Resolution indicates the smallest distance that can be distinguished on a map with a given scale. For example, a map with a scale of 1:100,000 has the smallest distinguishable distance of 0.5 mm. Therefore, the resolution would be 50 m. The larger the map scale, the higher the resolution. A map with a larger scale of 1:10,000 would have a resolution of 5 m, a higher resolution than a 1:100,000 scale map. According to Gillings and Wise (1998:16), it is important to be aware of the scale of a data source because, as the scale decreases, so too does the resolution. This is interpreted to mean that the accuracy decreases, causing generalization of the data source.

Additional considerations that need addressing are discussed at length in other publications, most notably Archaeological Data Service's *GIS Guide to Good Practice* (1998) and Burrough and McDonnell's *Principles of Geographic Information Systems* (1998). Some of these considerations include the currency of the data (purpose of original data creation), the geo-referencing system used, data collection techniques, and the data classification and interpolation methods used.

Archaeological Data as Spatial Data

Chapters four through six focus on Natufian sites in the study region and their associated material culture. Although not explicitly stated in these three chapters, this data is considered to be spatial data. To be considered as spatial data, the sites and their information must have spatial coordinates. All sites used for this research have recorded geographical coordinates. A problem encountered when recording these geographical coordinates concerns the referencing system used. Some sites were recorded using the geographic coordinate system of latitude and longitude, while others were recorded using Universal Transverse Mercator (UTM) coordinate system. Furthermore, some sites using the geographical coordinates system recorded latitude and longitude in degrees, minutes and seconds while other sites used decimal degrees. To confuse matters more, some sites are recorded using projected coordinate systems. A projected coordinate system uses geographic coordinates that are built on a sphere or spheroid. In other words, these coordinates are based on the premise that the earth is not flat. The projections used in recording Natufian sites include the Palestine 1923 (Palestine Belt, Palestine Grid, Israel CS Grid), GCS 1980 (Israel TM), and WGS 1984 (UTM 35N and 36N). Some site reports never state which projection was used.

The solution to these problems is to convert all coordinates to one universal coordinate system using decimal degrees. The World Geodetic System 1984 (WGS 84) is used. Essentially, WGS is an earth-fixed global reference frame defined by primary and secondary parameters. The primary parameters define the shape of an earth ellipsoid, its angular velocity and the earth's mass; while the secondary parameters define a gravity model for the earth (http://www.wgs84.com accessed Jan. 31, 2005). The advantage to using WGS 84 is that it is a global system that provides a common reference for all sites. A second advantage to using this system is the fact that all other spatial data used in this research is already in WGS 84 format.

There are several routes that can be used for this data conversion. Steven Savage[3] developed a program called "ReprojectME!" specifically for the re-projection of the various geographical coordinate systems used in Southwest Asia. Alternatively, many GIS programs, such as ArcGIS v. 9.0, have conversion, or transformation, programs built into the system. These programs worked well, when the map projection for the site was known. When the projection is unknown, a more *primitive* tactic is used. This tactic involves locating the archaeological site on a paper map, then calculating the latitude and longitude (always expressed in degrees, minutes and seconds), then converting the latitude and longitude to decimal degrees. Conversion to decimal degrees is relatively simple. There are several web-based conversion programs from very reliable sources such as the United States Federal Communications Commission[4]. Once the coordinate is in decimal degrees, it can be transformed to WGS 84. Figure 7.3 demonstrates the results of this

---

[3] http://archaeology.asu.edu/jordan/Reproject.html
[4] http://www.fcc.gov/mb/audio/bickel/DDDMMSS-decimal.html

transformation of Natufian site coordinates into a common system, and then transferred to a GIS.

The Natufian sites are in vector format, represented as points. Each point has a series of associated attributes that define the characteristics of the point. These characteristics include the geographical location of the site, the material culture associated with the site, the excavation history and specifications of the site, as well as the results of the first stage of analysis for this research, cluster information. The inclusion of attribute data is a unique characteristic of GIScience that cannot be adequately represented through traditional paper mapping.

Figure 7.3 Natufian sites in their geographical context.

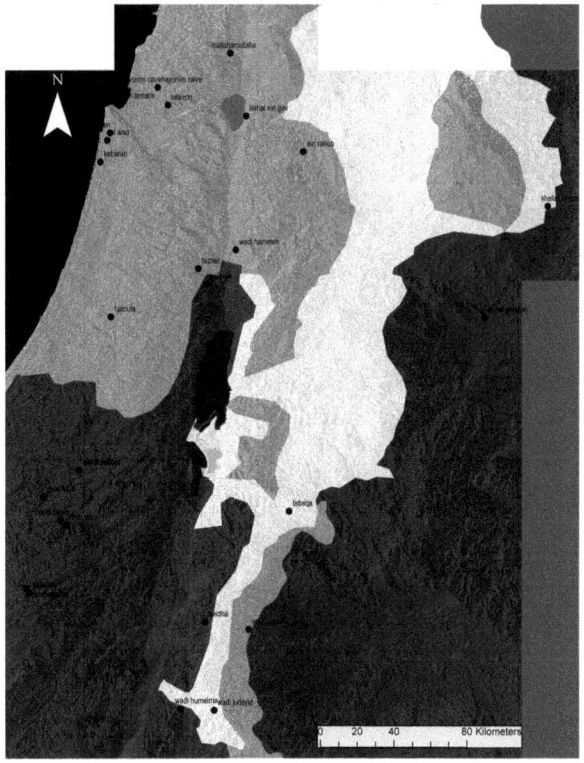

Elevation Models and Their Offspring

Digital elevation models (hereafter known as DEMs) and digital terrain models (hereafter known as DTMs) are continuous raster data layers where a grid of cells is superimposed over a map region. Each cell contains an elevation value. The data is continuous in that there is variation over the earth's land surface and is usually "a topographic height of the terrain, normally expressed in meters above sea level" (Wheatley and Gillings 2002:107). An alternative to the raster-based DEM and DTM is a vector data layer known as a triangulated irregular network (hereafter known as TIN). A TIN consists of a "sheet" of triangles, produced from Dalaunay triangulation of irregularly spaced points (Wheatley and Gillings 2002:112). Although DEMs/DTMs and TINs are produced by different means and stored as different structures, their function is essentially the same. Elevation models and their by-products have several uses in archaeological spatial analysis including (Wheatley and Gillings 2002:107):

- Visualization of topography and of other data in relation to terrain;
- cost-distance and least-cost pathway analysis;
- predictive modeling for research or management;
- analysis of visibility and inter-visibility;
- simulation of natural processes such as flooding and erosion; and
- virtual reality and the visual re-creation of archaeological landscapes.

More information on the use of elevation models is discussed in the next chapter.

All three elevation models can produce other forms of data, such as slope, aspect and hill-shade. Slope is another way of referring to the gradient of the land (steepness). Slope is expressed in one of two ways: in degrees (0°- 90°) or in percentages (0 – 100 %). Aspect, related to slope, refers to the direction or "surface orientation" of the slope (Wheatley and Gillings 2002:120). Aspect is also known as exposure. It can be represented in degrees (0° to 360°) or it can be represented in compass direction (N, NE, E, SE, S, SW, W, and NW). Hill shade, based on both slope and aspect calculations, represents the shading of the terrain as if you were situated perpendicular to the earth. The purpose of hill shade is mainly visual, for use in interpretation of landform (Wheatley and Gillings 2002:201). One other derivative of the elevation model that needs to be discussed because of its growing popularity and equally large complexity is hydrological or flood modeling. Hydrological modeling uses elevation models to delineate possible drainage systems then attempts to quantify the characteristics of these systems (ArcObjects Online 2003). In essence, you are modeling the *behavior* of water. Hydrological modeling not only requires an elevation model but also relies on derivatives of the elevation model, such as slope and aspect.

In support of military applications, the National Imagery and Mapping Agency (NIMA) developed a standard digital dataset Digital Terrain Elevation Data (DTED®). This DTED product is a uniform matrix of terrain elevation values that provides basic quantitative data for systems and applications that require information on terrain elevation, slope, or surface roughness. DTED Level 1 elevation data cell resolution is 3 arc seconds (nominally 90 m). This means that, for 1° of latitude, 1201 elevation points are recorded. The information content is approximately equivalent to a 1:250,000 scale resolution. Accuracy statements are individually calculated for every DTED. Accuracy objectives are: *Absolute Horizontal* - 90% Circular Error (C.E.) World Geodetic System (WGS) $\leq$ 50 m; *Absolute Vertical* - 90%

Linear Error (L.E.) Mean Sea Level (MSL) ≤ 30 m. This means that the relative vertical accuracy - point to point - is 90% L.E. MSL ≤ 20 m over a 1° cell. The individual calculated DTED cell accuracies are usually better than those cited in the documentation (NIMA 2000:3). The coordinate reference system used is the World Geographic Reference System (GEOREF) and the horizontal datum is the World Geodetic System (WGS84).

I was able to acquire DTED Level 1 data from the United States Geological Survey (USGS) for a relatively small cost (US $115). DTED Level 0 data is accessible from USGS for free, but its elevation post spacing is 30 arc seconds (nominally 1 km). This means that, for 1° of latitude, 121 elevation points are recorded. The information content is approximately equivalent to a 1:1,000,000 scale resolution. Unfortunately, DTED Level 2 data is not available for the study region to date. This data would provide elevation post spacing every 1 arc second (nominally 30 m). This means that for 1° latitude, 3601 elevation points are recorded. The information content is approximately equivalent to a 1:50,000 scale resolution. As the level of resolution scale decreases, the need for additional computer power and memory to display and manipulate the geological data increases exponentially.

The DTED data, in its original format, is a 16-bit grayscale image. Figure 7.4 illustrates the original data. In order to make this data useful for research, it is necessary to reclassify the data into meaningful values. Figure 7.5 demonstrates the results of reclassifying the 16-bit gray scale data into DEM with 100 m intervals. From this map, it is possible to produce slope and aspect data. Figures 7.6 and 7.7 show calculated slope and aspect for the region respectfully. The DEM, slope and aspect data are the primary spatial data used for this research.

It is important to realize that the use of modern DEMs to study prehistoric populations does have limitations. The present physical environment is not always indicative of the past. Climatic changes can affect vegetation growth, water levels, and soil deposition or erosion. The ideal solution is to reconstruct the environment for the period of interest, then create a DEM based on paleo-environmental research. For the Near East, there is no shortage of research on this topic. However, most research is limited to specific areas such as the Ghab in Syria, the Hula in the northern part of the Syrio-African Rift (northern most Israel), or to specific archaeological sites and no synthesis of this research has been conducted (Bartov et al. 2000; Baruch & Bottema 1991; Cordova et al. 2005; Goldberg 1980; van Zeist & Bottema 1982; Zohary 1973). TAVO (Turbinger Atlas des Vorgeren Orient 1991) has published vegetation maps for the Near East but they are general in that they are not spatially referenced.

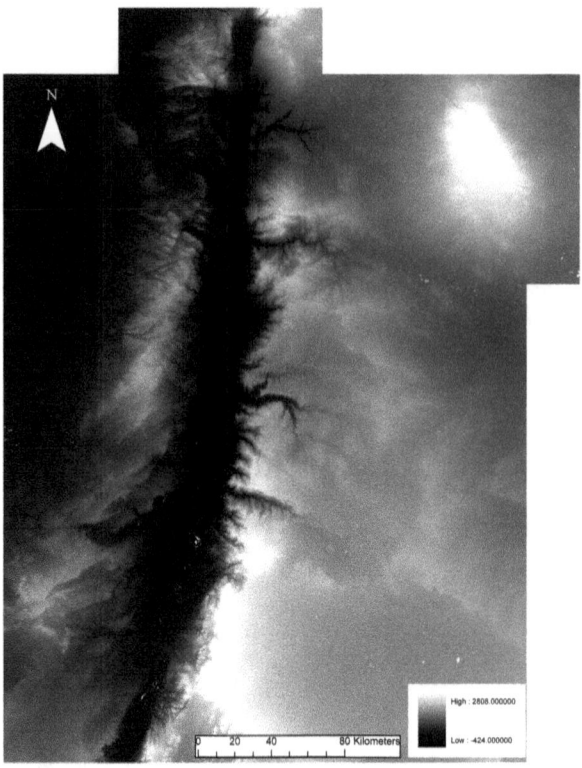

Figure 7.4 Original digital terrain elevation data (DTED).

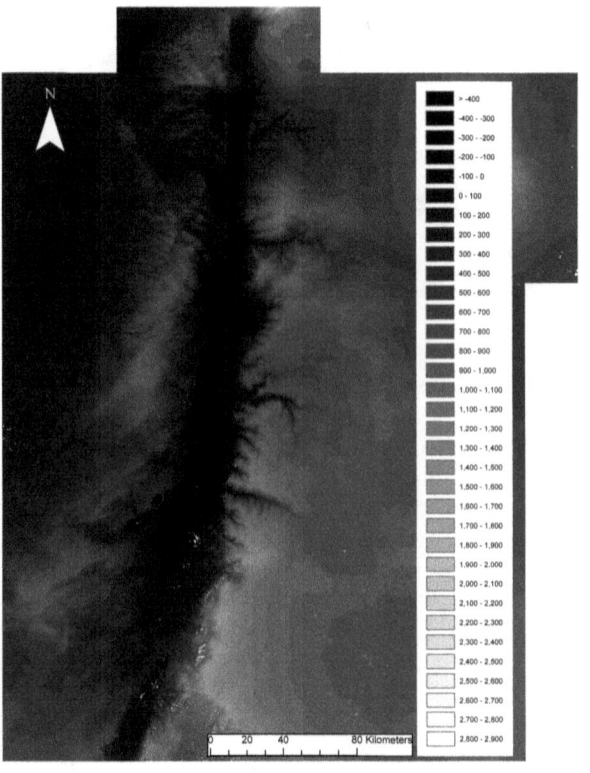

Figure 7.5 Digital elevation model (DEM) for the study area in 100 m intervals.

Figure 7.6 Slope values for the study area.

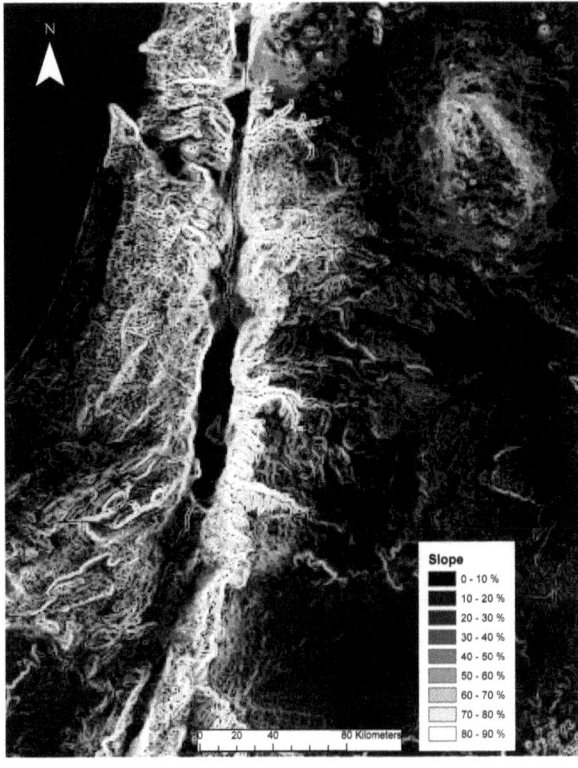

Figure 7.7 Aspect values for the study area.

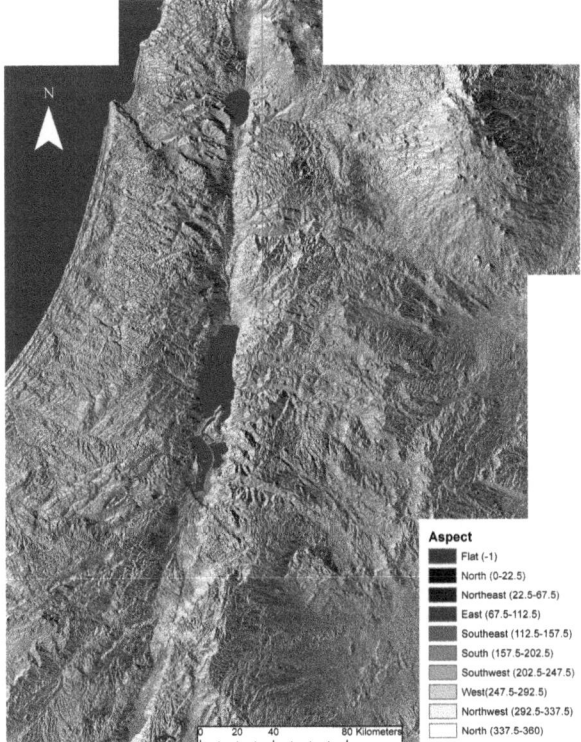

Present Ecological Data

Vector polygons data, produced by ESRI for the World Wildlife Fund and representing global terrestrial eco-regions, is used for this research. Eco-regions are "relatively large areas of land or water in the world containing a characteristic set of natural communities that share a large majority of their species, dynamics, and environmental conditions" (ESRI Data & Maps 2003). This data set contains all terrestrial eco-regions, which include a collection of the Earth's most outstanding and diverse terrestrial, freshwater, and marine habitats. The data is based on the Digital Chart of the World as a scale of 1:1,000,000. The data is recorded using decimal degree geographic coordinate units and uses the WSG 84 geodetic model. Although the data is generalized and the tolerance was not recorded so the positional accuracy is not known, it can be used for geographic display and analysis at national and world levels. According to the creators of the data (ESRI Data & Maps 2003):

> We began by accepting the biogeographic realms of Pielou (1979) and Udvardy (1975) and modifying the biome systems of Dinerstein et al. (1995) and Ricketts et al. (1999). We then consulted existing global maps of floristic or zoogeographic provinces, global and regional maps of units based on the distribution of selected groups of plants and animals, the world's biotic province maps, and global maps of broad vegetation types. These were useful for evaluating the extent of realms and biomes, the first two tiers in our hierarchical classification. We then identified published regional classification systems to be used as a baseline for eco-region boundaries. Data and consultations from regional experts were also important for final eco-region delineations.

The attributes extracted from this data are the Eco-Name and the Biome. The Eco-Name is the descriptive name for the eco-region. Figure 7.8 shows the Eco-Names for the eco-regions in the study area. The Biome is a broad eco-region that: a) experiences comparable climatic regimes; b) has similar vegetation structure; c) displays similar spatial patterns of biodiversity; d) contains flora and fauna with similar guild structures and life histories; e) has similar minimum requirements and thresholds for maintaining certain biodiversity features; and f) has similar sensitivities to human disturbance. Figure 7.9 shows the Biomes present in the study area.

As with the limitations discussed in using modern DEMs to study prehistoric events, the use of present day ecological data also has limitations. To test if there is a significant difference between modern an ancient ecological biomes, I conducted a comparison between modern vegetation (Figure 7.8) with vegetation outlined in the TAVO map publication. TAVO indicates that at approximately 12,000 BP, the Mediterranean biome was predominantly mixed dwarf-scrub and broad-leaved forests; the Irano-Turanian forest steppe and mixed xeromorphic dwarf-shrublands and grasslands; and the Saharo-Arabian mixed xeromorphic dwarf-shrublands and grasslands as well as scarcely vegetated sand dunes (particularly in the Negev/Sinai) (TAVO 1991). This comparison suggests that modern vegetation does not significantly differ from vegetation at 12,000 BP.

Data Produced through Remote Sensing

Remote sensing is the science of acquiring information about the Earth's surface without actually being in contact with it. This is done through detection and recording of reflected or emitted energy (electromagnetic radiation) by sensors onboard aircraft and satellites (Burrough & McDonnell 1998:77). Remotely sensed data, once processed, can be in analog or digital format. Digital data is recorded as a series of cells or pixels, each coded with a value representing the electromagnetic radiation detected by the sensors (Burrough & McDonnell 1998:77). The remotely sensed data used in this research is digital because the data was obtained from sensors mounted on satellites.

Figure 7.8 Ecological regions for the study area.

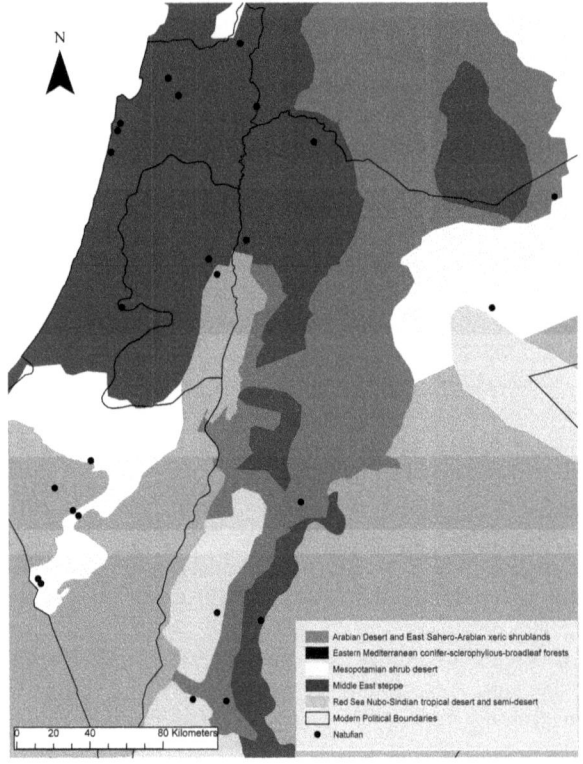

Figure 7.9 Terrestrial biomes for the study region.

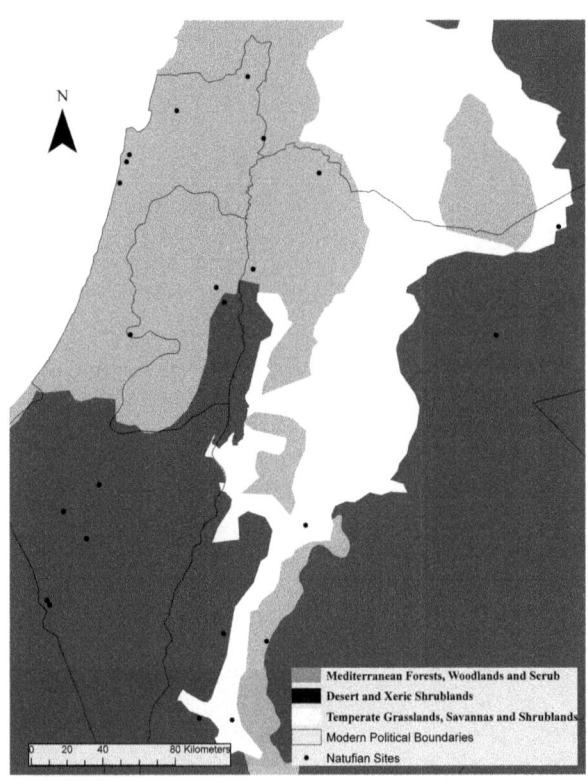

NIMA-SPOT Images

This remotely sensed data is provided by the National Imagery and Mapping Agency (NIMA). It contains 10 m resolution Digital Orthorectified Imagery (DOI-10M) derived from data obtained from the SPOT Image Corporation under an unrestricted license. The unrestricted license means that information extracted from DOI-10M does not require copyright notices. A series of 39 tiles in the region from 35 N, 34 E (northwest corner) to 29 N, 40 E (southeast corner) which contains Jordan, Israel and parts of their neighbors, were collected and made available for download through Stephen Savage's web site at Arizona State University[5]. The original source is found at the National Geospatial Intelligence Agency[6]. Most of the 39 tiles cover an area that is one degree east-west (a few are 1.1°) and one-half degree north-south. The images are panchromatic, digitally orthorectified (scale-corrected), 10 m resolution, GeoTiff, using the WGS 84 coordinate system. They can be loaded directly into a GIS program and used as background images or as overlays for DEMs. However, SPOT images are limited in their function for creating new information for comparative analysis.

LandSat 28m resolution

The LandSat (Land remote sensing satellite program) satellites observe the Earth, and the data collected have been used for almost 30 years to study the environment,

---

[5] http://archaeology.asu.edu/jordan/nimasat.html

[6] http://geoengine.nima.mil/geospatial/SW_TOOLS/NIMAMUSE/webinter/rast_roam.html

resources, and natural and man-made changes on the Earth's surface (http://LandSat.gsfc.nasa.gov/, accessed May 21, 2004). The 28m resolution LandSat images used in this research are processed from the MrSid images available on the NASA MrSid Image Server web site. Those images are in UTM projection, and do not include the header information, which made it necessary to re-project. Fortunately, Steven Savage went through a "twelve-step program" to convert the UTM projection into WGS84, decimal degree format[7]. According to Savage, the MrSid images are first converted to .tif files, and then header information is written into the .tif image. Once complete, the images can be re-projected to WGS84 decimal degree format. Once again, I was fortunate to have this re-projected data available for download from Savage's web site. The LandSat images contain five-band color information in the image, which makes them suitable for analysis with an image analysis program.

Both SPOT and LandSat images are used here to illustrate the current topography of the landscape. The usefulness of satellite images for this research will be to render them in 3D. To do so, the images are used as an overlay for DEMs to create a 3D perspective of the research area. Figures 7.10 and 7.11 contrast SPOT with LandSat images of the region.

Figure 7.10 SPOT image for the study area.

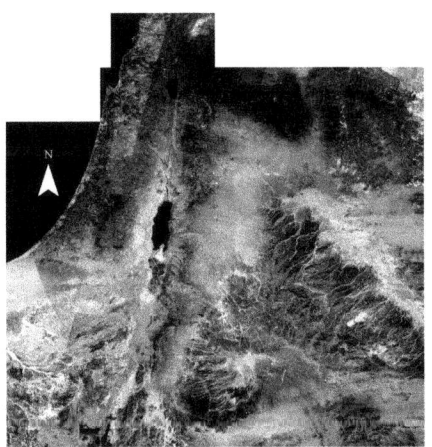

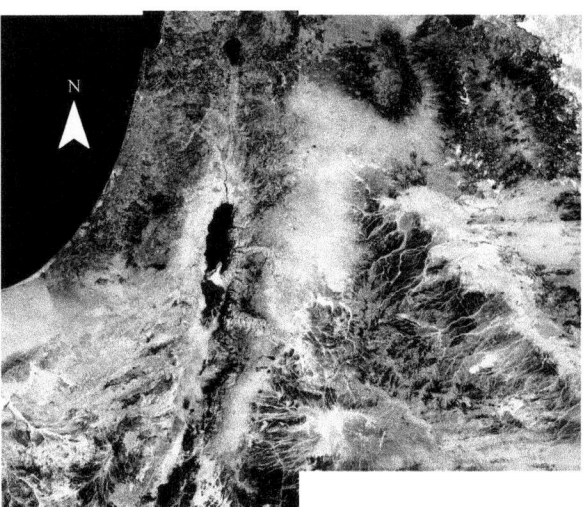

Summary

This chapter introduced the concepts of spatial data and GIScience. Spatial data represents the second data source used in this research. It is clear that archaeological data are included in the category of spatial data in that it is geographically referenced. Other spatial data used represents topographical and ecological characteristics of the study region, including elevations, slopes, aspects, ecological zones, and biomes. The combination of spatial data that is archaeological and environmental represents structure that both enables and constrains agency in that this data represents the social and ecological structures for a population.

The implementation of GIScience in recent archaeological research is described as positivistic in the sense that (1) techniques direct research questions rather than the archaeological data, (2) there is a tendency towards an environmentally deterministic interpretation of the archaeological record, and (3) cognition and perception of past human populations are unrecognized. These are briefly addressed in this chapter and explored further in the following chapter.

The next chapter introduces the second part of the methodology for this research. Keeping in mind this socio-theoretical critique of GIScience-driven archaeological research, the second part of this research will focus on spatial analysis that is theoretically driven.

Figure 7.11 LandSat image for the study area.

---

[7] http://archaeology.asu.edu/jordan/LandSat.html

CHAPTER 8
DATA ANALYSIS PART II – CREATING SPATIAL DATA MODELS

Introduction

Chapter seven discusses the concept of spatial data as well as the spatial data used for this research. This chapter illustrates the methods used to analyze spatial data in order to create a spatial data model. Spatial data models, also known as geographical data models, formalize how space is divided into components for analysis and communication. A spatial model also "assumes that phenomena can be uniquely identified, that attributes can be measured or specified and that geographical coordinates can be registered" (Burrough & McDonnell 1998:21). Spatial data models are categorized as either representation models – those that represent objects in a landscape; or process models – those that attempt to simulate processes in the landscape (ESRI 2003:56). Representation models are illustrated in chapter seven through discussion of digital elevation models and their derivatives. Process models are illustrated in this chapter through cost-surface analysis.

It is accepted that traveling by foot or any other form of transportation from one location to another can be measured in distance. However, measurement can also take the form of time or energy exerted. It is also recognized that distance, time and energy exertion are not always equal in magnitude. For example, the distance required to reach a given location from two different points may be equal but the time and energy required may be different because of terrain. Human travel tends to minimize both time and energy but one measure may, at times, be sacrificed over the other. Movement within a landscape is influenced by both physical and symbolic resources (Wheatley & Gillings 2002:155).

Geographers initiated interest in what Aldenderfer (1998:11) terms "models of movement," - the measurement of cost (time, energy, or both) in traveling from one location to another. Models of movement are interested in locating the optimal routes for traveling over a given landscape. The second part of this analysis introduces the method used to model movement for the Natufian. This model includes the movement of people, materials, ideas, and information. To analyze this movement, cost-surface analysis is used in a GIS environment. The basic concept for cost analysis is that there is a price one must pay to move from one location to another and that the objective is to select a route with the minimum price, or the least expenditure of time and/or energy.

This chapter comprehensively presents the principles of cost-surface analysis and the techniques employed in a GIS. It also appraises their advantages and limitations and illustrates examples of this methodology in an archaeological context are illustrated. According to Van Leusen (1999:218), cost-surface analysis is "the generic name for a series of GIS based techniques based on the ability to assign a cost to each cell in a raster map, and to accumulate these costs by traveling over the map." By the conclusion of this chapter, it will be understood that cost-surface analysis goes beyond this definition.

History of Cost-Surface Analysis and Models

Cost-surface analysis is historically linked to spatial models in geography. Those models most noted for shaping cost-surface analysis include location theory, central-place theory and site-catchment analysis. Elaborations of these historical models are not discussed at length here because others (Clark 1977; Haggett 1965) have thoroughly covered this subject. Therefore, only a brief summary will be outlined.

Location theory, first developed by Von Thünen (1826), states that concentric zones (circles) of human land use and activity have a tendency to develop around isolated site centers. Weber (1909) elaborates this theory by speculating that the locations of these sites are not isolated but rather, there is a connection between site location and the movement of resources. Furthermore, he hypothesizes that sites are selected to minimize unnecessary movement so that "sites represent minimum-energy least-cost locations" (Clark 1977:22). A constant theme in these early location models is the focus on the individual site.

Christaller (1933) developed the first model that integrates the "relationship between the area served by sites" with the "site's functions and the network of sites" (Clark 1977:23). This model is known as *central-place*. Effectively, this is the first model that examines a collective of sites, rather than single sites, thus moving the level of analysis from individual to the local and regional. Others (Lösch 1944; Haggett 1965) further indicate expansion of this model by incorporating hierarchies of site location and spheres of influence.

Built upon location and central-place models, *site-catchment analysis* suggests that site location and the proximal resources are distant-dependant. First introduced in anthropology by Vita-Finzi and Higgs (1970:5), the site-catchment model is defined as "the study of the relationships between technology and those natural resources lying within economic range of individual sites." This model is unique in that it includes the topography of the land as a variable affecting the relationship between technology, natural resources and site location. Recalling chapter three, the site-catchment model is used in early settlement pattern analysis of Natufian sites. Figure 8.1 illustrates a hypothetical site-catchment model for the Natufian sites used in this research.

Incorporation of archaeological site-catchment analysis in a GIS environment is demonstrated through a method known as tessellation. Tessellation is a form of spatial allocation in that this method assigns an area to a point, or site in the case of archaeology. In this sense, an area such as an archaeological region is divided into smaller neighboring units with no break between them (Burrough & McDonnell 1998:114). Common forms of tessellation include Thiessen Polygons (Voronoi tessellation), and Delaunay Triangulation. These two forms differ in that Thiessen polygons allocate space around a point (such as an archaeological site), whereas triangulation joins the points using nearest neighbor as a factor, thereby creating triangulation. Figure 8.2 demonstrates tessellation of Natufian sites through Thiessen polygons. Although tessellation and triangulation are expedient methods for relating data points to space, they can only be used for preliminary analysis of qualitative data. According to Wheatley and Gillings (2002:151), "tessellation is a solely geometric allocation method and, as such, it assumes that the social and geographic features of an area have no impact on the allocation of space...instead of tessellations, contemporary archaeologists have more frequently turned to variants of what is termed *cost surface* modeling."

Figure 8.1 Hypothetical site-catchment model for Natufian sites.

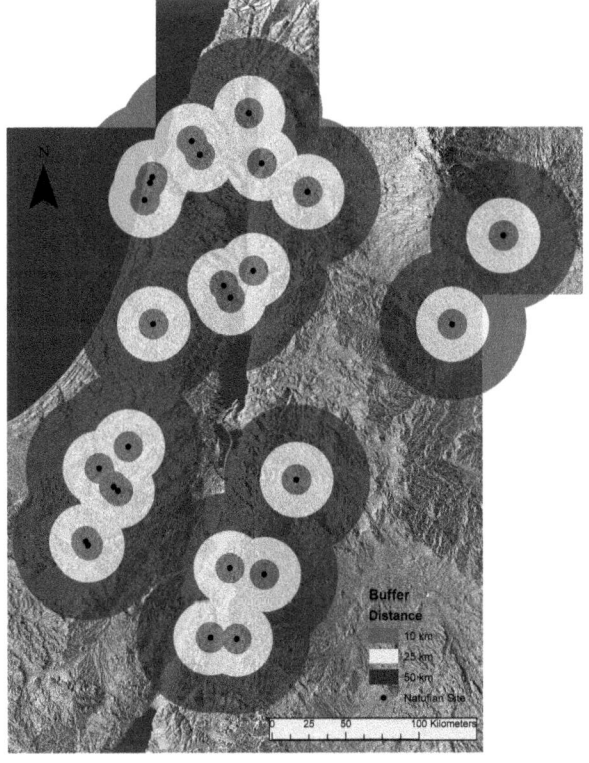

Figure 8.2: Tessellation of Natufian sites through Thiessen polygons.

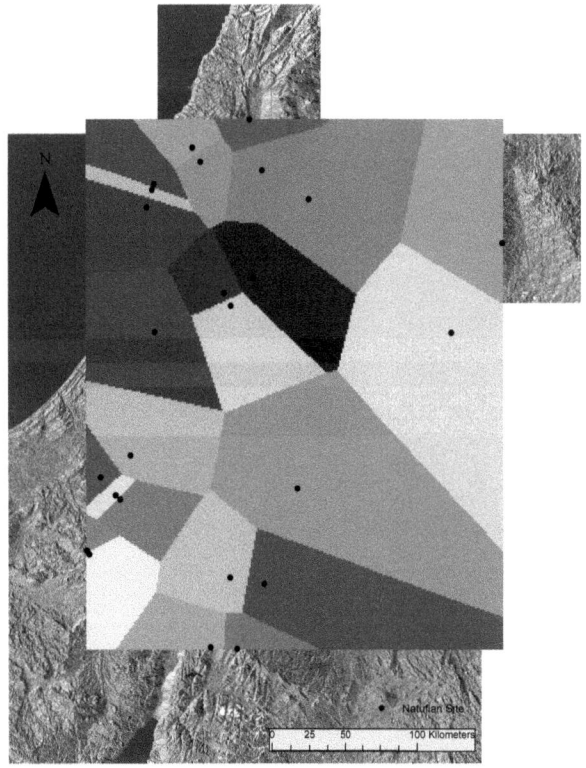

Cost-Surface Analysis

As I state earlier, cost-surface analysis is a GIS based technique that assigns a cost to each cell in a raster setting on the basis of the notion that one must pay a price to move from one location to another. This price may include, but is not necessarily limited to, distance, time and energy. Cost-surface analysis is comparable to "earlier attempts to provide site-catchments based on time contours derived from ethnographic studies of hunter-gatherers or simple farming societies" (Stančič, et al. 1995:163). These earlier attempts were difficult to carry out because they were extremely time-intensive. However, with the introduction of GIS, there is a great reduction in the time involved in this procedure.

Essentially cost surfaces are mathematical models, also known as friction surfaces, to determine the route of movement. These mathematical models use either isotropic or anisotropic algorithms to create these surfaces. Isotropic algorithms incorporate the distance required to travel from one location to another as well as an additional relative cost based on a particular quantifiable element of the landscape, such as slope (Bell & Lock 2000:86). Figure 8.3 illustrates the fundamental characteristics of an isotropic algorithm by comparing walking velocity to slope of a landscape. To accomplish this, two layers of information are required: (1) a file containing the location of features from which the distance is calculated (seed locations) and (2) a file which contains the cost of travel across each landscape unit (friction surface) derived from slope data (Wheatley & Gillings 2002:152). An important issue concerning isotropic algorithms is that, while they illustrate the cost of moving across a heterogeneous surface, they do not consider the direction of movement. In this sense, isotropic algorithms are symmetrical.

Figure 8.3: Representation of hypothetical walking velocity compared to slope.

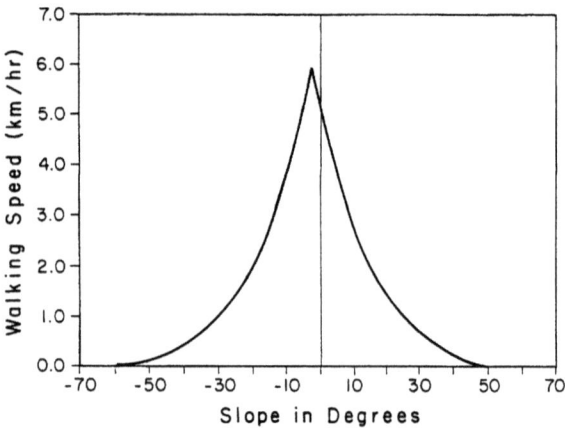

Anisotropic algorithms not only incorporate the distance and costs, in terms of friction, required to travel from one location to another, but also address direction of movement (Wheatley & Gillings 2002:152). There are several algorithms that can be used to create an anisotropic cost surface. The only real difference between these algorithms is how they deal with direction. Figure 8.4 demonstrates the component of direction included in anisotropic algorithms. Some use a single cost, such as aspect, while others (Dean 1996) use multiple direction-specific maps. In debating which method to use, Valdez and Dean (2000:4) state that regardless of how the directionality of unit costs is handled, all anisotropic algorithms build their outputs by iteratively searching for the least costly routes.

Figure 8.4: Graphical representation of Tobler's hiking algorithm.

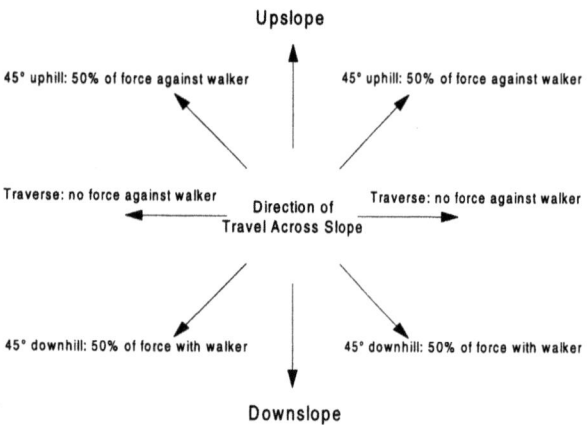

One anisotropic method used in archaeological as well as environmental research is Tobler's hiking function algorithm (Tobler 1993). According to this algorithm, for walking on footpaths in hilly terrain:

$$W = 6 \exp \{-3.5 * abs (S + 0.05)\}$$

Where W is the walking velocity, S is the slope of the terrain, calculated as vertical change divided by horizontal change measured in the same units. The velocity is given in km/hr. As Tobler (1993:2) indicates, to use this function, "one simply calculates the slope of the terrain and then converts this to a walking velocity" via the algorithm. The velocity on a flat terrain is 5 km/hr whereas 'off-path' travel times can be estimated by multiplying any walking velocity by 0.6 (Tobler 1993:2). The algorithm is used because it is symmetric but slightly offset from a slope of zero. Therefore, velocity is greatest when walking down a slight incline with velocity reduced for both increases and decreases in slope (Gorenflo & Gale 1990:244). Figure 8.4 graphically represents the hiking function where walking speed is determined by slope.

The characteristics of isotropic and anisotropic algorithms as well as the decision to use one over the other are the subject of debate. In reference to Tobler's hiking function, Van Leusen (1999:217) states that this function remains symmetric even if it is slightly offset from a slope of zero (so the estimated velocity will be greatest when walking down a slight incline) and it is still isotropic. However, Marble (1996) asserts that the function relating physiological expenditure to slope is appropriately symmetric and that travel costs have both isotropic and anisotropic components. Aldenderfer (1998:12) asserts that the hiking algorithm can be applied to any walking situation in which the slope can be defined as a change in elevation over a change in distance traveled and "is used appropriately when it is possible to break the different segments of the trip into positive or negative slopes." Most authors agree that travel costs have both isotropic and anisotropic components. However, this debate is further extended to include questioning the use of cost-surface analysis.

Tobler's algorithm is not the only pedestrian cost surface model that can be considered. Two other models, one proposed by McDonald (1961) the other by Pandolf et al. (1977), take into consideration the costs of walking over a landscape. Both models are physiological in that they consider the weight of the pedestrian as well as the potential load the individual may be carrying. Pandolf's algorithm measures degree of slope against the metabolic rate in watts per step, while McDonald's algorithm measures degree of slope against Kcal per step.

For this research, physiological information is not available. As well, the distances traveled are potentially large and may not be representative of a daily journey. Rather, the routes I am interested in may be indicative of seasonal, yearly or even greater lengths of time. Finally, the routes or paths that I am interested in finding may not be indicative of routes used for trade of physical materials. Rather, the exchange may merely be that of information. In this sense, I will not account for the potential loads that pedestrians are carrying. On the basis of interests of this research, I will use Tobler's algorithm.

Critique of Cost-Surface Analysis

According to Boaz and Uleberg (1995:257-258), the use of cost-surface analysis is questionable on both theoretical and methodological grounds.

> The use of cost-surface analysis presumes that the occupant's perception of the area was based upon the single economic variable of transportation costs. While such considerations are an aspect of cognition, focusing on a single economic variable is clearly an oversimplification. Methodologically, cost-surface analysis ignores the importance of unknown or seasonable variable factors affecting transport costs.

This critique is legitimate given the high value placed on transportation cost while the unknown and seasonable factors are ignored. Theoretically, this is a principle concern when the focus of research is past human perceptions of a landscape. However, if the research question focuses on social interaction at a regional level, transportation cost plays a primary factor in degree or level of interaction. The dismissal of unknown or seasonal variables in the creation of cost surfaces is a concern, regardless of the focus of research. Boaz and Uleberg (1995:258) make the point that "concepts of distance and travel costs are culturally bound and are more complex than are allowed for in cost-surface analysis". I agree that these concepts are culturally bound in that the notion of cost for the individual and the group is related to the shared perceptions within a given society. To address this issue, one must look to other sources of information, such as ethnography, oral or written history, to factor in the culturally bound concept of distance. In the absence of such information, as is the case in most prehistoric studies, this limitation must be acknowledged, but cannot necessarily be rectified.

Van Leusen (2002:68) also draws attention to the prominence of resource-centered networks created through cost-surface analysis, with little attention paid to "the importance of day-to-day social networks by which neighboring families and villages form and maintain a community." To address this concern, Van Leusen suggests combining resource and social networks. Again, I agree with the point Van Leusen makes but I believe that, in archaeology, the use of cost-surface analysis is overwhelmingly directed at answering questions related to social networks. The following section, highlighting examples of cost-surface analysis in archaeology, addresses this critique.

A second concern is directed at the algorithm used to generate the cost surfaces. For example, Bell and Lock (2000:89) note that traditional (isotropic) slope-derived cost surfaces use uniform slope values, meaning that the cost value would be the same for "modeling a movement *down* a 20° slope and *up* the same." In a 1996 unpublished report, Marble suggests that, since the function relating physiological expenditure to slope is approximately symmetrical, we can safely ignore the whole problem of anisotropy (Van Leusen 2002:6.7).

A third concern, or more appropriately realization, when doing cost-surface analysis is that the costs calculated are relative rather than absolute costs. To address this issue, Van Leusen (2002:6.8) suggests that there be differential weighting of the sites used in the analysis. This does not, in itself, transform the costs into absolutes, but it does regulate the cost based on site importance. Others (Tomlin1990:170-176) suggest compiling multiple least-cost-path s into a 'least-cost network'. Bell et al. (2002) used this approach in their research on routes connecting Samnite settlements in Italy.

It must be stressed that the creation of cost surfaces is based on relative, not absolute costs. Taking into consideration the algorithm used to generate the cost surface, as well as applying various tactics, such as site weighting or compiling a series of cost-path models to create a least-cost network, or corridor, will address some reservations about cost-surface analysis.

Cost-Surface Analysis in Archaeology

Cost-surface analysis was first effectively applied in 1989 to an archaeological project in an attempt to define the territories of ancient sites through the use of site-catchment analysis on the island of Hvar (off the coast of central Dalmatia Croatia) (Gaffney and Stančič 1991). In this research, "Gaffney and Stančič employ GIS to develop a topographically-based cost surface, in which the cost is not simply based on distance, but on the slope that one must cross to reach that point and return" (Bell et al. 2002:174). This model is isotropic in that it does not consider direction of slope but its initial results were highly significant.

According to Gaffney, Stančič and Watson (1996:214), investigation of economic catchments of the largest defended sites on the island illustrate how GIS is used to establish the relationship between principal prehistoric sites on the island and their economic basis. They constructed cost surface catchments for each large defended site (hillfort) by using a timed and measured journey as a calibration factor (Gaffney et al. 1996:214-215). The results suggest that these sites might be interpreted as central-places of small prehistoric communities and that they were situated in order to control large expanses of fertile land (ibid. 1996:215).

In 1990, Savage used landscape archaeology to study of social organization in the Late Archaic in the Savannah River Valley of Georgia and South Carolina (Savage 1990:330). This research is considered innovative for its time in that its primary goal was to develop an understanding of Late Archaic social organization that provides a framework for studying the social and technological changes attending the period. Savage also attempted to develop a GIS-based methodology that can work hand-in-hand with anthropological theory to provide new avenues of research into past cultural systems (Savage 1990:331). This research includes a four-step methodology: (1) determining site function based on form, space and time; (2) deriving least-cost movement ranges from base camps; (3) creating habitual use areas with Thiessen Polygons; and (4) overlaying site types on Thiessen Polygons. Savage created a cost surface by using hydrology and terrain roughness (slope). Thiessen Polygon boundaries were then drawn by dividing the landscape along straight lines that run between areas of greatest equal distance between base camps. This model is based exclusively on isotropic cost surfaces.

Ruggles and Church (1996:158) illustrate the shortcomings for archaeologists when using Thiessen-based tessellations of space. They state that tessellations are space-filling, assume sites are contemporaneous, and are not truly hierarchical, and continue to operate under conditions of physical isotropia. Ruggles & Church (1996:158) further state that:

> A dramatic example of this in archaeology can be found in Savage (1990), where, after carefully reasoned exploration of the effects of topography on a group's interaction with a territory, he had to resort to a standard, isotropically defined Thiessen tessellation of space to approximate use areas.

Using an integrative approach to cost-surface analysis, Madry & Rakos (1996) use GIS for analysis of digital elevation models to study the interaction of two major cultural components and the landscape in the Arroux River valley, in the Burgundy region of France. The relationships between the location of hillforts and known roads are examined through line-of-sight and optimum-route-selection analysis. Results show a strong correlation of these routes with the visibility from the hilltop defenses (1996:104). This research is innovative for its time in that Madry and Rakos have shown that cost surface models need not be limited to the single variable of slope. They demonstrate this through generation of paths between hillforts, on the basis of maintaining the highest possible elevation and using the lowest angles of slope while remaining in view of the maximum number of forts (Bell & Lock 2000:87). Regardless, this model is limited because it does not choose the total least-cost-path but only the iterative least-cost-path (Madry & Rakos 1996:113). This limitation is a result of the algorithm used in this research (a limitation of the GIS program used – GRASS).

In research similar to that of Madry and Rakos, Llobera (2000) provides a model that illustrates the sociology of movement. This model demonstrates a relationship between monuments and linear ditches from an area of the Yorkshire Wolds in eastern England. The two important characteristics identified in this model are the retrieval of general patterns of movement rather than specific paths and the notion that these patterns are a vital piece in the socialization of people into a landscape (Llobera 2000:65). In this model, the likelihood that an individual would move into a specific location is defined in relation to the cost of reaching that location from any other one (Llobera 2000:70). The costs are based on both topographic cost and the effects of landscape features (soil, vegetation, and hydrology). In effect, costs associated with the landscape as well as perception of the landscape are considered. The results show that "the effect of each linear ditch on the landscape is proportional to the magnitude – that is the effect due to the presence of multiple ditches is much more noticeable that that for single ditches" (Llobera 2000:80).

The last five years have introduced an examination of the various algorithms used in cost-surface analysis and realization that some are more efficient than others (Bell & Lock 2000; Bell, Wilson, & Wickham 2002; Jennings & Craig 2001). For example, Bell and Lock (2000) explore the origins and route of the prehistoric Ridgeway in Oxfordshire, England and its spatial and temporal relationships with a series of Iron Age hillforts located on and close to it. By considering movement and developing a new approach to cost-surface and least-cost-path analyses, the authors suggest an early origin for the trackway based primarily on topographic considerations. Interpreting the least-cost-path suggests that, when first constructed; the hillforts were located on the existing Ridgeway to establish a direct relationship with travelers along the track. However, their initial results indicated a problem with the technique (isotropic algorithm). According to Bell and Lock (2000:91), "The algorithm used conceives of downward movement, especially on steep slopes, as both preferable and entailing least-cost." To tackle this problem, they introduced a "topographical bias" into the algorithm's interpretation of slope and aspect by proportionally inverting the north-south aspect data to generate a topography in which the descent is no longer a descent but rather an ascent (Bell & Lock 2000:92). This research represents a new direction in cost-surface analysis in archaeology in that it "introduces anisotropy in slope-related costs by interposing an aspect-checking step – cutting costs by 50% for 'angled' ascents and benefits by 50% for 'angled' descents" (Van Leusen 2002:6.6).

Similarly, Jennings and Craig (2001) test a model for the political economy of the Wari Empire (AD 600–1000) of Peru. They test the model through a GIS in which two kinds of "distance from" layers cover the study area. These layers, or cost surfaces, were created using Tobler's hiking algorithm. Results from all distance measures show a trend for Wari administrative sites in politically complex valleys to be further from the center than one would expect (Jennings & Craig 2001:492) Furthermore, the application of Tobler's hiking algorithm shows that administrative sites in politically complex valleys are a greater walking time away from the center than all but one of the sites found in valleys exhibiting simple Early Intermediate Period political complexity (Jennings and Craig 2001:492-493).

This survey of archaeological research using cost-surface analysis demonstrates two points. The first is that, although a recent methodology, cost-surface analysis is receiving attention and is proving to be a valuable form of analysis. The second point is that, with this attention, comes critical evaluation as well as progressive improvements. In other words, problems with cost-surface analysis quickly attract attention and are promptly addressed.

Cost-Surface Analysis – Methods for this Research

In brief summary, two major considerations need to be addressed prior to initiating cost-surface analysis. The first involves the features from which the cost distance will be calculated (seed locations). The second is the algorithm used to create the friction surface.

The Natufian sites are considered the seed locations for this research. However, the first stage of analysis in this research (cluster analysis) suggests that the sites are grouped on the basis of their similarity in material culture not on their ecological environments. For this stage of analysis, cost surfaces for sites within each cluster will be calculated individually. The resulting cost calculations will provide a least-cost network for sites within their groups. This will give insights into the social network among *similar* Natufian sites. Alternatively, it is also beneficial to examine all Natufian sites in their spatial context. To do so, cost calculations for the totality of Natufian sites are also conducted. These calculations are then compared to the cost calculations generated for the individual clusters.

In considering the algorithm used to create the friction surface, it is apparent that anisotropic algorithms are preferable to isotopic algorithms. The choice to use an anisotropic algorithm becomes more complex when considering the diversity of functions as well as the capacity of the GIS program. Although travel costs have both isotropic and anisotropic components, built-in cost-surface analysis functions in GIS programs usually do not allow users to select one algorithm over another. For example, the GRASS cost-analysis function is isotropic and iterative so that it does not choose the total least-cost (Madry & Rakos 1996:113). IDRISI uses the following equation:

$$\text{Cost} = \text{Cost}_{base} \times F_{max}^{\cos k(\alpha)}$$

$Cost_{base}$ is the base cost, F_{max} is the maximum magnitude of the cost surface, α is the angle between the direction of travel and the direction of cost and k is a constant used to effect the costs between $\alpha = 0°$ and $\alpha = 180°$. This function is anisotropic.

Alternatively, ArcGIS version 9.0, the program used in this research, contains a suite of tools that make the application of this function very simple through ArcToolbox distance function Path Distance. The **PathDistance** function calculates, for each cell, the least-accumulative-cost distance over a cost surface from a source cell or a set of source cells while accounting for surface distance and horizontal and vertical cost factors. The formula used by PathDistance to calculate the total cost from one cell another is:

Cost_distance = Surface_distance * Vertical_factor * ~ (Friction(a) * Horizontal_factor(a) + ~ Friction(b) * Horizontal_factor(b)) /2)

The **Surface Raster** is used to determine the actual surface distance that is traveled from one cell to the next. Elevation is usually the input surface raster. The **Vertical factor** takes into account the cost necessary to overcome the slope between two cells. The vertical slope or angle is first calculated between cells from the elevation values assigned to each location on an input vertical-factor raster, and then the slope is correlated to a vertical factor on a graph. The **Horizontal factors** determine the difficulty of moving from one cell to another. To determine the horizontal factor for moving from one cell to the next, the horizontal direction must be established from the horizontal-direction raster. To accomplish this, the horizontal relative moving angle, the relationship between the moving direction with respect to the horizontal direction, is calculated to determine the horizontal factor. The resulting value is the horizontal factor from the originating location (the FROM cell) to the destination location (the TO cell).

The PathDistance tool in ArcGIS can accomplish anisotropic distance calculations by supplying a vertical factor table. Nicholas Tripcevich[8] generated a vertical factor table in Excel that reflects Tobler's Hiking Function by using the reciprocal of Tobler's function and applying it to the unit distance of the raster 1 meter (thus, it finds hours/meter). This vertical table also emphasizes the peak of Tobler's function by increasing in 1/100th of a degree increments between -3 and -2. According to Tripcevich, this function calculates costs going **away** from the source cells. An inverse of this function can also be used to calculate costs associated with going **towards** the source cells. These two tables represent the horizontal factors. The PathDistance tool and the vertical tables provided by Tripcevich will create a cost-surface analysis that is anisotropic.

Alternatively, one can forgo the PathDistance tool in ArcGIS in favor of map algebra calculations. This is especially favorable because Tripcevich reported that the custom tables did not work in the PathDistance tool. Essentially, this method of calculating least-cost-paths is the same as the PathDistance tool, except the operator is in charge of the calculations. The first step is to calculate

---

[8] http://www.uweb.ucsb.edu/~nico/comp/cost_surf.htm

the cost distance. The formula needed to perform this calculation is as follows:

CostDistance(<source_grid>, <cost_grid>, {o_backlink_grid}, {o_allocate_grid}, {max_distance}, {value_grid})

where the <source_grid> is the Natufian site clusters and the <cost_grid> is the cost surface produced from Tobler's algorithm. The results of this equation are distance and direction surfaces. These surfaces are then used to calculate the shortest path. The equation required to perform this calculation is as follows:

CostPath_sa <in_destination_data> <in_cost_distance_raster> <in_cost_backlink_raster> <out_raster> {EACH_CELL} {destination_field}

An explanation of the expressions used in the cost path equations are found in Table 8.1.

Table 8.1: Map Algebra expressions for cost-surface analysis (ESRI 2004).

Expression	Explanation
<in_destination_data>	A raster or feature dataset that identifies those cells from which the least-cost-path is determined to the least-costly source.
<in_cost_distance_raster>	The name of a cost distance raster to be used to determine the least-cost-path from the <in_destination_data> cell locations to a source.
<in_cost_backlink_raster>	The name of a cost back link raster used to determine the path to return to a source via the least-cost-path. For each cell in the back link raster, a value identifies the neighbor that is the next cell on the least accumulative cost path from the cell to a single or set of source cells.
<out_raster>	The raster to be created.
{EACH_CELL}	EACH_CELL - For each cell with valid values on the <in_destination_data> a least-cost-path is determined and saved on the output raster of the CostPath function.
{destination_field}	The field used to obtain values for the destination locations.

Summary

Models demonstrating movement are not new in archaeology but the methods used have changed greatly in the last 10 years. This chapter discussed one of the more recent advances. Cost-surface analysis is made possible through geographic information systems. Of the various algorithms that could be used in cost-surface analysis, all can be classified as either isotropic or anisotropic. Both isotropic and anisotropic algorithms are used in archaeological research but anisotropic algorithms, which take direction into account, are preferable. The anisotropic algorithm that is discussed in length and used for this research is Tobler's hiking function.

Aldenderfer (1998), in an experiment testing Tobler's hiking algorithm in the Andes montane region, concluded that it models reality. The region considered in this research is diverse in terrain (Figures 7.5 and 7.6). It would be erroneous to define the region as mountainous but it is also far from flat. It would be correct to categorize the terrain as a hilly macro-region, with characteristic mountainous and flat micro-regions. Because of this diversity, Tobler's hiking function is an ideal algorithm for creating a cost surface. The following chapter illustrates the results of cost-surface analysis.

CHAPTER 9
RESULTS PART II – SPATIAL ANALYSIS

Introduction

This chapter presents the results of the second part of analysis for this research. These results are the product of the results first presented in chapter six, cluster analysis of material culture, applied to spatial analysis methods discussed in chapter eight. This chapter is divided into four parts: first-level analysis, second-level analysis, considerations and lithic data. When conducting analysis, regardless of whether it is statistical, as is the case for chapters five and six, or spatial, as is the case for chapter eight and the current chapter, it quickly becomes clear that analysis can take on a "life of its own." This means that the methods and procedures initially set in the research design tend to produce more questions than results. These questions lead to further inquiry of the data and hence, greater results. This is the case for the spatial analysis presented here. It became clear to me, when conducting first-level analysis that producing one *set* of least-cost paths based solely on the clusters of Natufian sites is insufficient. However, this insufficiency has led me to consider other areas of analysis, such as routes between clusters and other characteristics of the Natufian sites themselves, such as temporal and size factors.

First-level analysis: Least-Cost-Paths for Each Cluster

The first step in the analysis of the clusters is to import them into a GIS environment. Once the table is imported into the GIS environment, the data can be queried to highlight the desired information. Figure 9.1 illustrates this function, where the data is queried to identify clusters. This information can be saved as a map layer for use at a later time. Alternatively, the data can be imported once more and a different query can be performed to highlight another area of the data. Figure 9.2 illustrates this function, where the query is applied to highlight clusters created for lithic data. Once again, it is saved as a map layer for future analysis. These two layers are used in cost-path analysis.

The second step in this analysis is to create the cost-surface. As I indicate in chapter eight, Tobler's hiking algorithm is used. Calculation of this algorithm requires a digital elevation model of the research area. From there, I calculate the slope of the area using the *surface analysis* feature in ArcMap. Using the raster calculator, a map calculator function in ArcMap, the following equation is calculated:

$$((Exp(((Abs([Slope]/100))+0.5)*-3.5))*6)$$

The result of this calculation - [Cost_Map] - undergoes one further transformation:

$$([Cost\_Map]/0.3)/30$$

Figure 9.1: Geographical location of non-lithic artifact clusters of Natufian sites in the study region.

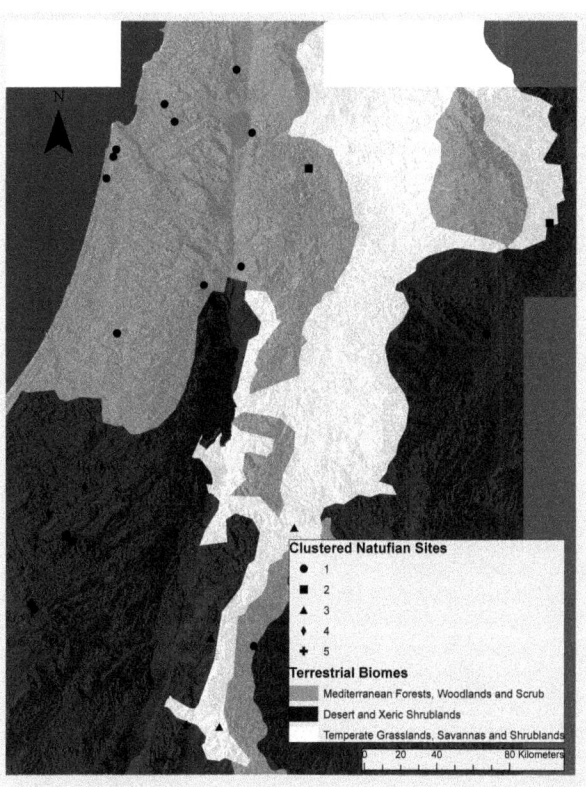

Figure 9.2: Geographical location of lithic artifact clusters of Natufian sites in the study region.

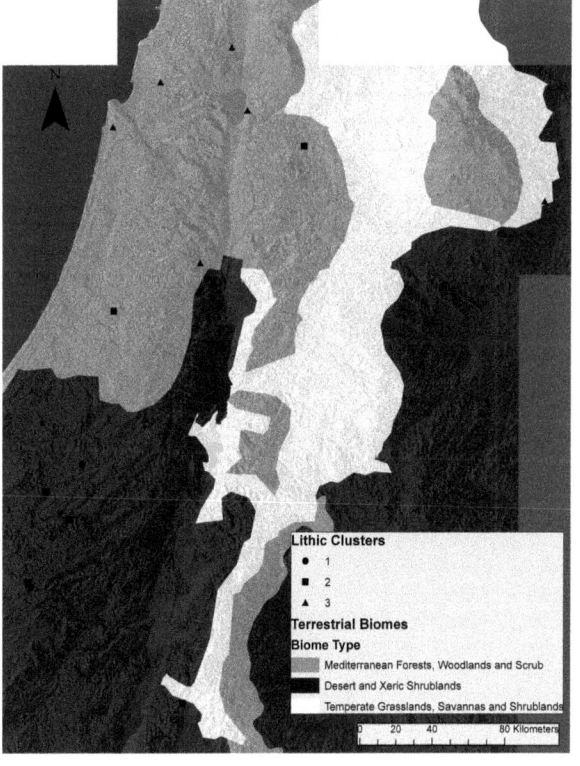

The result of these calculations is an anisotropic cost raster that calculates the walking velocity, taking slope into account. Figure 9.3 illustrated the resulting map produced from Tobler's hiking algorithm.

Figure 9.3: Calculation of Tobler's Hiking Algorithm (walking velocity) for study area.

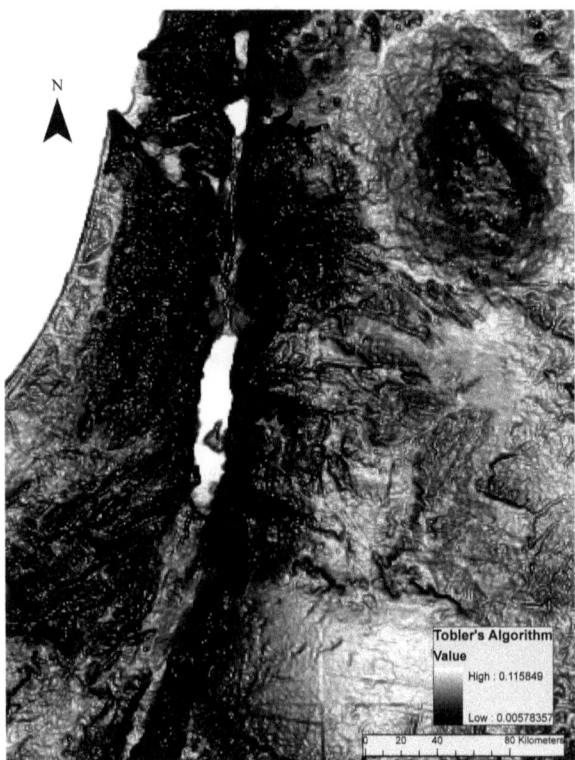

The third step in determining the least-cost-path to and from Natufian sites it to calculate the cost-weighted distance. This geoprocessing function is available in ArcMap using the cost-weighted distance function. To perform this function, two sets of data are required, a feature class of data, such as Natufian sites, from which to measure the distance, and a cost raster. The cost raster could be as simple as the slope created through a DEM but, because I am interested in the *realistic* costs when traveling by foot, the Tobler's hiking algorithm is a good measure. The results of the cost-weighted distance function are two maps - a cost-distance and cost-direction map. A cost-allocation map (similar to Theissen polygons described in chapter eight) can also be calculated as an option but is not necessary for this analysis. The process of calculating the cost-weighted distance is conducted for each Natufian site cluster. The result is a cost-distance and cost-direction map for each cluster of Natufian sites.

The final step is to calculate the least-cost-path based on the cost-distance and cost-direction maps. Once again, this step is conducted for all clusters. Figures 9.4 through 9.7 illustrate (a) the cost-distance, (b) cost-direction, and (c) least-cost-path for each cluster of Natufian sites. The least-cost-paths for all clusters are illustrated in Figure 9.8. I identify these paths as *first-level paths*.

Figure 9.4(a): Cost distance, cluster 1.

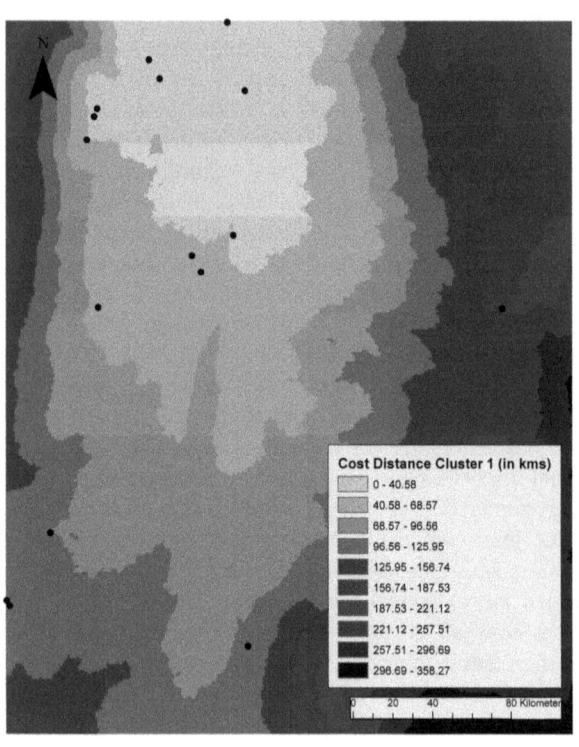

Figure 9.4(b): Cost direction, cluster 1.

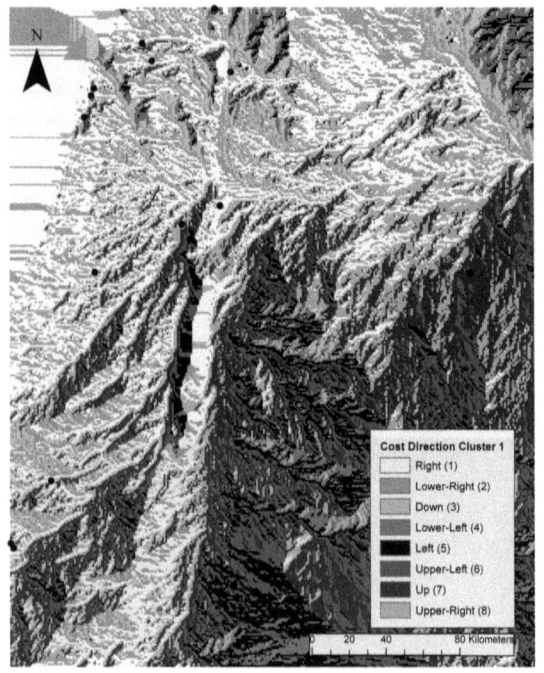

Figure 9.4(c): Least cost path, cluster 1.

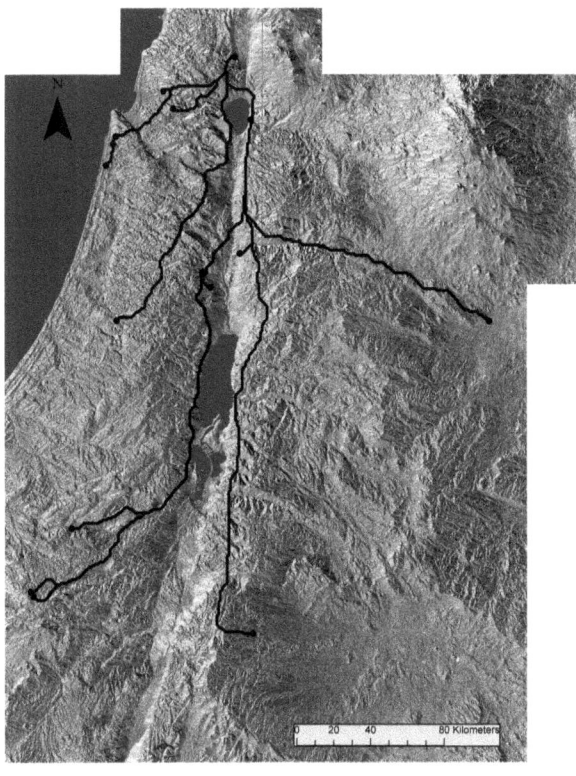

Figure 9.5(a): Cost distance, cluster 2.

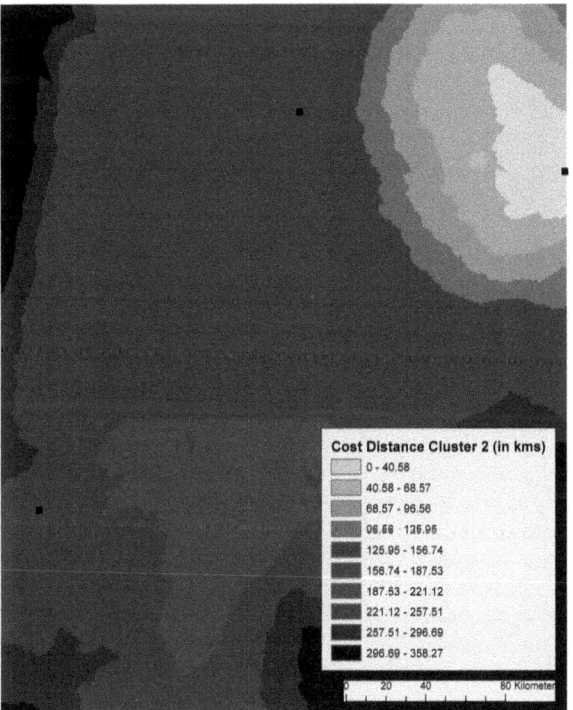

Figure 9.5(b): Cost direction, cluster 2.

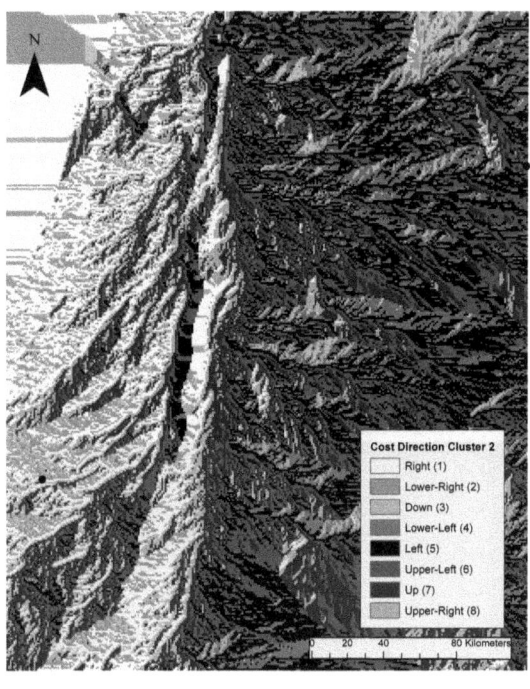

Figure 9.5(c): Least cost path, cluster 2.

Figure 9.6(a): Cost distance, Cluster 3.

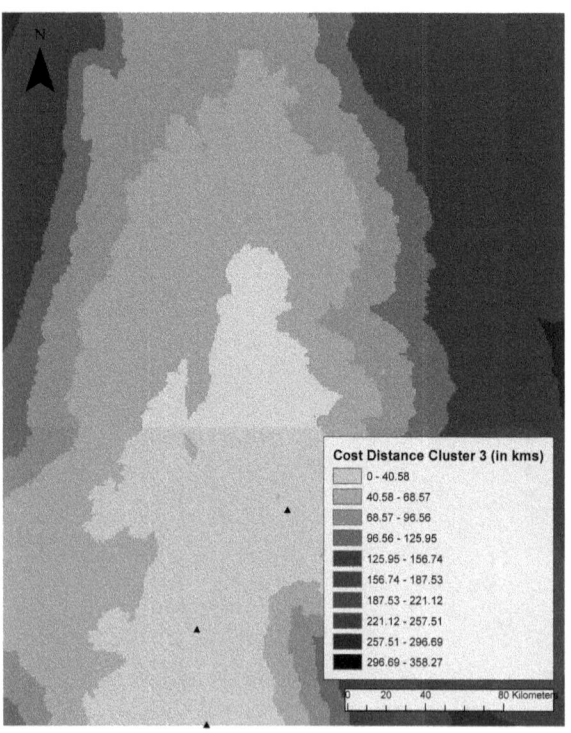

Figure 9.6(b): Cost direction, cluster 3.

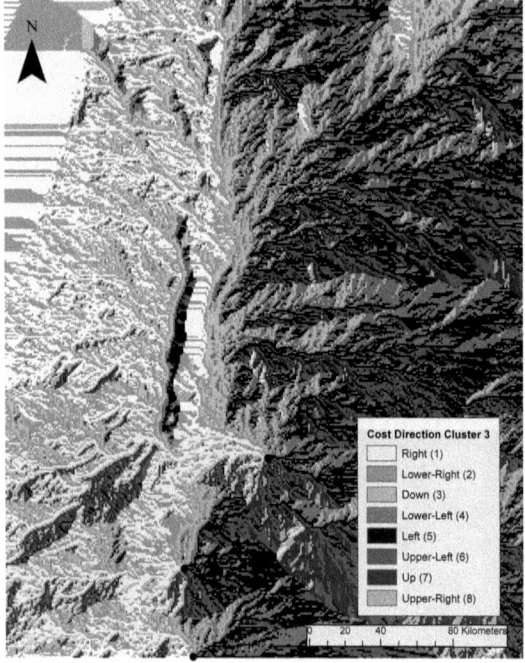

Figure 9.6(c): Least cost path, cluster 3.

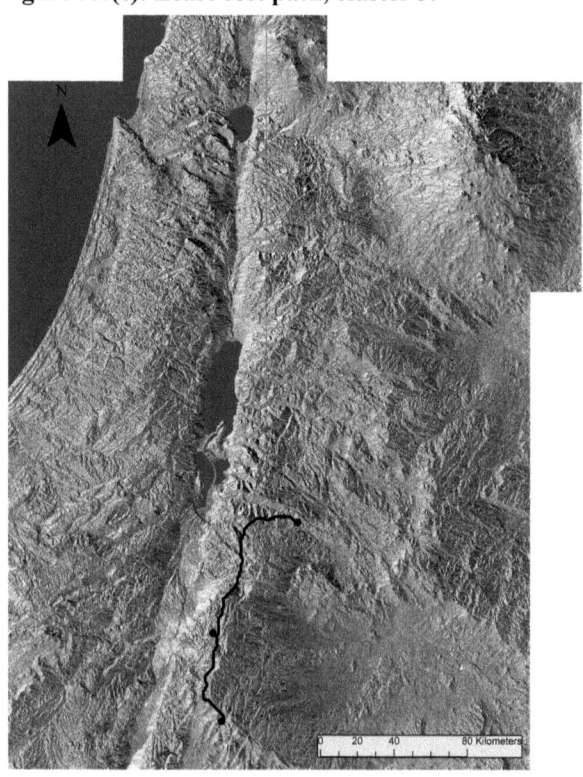

Figure 9.7(a): Cost distance, cluster 4.

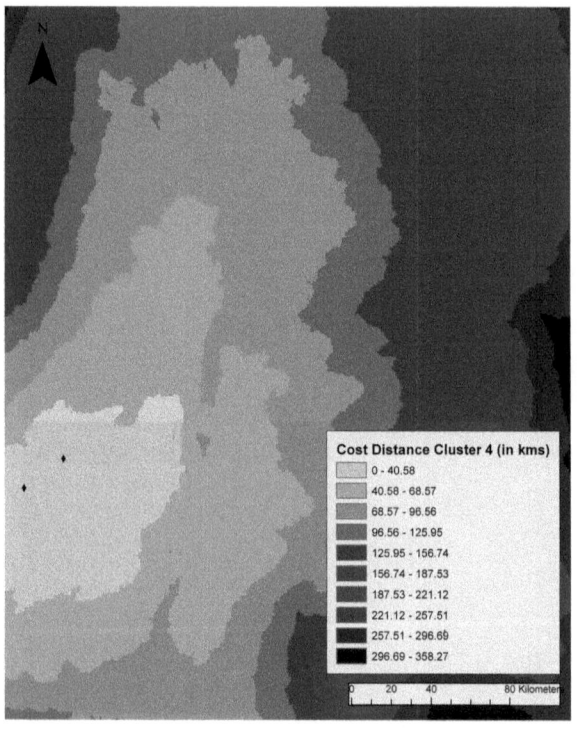

Figure 9.7(b): Cost direction, cluster 4.

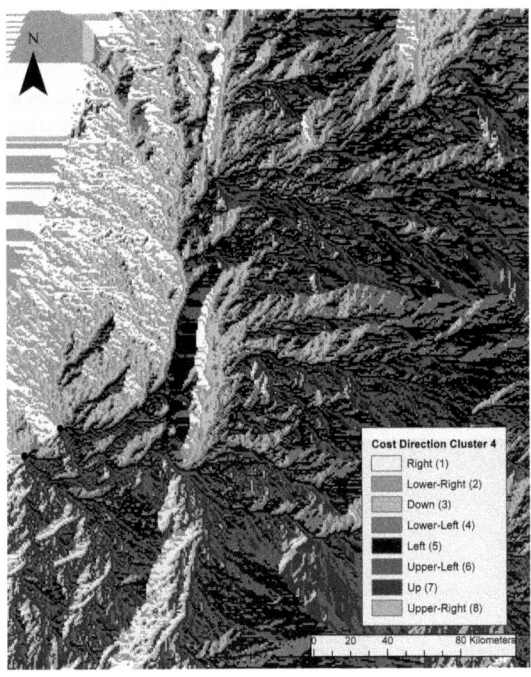

Figure 9.8: Combined least cost path.

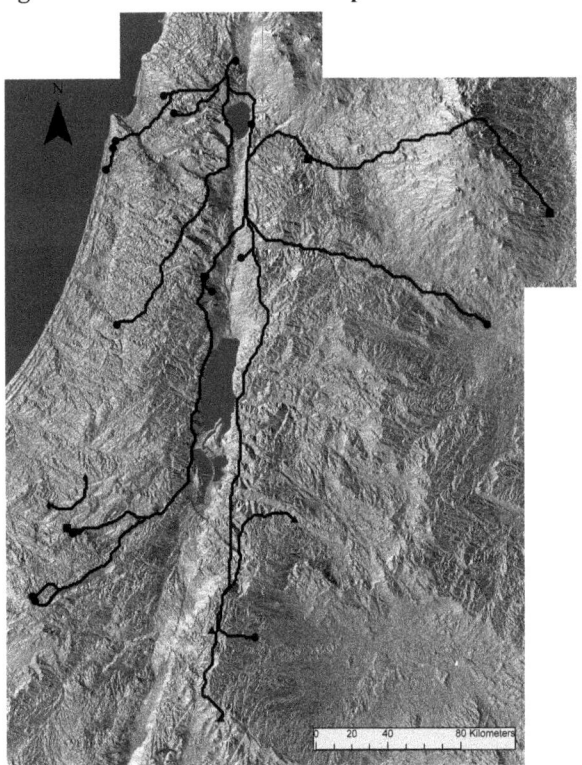

Figure 9.7(c): Least cost path, cluster 4.

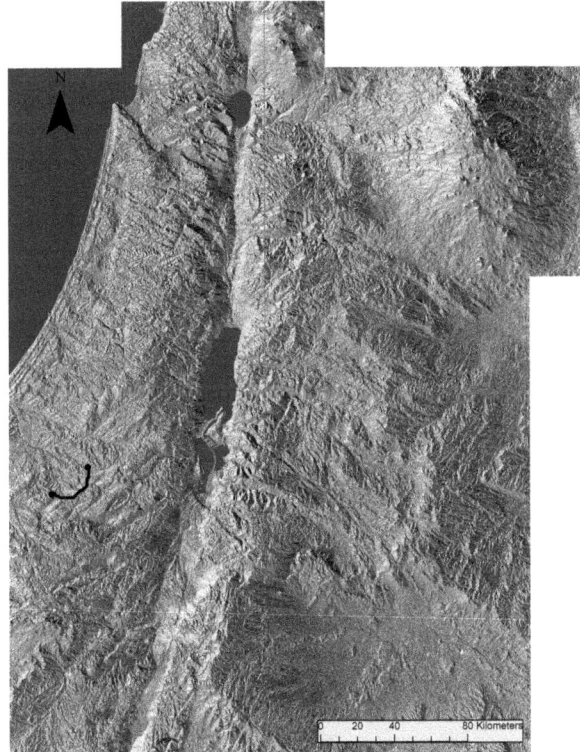

Looking at the geographical distribution of the clusters (Figure 9.1) as well as the ensuing least-cost-paths, several observations can be made. The first set of observations concerns the generated least-cost-paths. One of the more obvious patterns detected is the general north-south direction, regardless of the length of these paths. A second observation, also concerning this pattern, is the fact that this north-south direction runs along both the west and east sides of the Jordan River Valley. Coinciding with this observation is the noticeable crossing point for the Jordan River Valley that is located in the north.

The second set of observations concerns the geographical distribution of clusters. In this set of observations we see that three of the clusters - 3, 4 and 5, are restricted to the southern part of the study region. Clusters 3 and 5 are restricted to the southeastern area while cluster 4 is restricted to the southwestern area. The remaining two clusters, 1 and 2, are concentrated in the north with *pockets* in the south of the study region.

Cluster 5 is not included in the calculation of these least-cost-paths because only one site, Wadi Humeima, comprises this cluster. As discussed in chapter six, regardless of the number of clusters used, Wadi Humeima would remain in its own cluster.

When examining Figure 9.8, it becomes clear that some of the paths overlap, or intercept each other. To outline these intersections, I ran an intersect geoprocessing function. The results of this function are illustrated in Figure 9.9. In this figure there are two areas of intersection, one running north-south on the west side of the Jordan Valley, the other restricted to the southern part of the region on the east side of the Jordan Valley. What is of interest to note is that both intersections involve the least-cost-path of cluster 1.

Figure 9.9: Identified areas where least cost paths intersect

Second-level analysis: Least Cost-Paths to Each Cluster

The calculation of the least-cost-paths, illustrated in Figure 9.8, shows the optimal route to travel from one site to another within a given cluster. However, in an attempt to understand social interaction between different groups within the same culture, it is also of interest to calculate the least-cost route to travel from one cluster of sites to all other site clusters. To calculate these paths, I selected all sites within a particular cluster, calculated cost-distance and direction maps for the sites, and then ran a least-cost-path for all sites, regardless of their cluster affiliation. I repeated these steps for each cluster. Figures 9.10 through 9.13 illustrate the least-cost-paths to travel from one cluster of sites to all other clusters of sites. I identify these paths as *second-level paths*. I also identified interceptions of the paths. Figure 9.14 shows the location of these interceptions. The difference between these intersections and those intersections found in Figure 9.9 is that these include all clusters. In other words, these intersections are locations where all second-level least-cost-paths, regardless of the initial cluster affiliation, intercept. While all sites are used in the calculation of second-level paths, there is variability in the paths created, depending on the location of the point of origin but there are some paths that reoccur.

Figure 9:10: Cluster 1 second level least cost paths with corresponding biome.

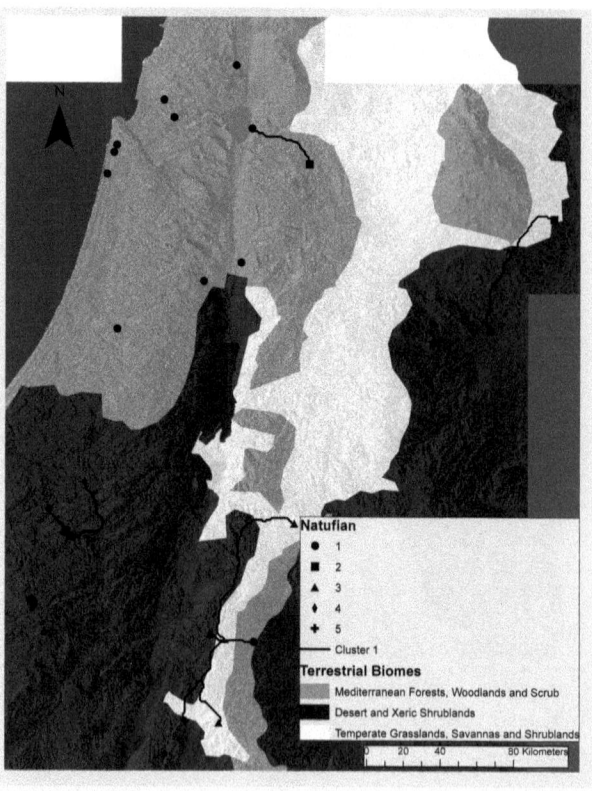

Figure 9.11: Cluster 2 second level least cost paths with corresponding biome.

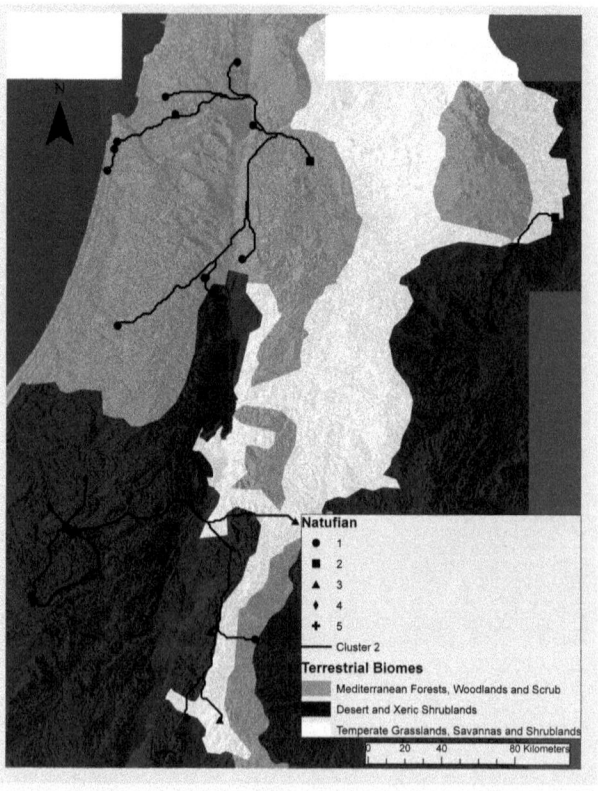

Figure 9.12: Cluster 3 second level least cost paths with corresponding biome.

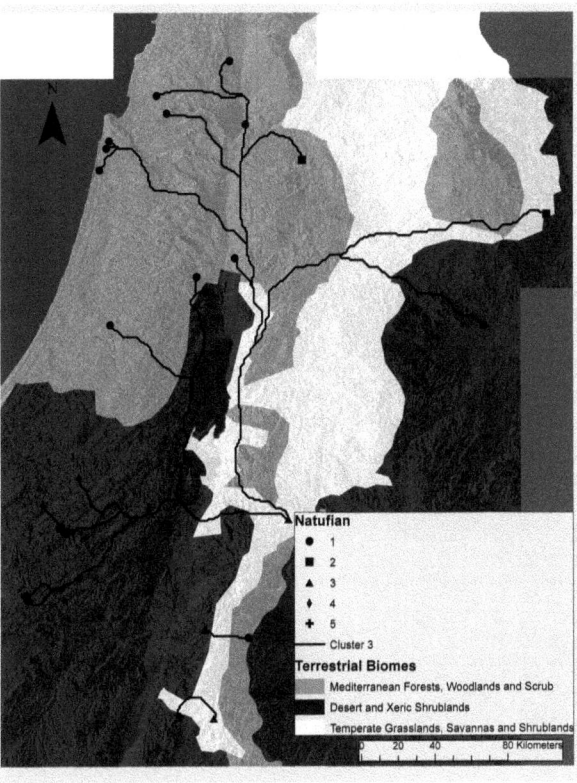

Figure 9.14: Identified areas where second level least cost paths intersect.

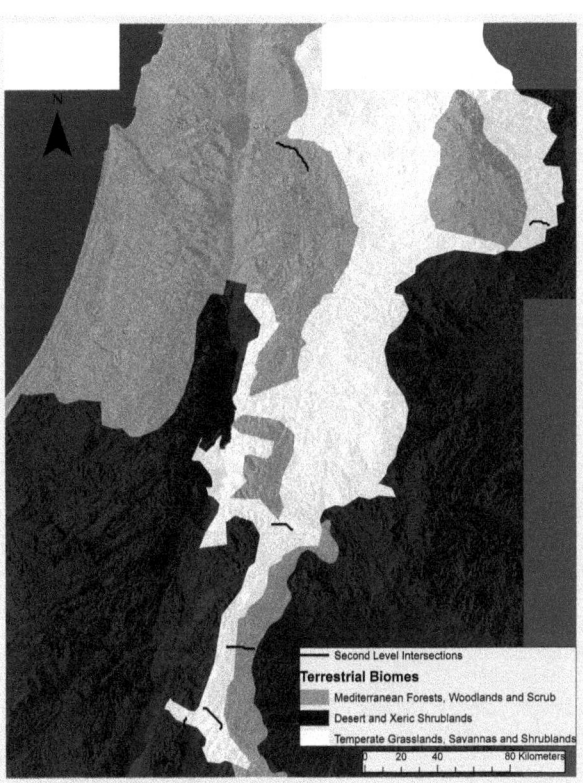

Figure 9.13: Cluster 4 second level least cost paths with corresponding biome.

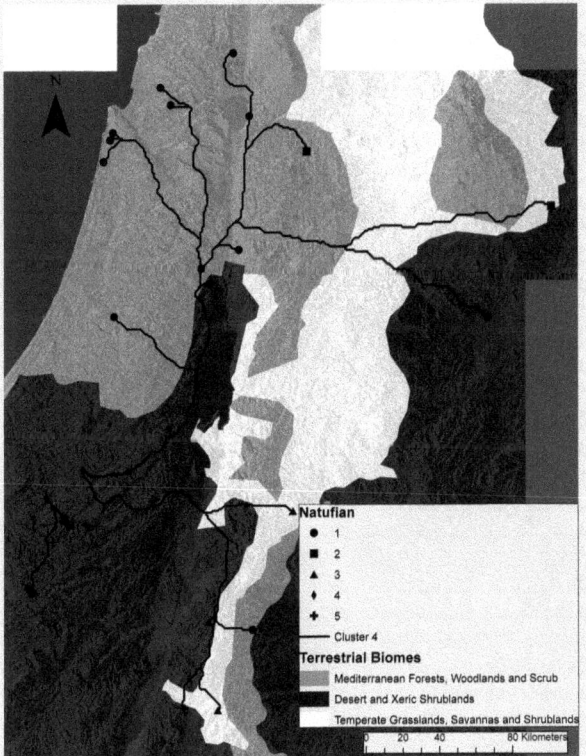

Examining the second-level paths shows that all sites within the five clusters do not necessarily link with other sites. For example, not all cluster 1 sites show a connection to all other sites. This occurrence could be because only certain sites within the cluster serve as *intermediary* sites, connecting to both sites within their cluster as well as to one or more other sites in other clusters. For example, Nahal Ein Gev, a site in cluster 1, has a direct path leading to 'Ain Rahub, a site in cluster 2. 'Ain as-Saratan, also a cluster 1 site, has a direct path leading to Khallat Anaza, a site in cluster 2. What is interesting to note about these two examples it that, when comparing the reverse routes, movement from cluster 2 with those sites from cluster 1, the paths are not always the same. For example, when looking at the routes traveled between Khallat Anaza, a cluster 2 site, and 'Ain al-Saratan, a cluster 1 site, we see that the travel route is the same, regardless of direction and that there is no additional routes linking other sites to these two sites. On the other hand, 'Ain Rahub is not limited to Nahal 'ain Gev. Rather, this cluster 2 site connects with all cluster one sites in the northwestern area of the region. It is possible to interpret this site as a *node* in a communication network (see Figs 9.15 and 9.16).

Other possible sites that can be interpreted as *nodes* include Wadi Mataha, a cluster 1 site; Upper Besor, a cluster 2 site, Tabaqa; a cluster 3 site; and both Givat Hayil and Nahal Seker, cluster 4 sites. Figures 9.15 through 9.18 illustrate all possible nodes and the sites they network for each cluster.

When comparing second-level to first-level intersections, it becomes clear that there is no overlap. In comparing the second-level intersections with the first-level paths, it appears that these intersections tend to extend the paths (Figure 9.19). Six of the eight second-level intersections connect with the first-level paths. Of the remaining two, one overlaps the path created for cluster 2 while the second stands alone.

Figure 9.15: Cluster 1 nodes and potential site networks.

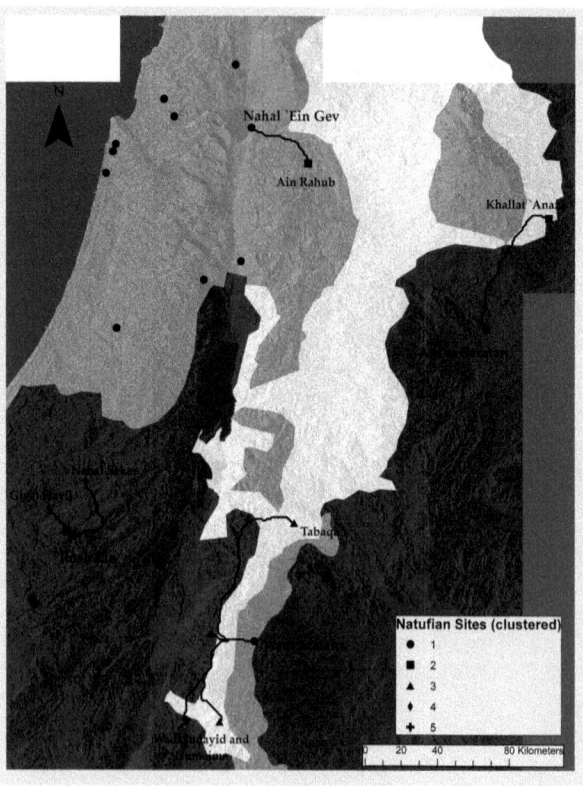

Figure 9.16: Cluster 2 nodes and potential site networks.

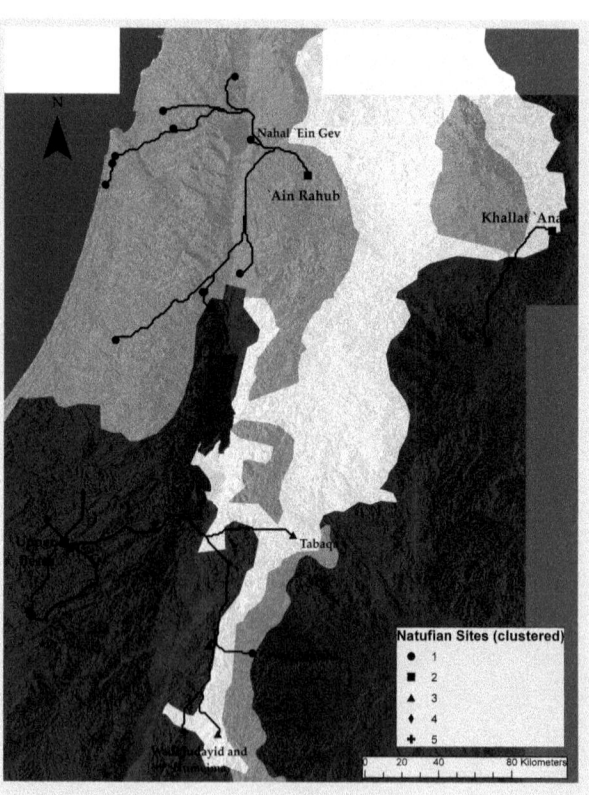

Figure 9.17: Cluster 3 nodes and potential site networks.

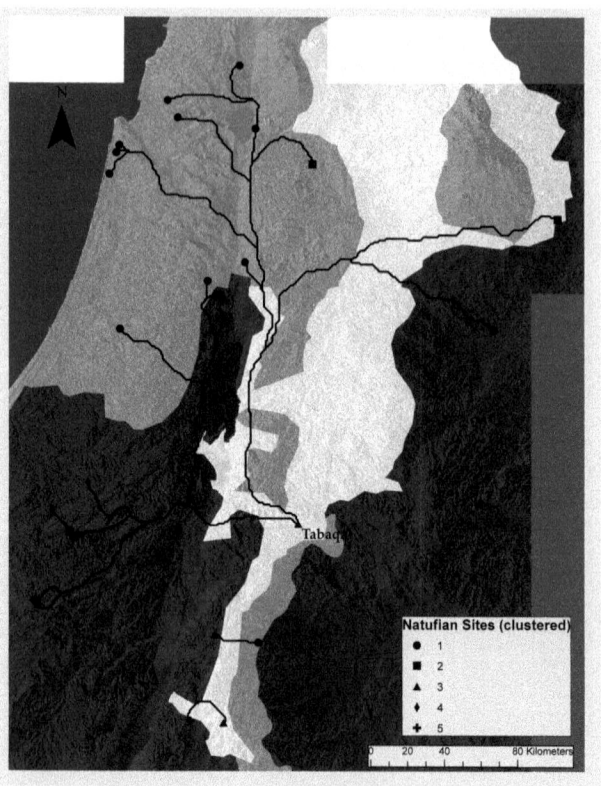

Figure 9.18: Cluster 4 nodes and potential site networks.

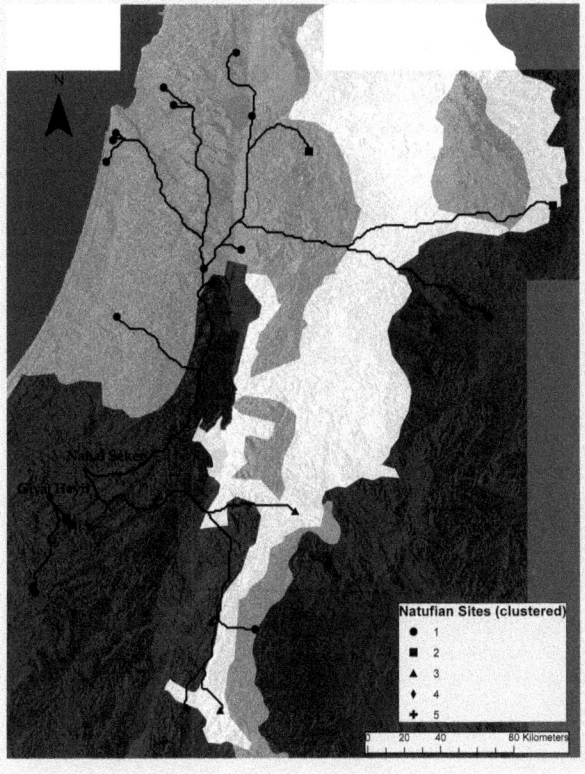

Figure 9.19: Second level intersections as extension of first level paths.

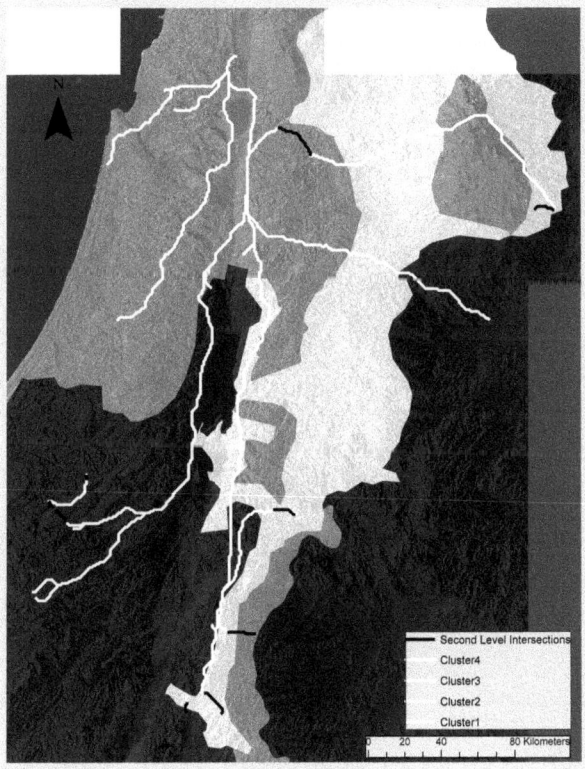

In summarizing the first- and second-level of analysis, some observations can be made. With respect to the paths themselves, the second-level paths are much more complex compared to the first-level paths. The reason for this is because the paths being calculated are greater – rather than remaining in a single cluster, they are actually connecting clusters. Both paths travel in a north-south direction along both the west and east sides of the Jordan Valley. While the first-level paths show Jordan Valley crossings in the northern area, level-two paths show these crossing in both the north and south.

Other Possible Considerations

In examining the first- and second-level paths, it becomes clear that to calculate least-cost-paths of the various clusters of sites does not give the full story of possible social interactions in the Natufian. One cannot create paths without taking into consideration the time period of the site. Further consideration of the size of the sites is also necessary.

To understand how time period and site size can be incorporated into the current methods, I first need to isolate the sites by (a) cluster; (b) phase; and (c) size. Phase is divided into Early or Late and size is divided into three categories - <1000, <2000, and >2000 m^2. I do this by querying the data from Natufian sites through ArcMap. I then incorporate the results into a least-cost-path analysis. For this analysis, I calculate the shortest distance, using the Tobler's algorithm cost-surface, for Natufian sites greater than 2000 m^2 in size in each cluster. Each cluster is also divided into Early and Late phases. If a cluster does not contain a site greater than 2000 m^2, I do not produce a least-cost-path. Figures 9.20 and 9.21 illustrate the results of this process. These results show that clusters 1 and 3 represent the Early phase while clusters 1 and 2 represent the Late phase.

I also conduct a second-level of analysis where all sites over 2000 m^2 for both the Early and Late phase, regardless of cluster, are incorporated into a least-cost-path. For this procedure, I select all sites greater than 2000 m^2 and calculate cost distance and direction surfaces. The shortest path is then created from sites less than 2000 m^2 to those greater than 2000 m. Figures 9.22 and 9.23 illustrate the results of this process. An interesting observation is that not all sites greater than 2000 m^2 are *connected* to sites of lesser area. Sites greater than 2000 m^2 in cluster 1 are the only ones that have paths connecting smaller sites, while the one site in cluster 2 has no path linking it to other sites.

Figure 9.20: First level paths for Early Natufian sites.

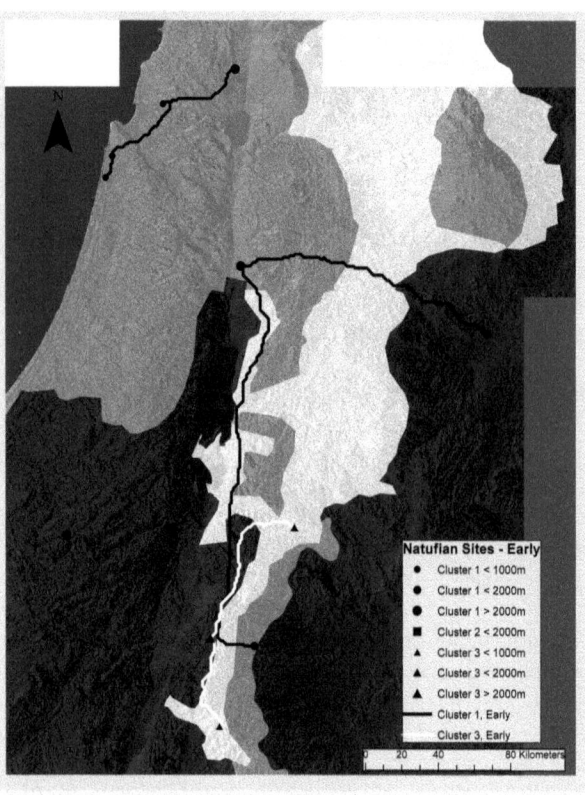

Figure 9.21: First level paths for Late Natufian sites.

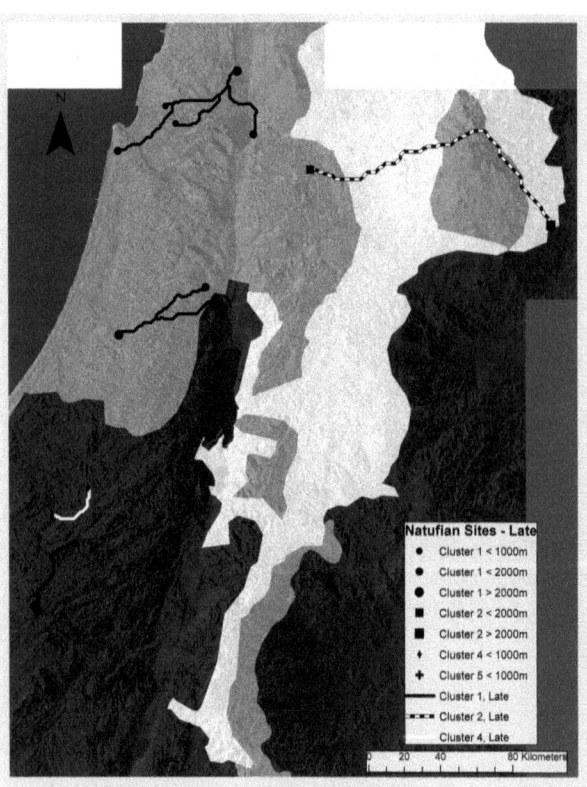

Figure 9.22: Second level paths for Early Natufian sites.

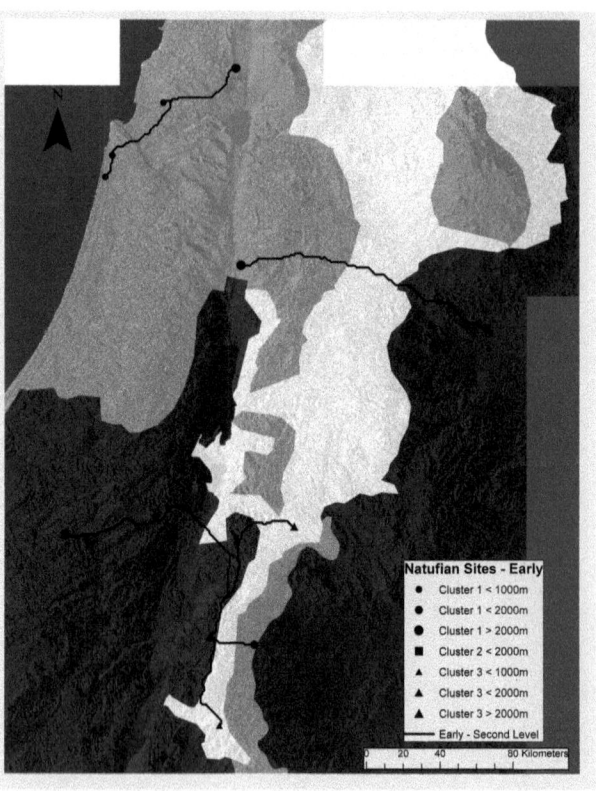

Figure 9.23: Second level paths for Late Natufian sites.

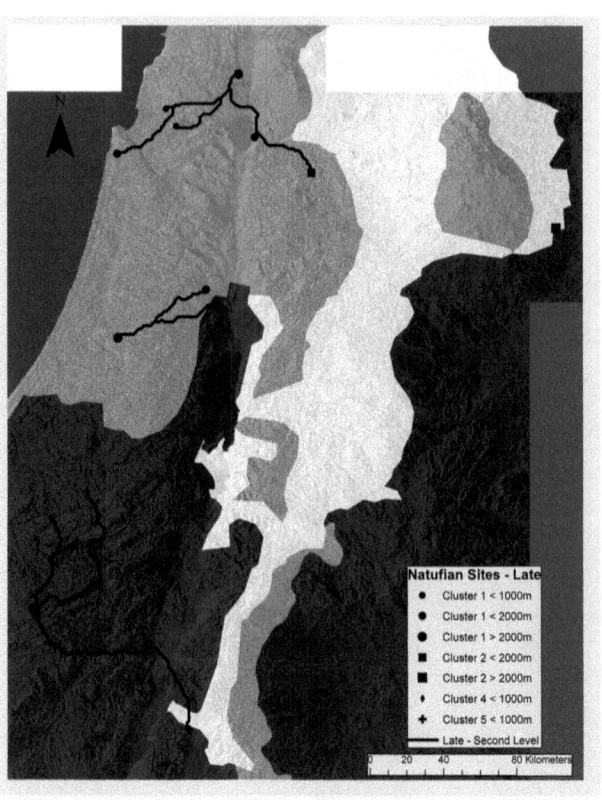

The Chipped-Stone Data

In chapter six I show the results of clustering the chipped-stone data exclusively. As I previously explain in the introduction to this research, the focus is on material culture related to exchange and artistic activities. I also state in chapter three that, in previous studies on the Natufian, the focus is on chipped-stone typology, rather than on other material culture. Furthermore, in chapter three, I also state that much of the cultural-ecological interpretations associate the chipped-stone industry with macro- and micro-ecological environments.

Curious to see if the results of those who compared variability in chipped-stone technology to the macro- and micro-environments can be replicated through the clustering methods used in this research, I decided to map the results of the cluster analysis performed on this data exclusively. Figure 9.2 illustrates the geographical location of these lithic clusters. The results show that there is a general geographic distribution of these lithic clusters – clusters 1 and 2 overlap each other and are located in the south of the archaeological region while clusters 3 and 4 are located in the north. There are outliers for clusters 1 and 2.

I am also curious to see what least-cost-paths would be produced for this data, so I produced least-cost-paths for the clusters, both first- and second-level (within and between clusters). The first-level paths are illustrated in Figure 9.24. Intersections of these paths are also identified and illustrated in Figure 9.25. As with the first-level paths for the other material culture, the intersections are particular to certain cluster combinations.

The second-level paths and their corresponding intersections are illustrated in Figures 9.26 and 9.27. Unlike the connection between first-level paths and second-level intersections for other material culture (Fig. 9.19), there do not appear to be any extension of pathways. Rather, the second-level intersections overlap the first-level paths.

Figure 9.24: Combined first level paths, chipped stone (lithic) data.

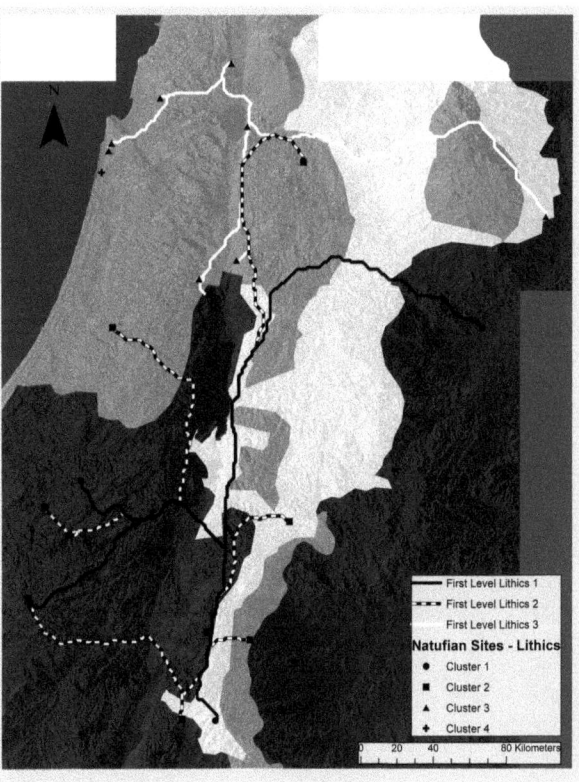

Figure 9.25: Areas of interest of first level paths, chipped stone (lithic) data.

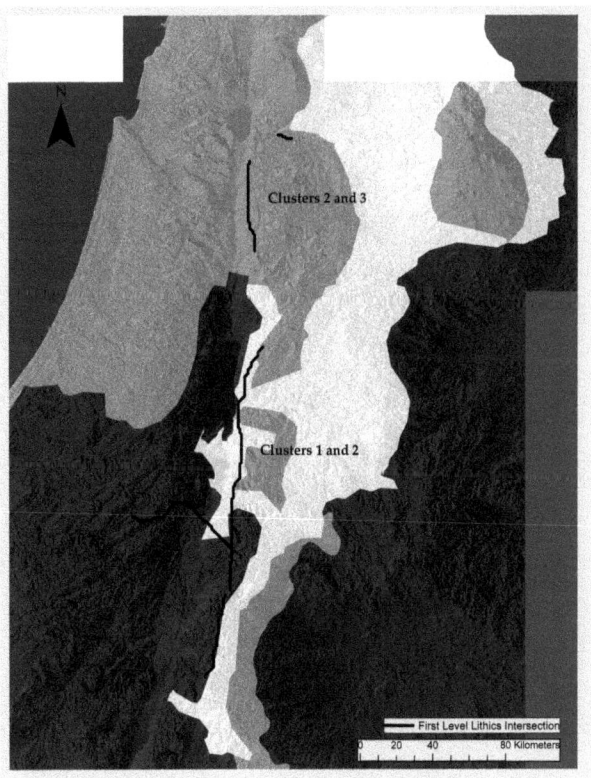

Figure 9.26: Combined second level paths, chipped stone (lithic) data.

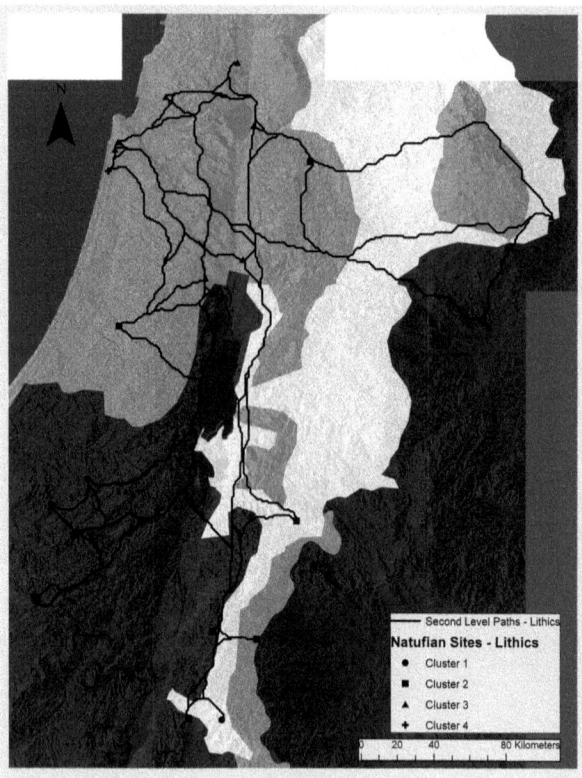

Figure 9.27: Areas of interest of second level paths, chipped stone (lithic) data.

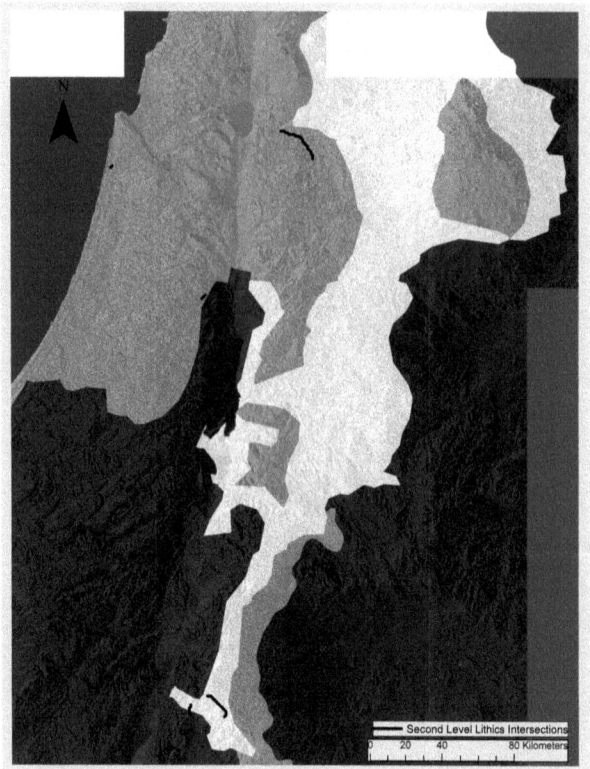

In considering the previous interpretations of Natufian sites in terms of macro- and micro-environments, I looked at the sites in light of the ecological biomes in which they are located. Figure 9.28 shows the clusters of Natufian sites based on the chipped-stone data in relation to the terrestrial biomes. Cluster 1 is found primarily in the Saharo-Arabian Desert; cluster 2 is represented fairly equally in all biomes; cluster 3 predominates in the Mediterranean area with the exception of two sites – Salibiya in the Saharo-Arabian Desert and Khallat Anaza in the Irano-Turanian shrublands and, lastly, cluster 4, represented by only one site, occupies the Mediterranean zone.

Figure 9.28: Clusters of Natufian sites based on chipped stone (lithic) data corresponding with terrestrial biome.

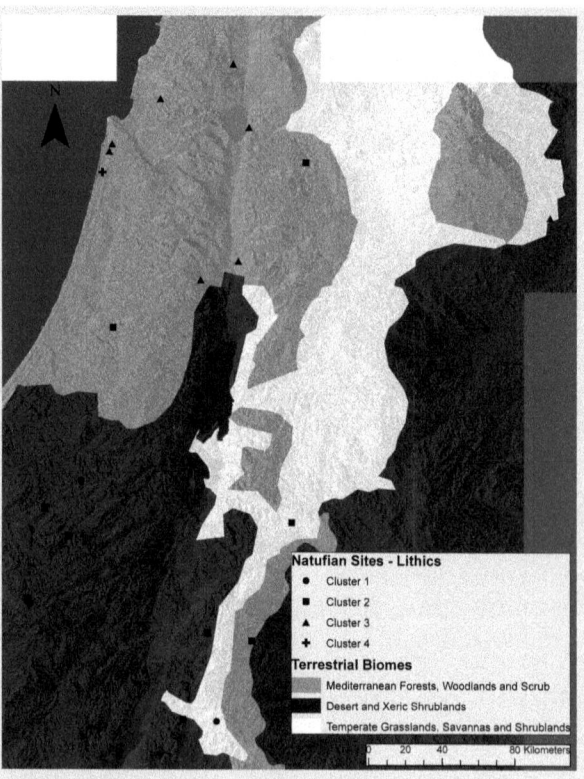

To maintain consistency and also to consider other pertinent characteristics of the Natufian sites, least-cost-path analysis is reevaluated using site phase and size as additional variables. This process is identical to the process described in the previous section, with both first- and second-level analysis. The results are illustrated in Figures 9.29 through 9.32. Natufian sites in clusters 2 and 3 are the only sites representing an area greater than 2000 m^2 and therefore, are the only clusters represented in the first-level of analysis. As with second-level of analysis described in the previous section, some sites greater than 2000 m^2 in area are not connected through paths to any other site in the archaeological region.

Figure 9.29: First level paths for Early Natufian sites based on chipped stone (lithic) data.

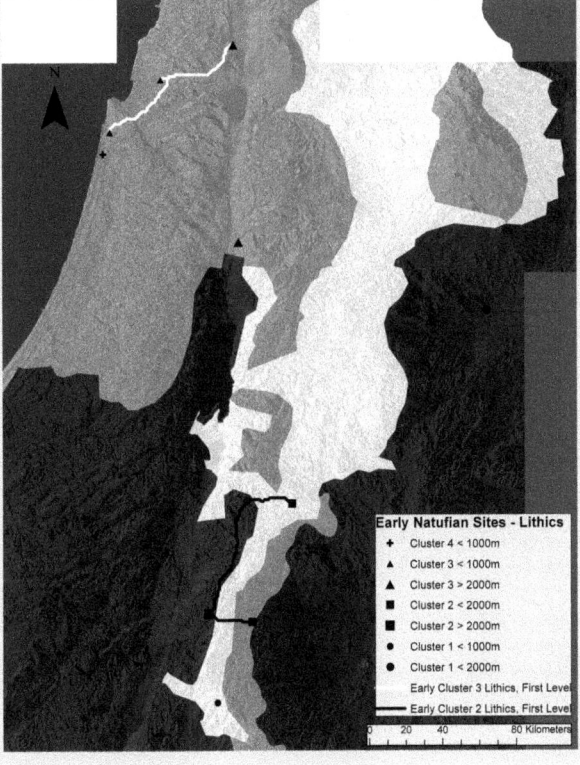

Figure 9.31: Second level paths for Early Natufian sites based on chipped stone (lithic) data.

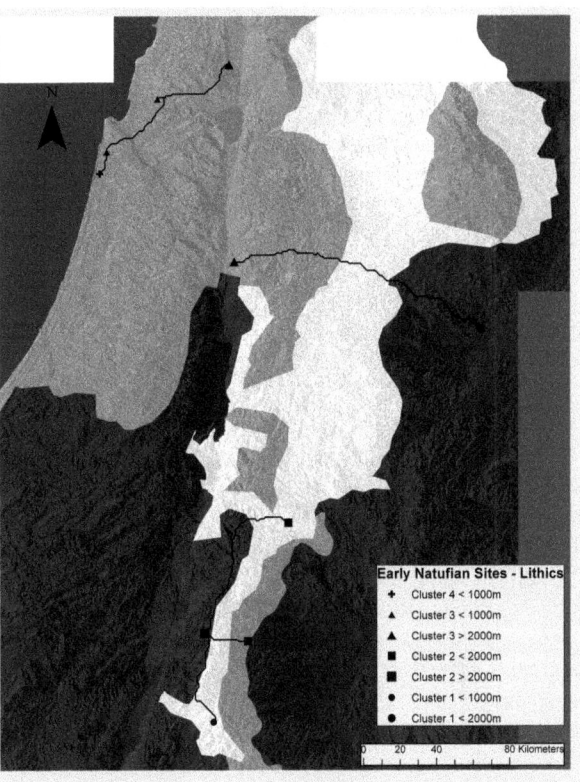

Figure 9.30: First level paths for Late Natufian sites based on chipped stone (lithic) data.

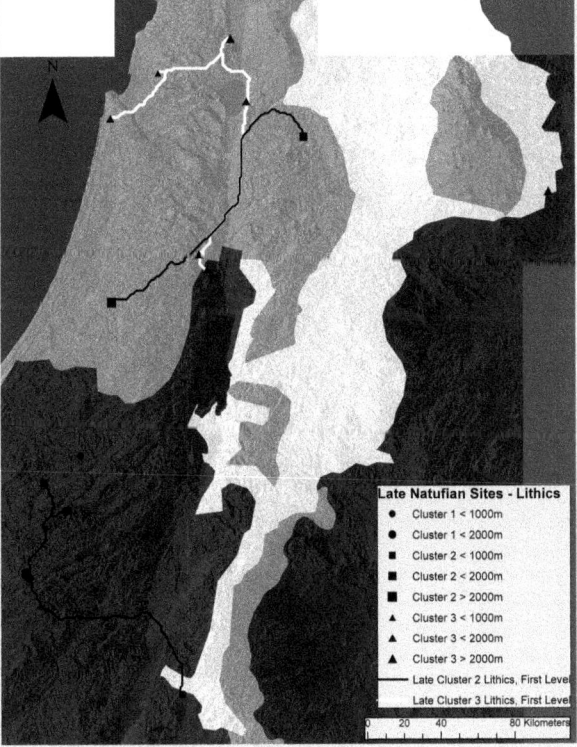

Figure 9.32: Second level paths for Late Natufian sites based on chipped stone (lithic) data.

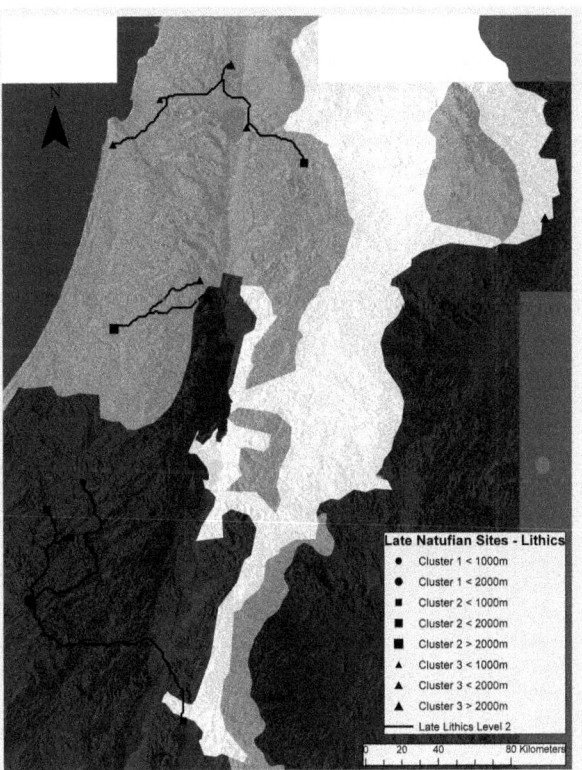

Summary of Results

Least-cost-path analysis is applied to the clusters of Natufian sites to create possible *routes of interaction* between sites within and between clusters. The clustering of sites gives initial evidence of similarity among groups of sites. Presenting these clusters in a geographical format gives initial evidence for the geographic distribution of the clusters. Creating a cost-surface using Tobler's hiking algorithm gives evidence for the time and effort required to traverse the geographical area in which these sites are located. Performing least-cost analysis gives evidence for the possible routes traveled in order to forward materials, information, and ideas between similar sites and between groups of sites.

This chapter demonstrates that it is possible to create potential *routes of interaction* through spatial analysis. First- and second-level least-cost-path analysis on the non-lithic data shows that there are routes of interaction within specific clusters of Natufian sites and between clusters of Natufian sites. Both levels of analysis also show that there are intersections where the path of one group overlaps the path of another group and that some sites may represent nodes or connectors between other sites.

This chapter also demonstrates that in developing these routes, the clustering characteristic of sites alone is insufficient. Time of occupation as well as size needs to be considered. The results illustrated in this chapter show the direct connections between groups of sites. Factors contributing to these connections include the initial clusters as well as the geographical location of these clusters. The results also show that there are definite divisions between groups of sites. These divisions are geographical rather than artifactual in nature. The following chapter will use these results to evaluate hypotheses described in chapter three and construct a model of social interaction for the Natufian.

CHAPTER 10

CONSTRUCTING A MODEL OF SOCIAL INTERACTION FOR THE NATUFIAN

Individuals are knowledgeable social actors and the ties they create through interaction both bind and bond – Gamble (1999:42)

Introduction

In the introduction to this dissertation, I state that the objective of this research is to investigate social relations of the Natufian through interpretation of regional and material-culture variability. I approach this objective from an agency-centered perspective. This perspective asserts that human thoughts and actions are influenced through structures. These structures are the relationships individuals have with other humans as well as with the environment they inhabit (Giddens 1984).

In chapter three, I discuss past approaches to understanding Natufian lifeways. Three themes predominate: chronology, culture-history, and ecology. Each theme is connected to a model of Perlès and Phillips (1991). The intention of the sequential analysis and results presented in chapters four through nine is to test these models. It is also the intention of this research to develop and test an agency-centered model. The purpose of this chapter is to put these hypotheses and proposed models to the test.

Each model is examined in light of the results of this research. The organization of this chapter is based on these individual models. In addition, I also explore an alternative model –the interactive agency model. The foundation of this model is the notion that humans are dynamic social beings whose actions are influenced by the enabling and constraining features of social and ecological structure.

Progressive Group-Splitting and Displacement

According to this model, common traits for all sites in all ecological zones reflect a common origin. However, as groups *split* in the Mediterranean core area to settle in peripheral areas, they interacted less and less. Eventually, sites outside the Mediterranean forest were no longer what we would consider to be Natufian. If this model is accurate, the clustered Natufian sites should reflect this through geographic differentiation. In other words there should be a primary cluster of sites in the Mediterranean core with one or more secondary clusters outside the Mediterranean core. The farther away the secondary clusters from the primary cluster, the more different the clusters.

This model can be tested using the result from chapter nine. In examining Figure 9.1, we see that no clusters of Natufian sites occur exclusively in the Mediterranean biome. This initial observation leads to the conclusion that this model is not valid. Upon examination of the first level of least-cost-path analysis (Figs. 9.4c, 9.5c, 9.6c, and 9.7c), it is clear that four of the five clusters (1 through 4) occur in at least two of the possible three terrestrial biomes. When comparing the terrestrial biomes to second-level analysis (Figs. 9.10 - 9.13), similar results are visible. If the distribution of sites as well as their clusters and corresponding paths are based on phase (Early vs. Late), we should see Early sites located in the Mediterranean with Late sites in the Irano-Turanian and Saharo-Arabian biomes. Looking at both the first-and second-level cost paths for Early and Late Natufian sites we see that this is not the case. Based on this evidence, the progressive group-splitting and displacement model is false.

Year-Round Settlement in the Mediterranean Forest

According to this model social interaction is limited, large permanently occupied sites in the Mediterranean are Natufian and, sites in the Irano-Turanian and Saharo Arabian biomes represent a different culture that did not interact with Natufian sites. It is possible that sites in the Irano-Turanian and Saharo-Arabian biomes may interact with one another. Once again, if this model accurately describes the case for Natufian sites, geographical representation should be available. In this model, as with the previous one, there should be one primary cluster of sites exclusively in the Mediterranean core and one or more secondary clusters outside of the Mediterranean core. The cluster in the Mediterranean should consist of primarily large (> 2000 m^2 in size) Natufian sites. Clusters outside the Mediterranean area may or may not overlap the peripheral Irano-Turanian and Saharo-Arabian Desert biome.

From the results demonstrated in chapter nine, once again it is possible to test this hypothesis. As with the progressive group-splitting and displacement model, it is evident that the clusters do not discretely organize themselves according to the terrestrial biomes. As well, neither the first- nor the second-level paths suggest that interaction was restricted to the peripheral biomes.

Because the premise of this model is based on the size of the site relative to its location, it is possible to organize the sites based on this attribute. We should see a high percentage of large sites (>2000 m^2) in the Mediterranean zone. Figures 9.20 to 9.23 demonstrate the distribution of Natufian sites on the basis of their size and show that, of the possible six sites that are >2000 m^2 in size, three (50%) are located in the Mediterranean zone. The remaining three (50%) are located in the peripheral areas, two in the Saharo-Arabian Desert biome and one in the Irano-Turanian. When comparing site size with the cluster membership and their corresponding paths, it is evident that sites greater than 2000 m^2 in size are represented in three clusters. It is also evident that two of the three clusters cross all three terrestrial biomes (clusters 1 and 2). Cluster 3 is the only cluster restricted to the peripheral biomes.

While I focus on those clusters with sites greater than 2000 m^2, I also need to address those clusters that do not contain large sites. Clusters 4 and 5 contain sites less than 1000 m^2 and all these sites are located in the Saharo-Arabian Desert biome. While cluster 3 contains a site greater than 2000 m^2, all sites in this cluster are located in the peripheral biomes. These three clusters provide some evidence that sites located outside the Mediterranean biome may represent different culture. However, the question remains, what about clusters 1 and 2? Both clusters and their paths, as I mention previously, cross all three biomes. Furthermore, sites greater than 2000 m^2 in size are represented in all three of these biomes. While this model is consistent with the evidence from clusters 3 through 5, evidence from clusters 1 and 2 indicate that it is false.

Semi-Sedentary Groups and Nomadic Groups

This model suggests that social interaction is based on aggregation and dispersion of Natufian social groups, with aggregation occurring in the Mediterranean forest and dispersion in the Irano-Turanian hills. Saharo-Arabian desert sites represent a different culture that did not interact with the former group. For this model, site clusters should be grouped geographically, with similarity of sites in both the Mediterranean and Irano-Turanian biomes and with larger sites in the Mediterranean and smaller sites in the Irano-Turanian zone. These sites will be inter-connected through paths. Separate clusters and their corresponding paths will be represented in the Saharo-Arabian Desert biome.

Once again, looking at Figures 9.4c through 9.7c as well as Figures 9.10 through 9.13, it is apparent that connections among sites cross-cut terrestrial biomes but there are no clusters or corresponding paths exclusive to the Mediterranean and Irano-Turanian biomes. Clusters 1 and 2 occur in all three biomes while cluster 3 occurs in both the Irano-Turanian and Saharo-Arabian Desert and clusters 4 and 5 occur only in the Saharo-Arabian Desert. Examining the cost paths at a second level of analysis, in general, no clusters of sites or their corresponding paths support this model.

When the clusters and paths are queried on the basis of site size as well as temporal factors, pattern does emerge. First-level analysis of Early Natufian sites (Figs. 9.20 - 9.23) shows that there are three main site groupings: (1) Mallaha (Mediterranean) connecting to other cluster 1 sites in the Mediterranean; (2) Wadi Hammeh (Mediterranean), connecting to Wadi Mataha, also in the Mediterranean and 'Ain as-Saratan in the Saharo-Arabian Desert, and (3) Beidha (Saharo-Arabian Desert) connecting to Tabaqa and Wadi Judayid, both in the Irano-Turanian. None of the three patterns for Early Natufian sites corresponds with the semi-sedentary and nomadic group's model. Reviewing the data for Late Natufian sites, four patterns are visible but, as with the Early Natufian data, they do not correspond with the proposed model. In fact, in one small group, the reverse is the case. The larger site Khallat Anaza is located in the Irano-Turanian biome while the smaller site with which it corresponds, 'Ain Rahub, lies in the Mediterranean biome. On the other hand, Rosh Horesha, a Saharo-Arabian site, corresponds with two other Saharo-Arabian sites, Rosh Zin and Saflulim. In this instance, the grouping of sites corresponds to the model, but not the main position of the model – of aggregation in the Mediterranean and dispersal to the Irano-Turanian. Rather, it corresponds to the later part of the model – the possibility that Saharo-Arabian sites represent an isolated culture. Looking at the potential site groupings in the second level of analysis for both Early and Late Natufian sites shows no change in pattern.

Semi-Sedentary Occupation of Large Settlements and Logistical Organization

This final model suggests that social interaction is based on a model of aggregation and dispersion of Natufian social groups whereby aggregation occurs in the Mediterranean forest with dispersal in both the Irano-Turanian hills and Saharo-Arabian desert. This model accepts that there was intensive interaction and all sites are Natufian. This model fits the theoretical perspective adopted for this research. It suggests that both ecological and social structures influenced social processes and behavioral strategies and that these influences are reflected in the material world. If this model accurately describes past interaction for the Natufian, large sites that are repeatedly occupied for a significant period of time will be located in the core Mediterranean area with smaller, seasonal or short-term occupation sites located in the Irano-Turanian hills and Saharo-Arabian desert.

The first level of analysis appears to validate this model in that there is a concentration of cluster 1 sites in the Mediterranean biome, with all other clusters distributed either exclusively in the Saharo-Arabian desert (clusters 4 and 5), or evenly distributed among all three biomes (clusters 2 and 3). The second level of analysis shows that there is extensive social interaction between all Natufian social groups (clusters) but there does not appear to be any pattern to indicate that aggregation occurred in the Mediterranean (see Figs. 9.15 through 9.18). Instead, there are several different patterns of aggregation and dispersal that occur outside of this model.

The data also suggest that large sites are concentrated in the Mediterranean, thus supporting the model's position of aggregation in this biome. Analysis based on phase and size of site (Figs. 9.20 through 9.23) indicates that the distribution of large sites (greater then 2000 m^2), is not limited to the Mediterranean biome. Of the six sites that are greater than 2000 m^2 in size, three are located in the Mediterranean, two in the Saharo-Arabian desert and one in the Irano-Turanian. While there appears to be a pattern of aggregation and dispersion, the ecological restrictions imposed by this model are not accurate.

Models and Chipped-Stone Data

Given that the results of this research have not validated the four previously proposed models for the Natufian culture, based on the non-lithic material culture, I will briefly examine the chipped stone data and its relationship to the models. Because previous research on lithic data are always placed in a temporal context (Byrd 1987; Henry 1982; Olszewski 1988), I limit my discussion to first- and second-level analysis of lithic material that is separated into Early and Late phases.

First-level analysis for Early Natufian lithic material shows two patterns. The first pattern (cluster 3 sites) is located in the northern Mediterranean biome. The second pattern occurs in the south. This second pattern consists of cluster 2 sites, with the largest site (Beidha) in the Sahara-Arabian biome while the two remaining sites are situated in the Mediterranean (Wadi Mataha) and the Irano-Turanian (Tabaqa) biomes. While the first pattern validates all hypothesized models, the second pattern does not correspond with any of the proposed models. The lithic data for the Late Natufian sites shows that there are three patterns: (1) clustering restricted to the Saharo-Arabian area (cluster 1); (2) clustering present in the Mediterranean and Saharo-Arabian (cluster 2) and; (3) a pattern represented by sites in all three biomes (cluster 3).

Second-level analysis reveals much the same information as the non-lithic second level of analysis. Three patterns emerge among the Early Natufian, one with all sites located in the Mediterranean biome, one represented by all sites situated in the Sahara-Arabian biome, and one in which the sites and their cost paths lie in both the Mediterranean and the Sahara-Arabian zones. Each of these patterns, if treated individually, can be used to validate all of the models but, when the patterns are combined, the models cannot be accepted.

Interactive Agency Model

Acknowledging that the results of this research do not satisfactorily confirm any of the previous models proposed to define and explain Natufian culture and behavior, this section will describe an alternative model – the **interactive agency model**. This model is different from the previous models in that (a) it focuses on the similar rather than variable characteristics of a culture; (b) it concentrates on behavioral strategies whereby people are viewed as dynamic actors in social processes such as interaction; (c) it appreciates that the behavioral strategies, and their material and ideological correlates, become part of the *environment* in which interaction occurs; and, finally (d) it advocates the importance of structures in individual or group decision-making and knowledge. While I concentrate on the Natufian, the interactive agency model is suitable for past cultures in which a hunting - and - gathering mode of subsistence and a non-sedentary mode of settlement are prominent.

According to this model, the locations of Natufian sites are not solely based on ecological aspects of the environment. Rather, these locations are places in a system of groups of people who interact with each other to some degree. The *extent* of interaction ranges from solitary interaction, where physical contact does not occur, to individual face-to-face contact among two or more individuals, to group interaction where more than one group interact with one another. These interactions also have a *temporal* component: contact can occur frequently, at a daily, seasonal, or yearly interval, or less frequently, perhaps only once or twice in an individual's lifespan. Finally, there is also a *spatial* component to the interaction; it can occur on either a large or small scale. The common thread that ties all these interactions together is their outcome: communication and the exchange of information, knowledge, and materials. This outcome affects the construction as well as the enabling and constraining natures of both social and ecological structure. Based on the foundation that interaction can be defined by extent, temporal framework, and spatial scale, three *spheres* of interaction can occur: within-group, between-group, and competitive.

Within-Group Interaction Sphere

The within-group interaction sphere (WGI sphere) is defined by exclusive contact among members of a specific group. The group is primarily identified through its similarity in social structure as expressed through similarity in material culture. Visually, this sphere is expressed as the location of sites within a group as well as the routes or paths used to travel from site to site. The spatial magnitude of this interaction sphere is primarily determined by the size of the group. The larger the group size, the larger the interaction sphere. However, at a general level this sphere tends to be large, crossing ecological and physical environmental boundaries. The extent of interaction is characterized by individual, face-to-face, contact and group interaction so that the entire culture comprising the group interacts. Face-to-face interaction may occur at a daily level, while the interaction of the entire group, within-group aggregation, occurs during a seasonal or yearly framework.

Between-Group Interaction Sphere

The between-group interaction sphere (BGI sphere) is defined by contact that occurs among two or more groups. This sphere contains all sites of a group of interest as well as the routes calculated to travel from these locations to sites of other groups. The spatial magnitude of this interaction sphere is quite different than that of the WGI sphere in that, (a) each group can have more than one interaction sphere and, (b) the spatial area and number of spheres is defined by group size. Large groups tend to have a greater number of interaction spheres with other groups and these spheres tend to be restricted in size. Small groups will have fewer BGI spheres but the spheres tend to be large. The number and size of the BGI sphere correlate with the number of ties one group has to another, but do not necessarily correlate to the extent and temporal framework of the interaction. For example, large groups will have several small BGI spheres and these may consist of as little as one other group. However, the extent of interaction may range from face-to-face interaction on a daily level to group interaction on a seasonal or yearly time frame. In contrast, small groups may be restricted to one BGI sphere but this sphere will expand over the entire region and involve all other groups. The extent of this interaction sphere ranges from face-to-face interaction to group interaction. It is within this sphere that the frequency of interaction ranges from daily to seasonal as well as very infrequent interaction, occurring rarely within an individual's lifespan.

Competitive Interaction Sphere
Essentially, the competitive interaction sphere (CI sphere) occurs where other spheres of interaction (WGI and BGI spheres) overlap. CI spheres are defined as the locations where the paths from interaction spheres intersect. There are two levels of competitive interaction because it takes place both in WGI and BGI spheres.

The first level includes the intersections of routes or paths contained in the WGI spheres. These competitive spheres are characteristically large in size and involve the only two spheres (two groups) in a region. These two groups have the opportunity to interact frequently with each other. Therefore, they have a greater opportunity to communicate and share information, ideas, and materials. Interaction is most likely to occur as face-to-face, individual contact but solitary interaction, where physical contact does not occur, is also a possibility. This solitary interaction may be a symbolic expression, such as pictographs or petroglyphs, or something less symbolic and obvious, such as refuse from artifact production or the remains of domestic activities. While it is possible that the two groups sharing this competitive sphere also share a similar social structure, they definitely share an ecological structure. In this sense, routing or scheduling competition may occur.

The second level includes the intersections of routes or paths contained in the BGI spheres. These second-level spheres are characteristically smaller and more fractured than first-level CI spheres because they involve all groups in a region. Because all groups living in the region are part of this sphere, the likelihood of face-to-face interaction of individuals from different groups is greater. A secondary result of the involvement of all groups is the increase in routing competition. This second-level CI sphere can be considered a high-competition area for access to both routes and resources near or on the routes.

Applying the Model to the Natufian

To illustrate the interactive agency model, I will apply it to the results of the cluster and least-cost-path analyses for the Natufian sites and their material culture. The results of the cluster analysis are the identified Natufian social groups within the study region. Although there is distinction through grouping of Natufian sites, it does not necessarily mean that these groups represent different cultures. These groups represent sites that are similar in their material culture.

WGI spheres are manifest in the clustering of archaeological sites and the first level least-cost-path analysis, where paths are created for each individual cluster of sites. The results show that there are four main WGI spheres (see Figs. 9.4c, 9.5c, 9.6c, and 9.7c). The spatial size of each sphere is correlated with the number of individual sites in each site grouping. For example, cluster 1 (Fig. 9.4c) consists of several sites and the spatial scale of its within-group sphere is large, while clusters 3 and 4 (Figs. 9.6c and 9.7c) contains fewer sites so their spatial scale is small. Cluster 2 (Fig. 9.5c) is anomalous in that it contains few sites yet, the spatial scale of its sphere is large. The temporal characteristic of these spheres may also differ. Because the within-group spheres for clusters 1 and 2 are large, interaction at a temporal scale can range from day-to-day interaction to seasonal or yearly contact. It is likely that clusters 3 and 4 interact more frequently within their interaction sphere because their spatial scale is much smaller. The extent is likely to be the same for all individual spheres in that it is characterized by face-to-face interaction or group aggregation. One further characteristic common to all WGI spheres is the general geographic tendency for a north-south sphere direction. Whether this is a further characteristic to be included in the model or a characteristic restricted to Natufian sites remains to be tested.

BGI spheres are evident through second-level cluster analysis in which the least-cost-path is calculated from one cluster of sites to all other sites, regardless of cluster (see Figs. 9.15 to 9.18). As the model indicates, the number of BGI spheres of a single cluster is correlated with the membership size of each cluster. For example, cluster one, containing the most sites, has four BGI spheres, while clusters 2 and 3, containing three sites each, have three spheres. Finally, cluster 4, containing only two sites, has two spheres. The size of the sphere is also correlated with the number created for each cluster. While cluster 1 has the most BGI spheres, the spatial scale of these spheres is small. In contrast, the spatial scale of clusters 3 and 4 are comparably large.

Applying this model to the Natufian, it is speculated that the individuals using sites in clusters 3 and 4 are more likely to have engaged in a form of BGI in which interaction occurred through group contact and from a temporal standpoint, this contact occurred infrequently because of the large spatial scale of these spheres. This interaction could be a "once in a lifetime" journey that has a strong symbolic connotation. On the other hand, individuals using sites in cluster 1 are more likely to have engaged in individual, face-to-face contact at more frequent intervals because of their smaller spatial scale. Cluster 2 is, yet again, anomalous because it does not have a large spatial BGI sphere but the cluster itself contains few sites. Based on the size of this sphere, it is speculated that interaction extent and frequency for the BGI sphere of cluster 2 is similar to that of cluster 1. Regardless of the size of BGI sphere, the potential for between-group aggregations is high.

CI spheres occur at both levels for the Natufian data (see Figs. 9.9 and 9.11). The first level occurs where the paths of WGI spheres intersect while the second level occurs when the paths from BGI spheres intersect. First-level CI spheres (Fig. 9.9) show that there are two potential spheres. The first includes clusters 1 and 2, while the second contains clusters 1 and 3. The total size of these two CI spheres occupies a large area of the region but the CI sphere for clusters 1 and 2 is larger than the CI sphere for clusters 1 and 3. This suggests that the potential for interaction and possibly conflict is greatest for individuals using sites and their corresponding paths in clusters 1 and 2. Second-level CI spheres (Fig. 9.14) show that although the number of spheres is greater at this level, their spatial extent is much smaller than at the first level. A second distinction is that all second-level CI spheres contain the BGI spheres for all Natufian site clusters. Because all clusters create these second-level CI spheres, and because they are relatively restricted to a small spatial scale, the potential for daily, face-to-face contact is high. Therefore, competition for resources and access to the route is greater. It is also possible that these second-level CI spheres indicate close proximity to sites where aggregation of all Natufian social groups, represented by the clusters, takes place.

While the interactive agency model is consistent with the results presented in this research, it does not address the issue of time period or site size. The data available for this research is by no means complete; it is a representative sample acquired from available resources. Because the amount of available data is not as great as ideally desired, it is difficult to derive WGI spheres based on site size and time phase. However, in examining the second-level least-cost-path analysis based on site size and phase (Fig. 9.23), similar BGI spheres form. There is no evidence for CI spheres at this level of analysis. The reason for this absence is possibly cluster size. Recalling from chapter nine, least-cost-path analysis is only carried out for sites greater than 2000 m^2 in size. This severely limits the number of potential paths created. Because estimated site size is never a true reflection of the size of the site when it was inhabited, I do not believe that site size should be included in research that incorporates the interactive agency model. Time frame, as indicated by phase whether Early or Late, is an issue that is not as easily resolved. It is possible to suggest that the interactions that took place in this region during the Natufian endured over time with slight deviations, but this remains speculative.

Alternatively, while I do not focus on the lithic data *per se*, the results of first- and second-level analysis (Figs. 9.24 though 9.27) can also be incorporated into the interactive agency model. Interestingly, when incorporated into the model, these results are very similar to results of the non-lithic material culture. WGI spheres are evident from the first-level least-cost-path analysis (Fig. 9.24) and BGI spheres are visible in the second-level least-cost-path analysis (Fig. 9.26). Both levels of CI spheres are also apparent (Figs. 9.25 and 9.27), illustrating first-level CI spheres as spatially large and consisting of only two groups, while second-level CI spheres are comparably small and contain all clusters.

Alternative Interpretations

The resulting clusters and least cost paths are used to construct the interactive agency model put forth in this chapter. Further questioning, with particular attention on the visible nodes illustrated in figures 9.15 to 9.18, results in possible alternative explanations for the clustering of Natufian sites and the paths created in second level least cost path analysis. One alternative explanation follows the forager and collector economic zonation model, put forth by Binford (1980), where the emphasis is on site function in relation to the natural environment. According to the forager model (Binford 1980:9), there are two types of spatial context for the discard, or abandonment of archaeological remains for foragers: residential bases and locations. Residential bases refer to the "hub" of subsistence activity but may vary considerably in both duration and spacing between sites. Locations are generally "low bulk" procurement sites, occupied for a short period. The collector model, on the other hand, recognizes five types of spatial context for the discard, or abandonment of archaeological remains for collectors: residential base, field camps - temporary operation centers, location - where procurement and processing of raw materials takes place, stations - sites where special purpose task groups are localized and engage in information gathering, and caches - temporary storage areas.

Based on consideration of the forager and collector models the question then becomes - are these sites and their resulting clusters the result of foraging or collecting activities? This is a difficult question to answer because all clusters exhibit features for both the forager and collector model. In addition, if we take into consideration the obvious nodes connecting one site to other sites belonging to different clusters, the interpretation becomes more complicated. Some of the previous models discussed in chapter three and at the beginning of this chapter correspond with the forager model but they do not correspond to the results produced through the cluster analysis and least cost path analysis, particularly with regard to spatial location of sites and corresponding ecological biome. For example, Henry (1977; 1983) applies the forager model to explain artifactual variability in the Natufian. According to Henry (1977:238), "the Natufian may be viewed as a homogeneous cultural entity, displaying two horizon styles with variations in tool kits corresponding to camp type differences and variations in macro-environment." However, Henry (1983:100) later argues, "given the environmental diversity of the region, some variation existed between adaptations to local settings and attendant cultural developments." Here, he sides with the cultural-ecological school of thought.

A second model that can be used as an alternative to the interactive agency model goes back to Julian Steward's (1936) band model where hunter-gatherers display one of three possible band formations: patrilineal, composite, or matrilineal. These band formations relate to the social organization of hunter-gatherers. Steward (1936) lists six main factors of a band:

> (1) The "social" aggregate is usually larger than the biological family;
> (2) Several families co-operate in some economic activity and frequently share food communally;
> (3) It is rare that land, if divided into family tracts, would provide a sufficient variety of foods;
> (4) Realignment of family tract boundaries each generation would entail serious practical difficulties;
> (5) Social activities tend to unite several families; and
> (6) A large group provides greater security in warfare of feuds.

Related to the concept of band, hunter-gatherers are also organized as either simple or complex. Again, the simple versus complex classification refers to social organization and the emergence of social institutions but it also categorizes hunter-gatherers in relation to environment, diet (and food storage), settlement size, mobility, demography, territoriality, political organization, and exchange. (Arnold 1996; Cohen 1985; Keeley 1988; Kelly 1995; Price 2003; Price and Brown 1985). Most complex hunter-gatherers exhibit several of the following characteristics: large settlement size with low mobility, a high population density, hierarchical decent groups, territoriality, competition, resource ownership (Keeley 1988).

Henry (1985) attempts to identify several common components of Natufian sites using both band and complexity characteristics for hunter-gatherers. According to Henry (1985:371), the Natufian practice a complex hunting-gathering strategy compared to earlier cultures, such as the Geometric Kebaran and Mushabian because the Natufian intensively exploited wild cereals (a storable resource), thus encouraging sedentary lifeways leading to "the emergence of various technological, demographic, social, and ritual elements common to more complex hunting-gathering societies." Henry further argues (1985:376) that it is possible that the Natufian represents a ranked society with a matrilocal residence pattern. Evidence to support this argument comes from attributes of burial.

Wright (1978:219) in his analysis of burial data also concludes that the Natufian grave goods, particularly Dentalium shell, symbolize a particular inherited status position and suggests that Natufian social structure is similar to that of settled agricultural communities. Bar-Yosef and Belfer-Cohen (1989) on the contrary, argue that there is no evidence of social inequality; rather, the differences in Natufian burials are a function of chronology. In a discussion on characteristics of complexity for hunter-gatherers and the Natufian, Wright (1978:220) further suggests that "alliances linked the Natufian groups, at least in part, to allow sharing of resources...such alliances would have been particularly important in terms of linking coastal groups to those further inland." Kaufman (1992:191) echoes Wright's argument by contending that evolving socio-cultural mechanisms played a significant role in the Natufian as complex hunter-gatherers where "alliances based on exchange and kinship, which began in the late Kebaran, allowed for the social agglomerations of the Natufians."

The work of Henry, Wright, and Kaufman form the foundation of the interactive agency model. Their work builds upon a large body of hunter-gatherer research on subsistence, settlement and social organization. However, their models do not fully explain how and where alliances occur and how this relates to the spatial patterning of Natufian sites. To complicate matters further, some anthropologists have questioned the concept of "band" at the regional level (Bird-David 1987; Myers 1986; Williams 1982) because regional organization is, as argued by Myers (1988:272), "not constituted through place" in the simple manner that band models imply. It is for this reason that the interactive agency model is of substantive importance when discussing social relations in the Natufian. The interactive agent model serves as a heuristic tool to further develop the concept of the Natufian as a practicing a complex hunter-gatherer strategy. It also provides the incorporation of agency and structure into the lives of the Natufian.

Final Remarks

This chapter integrates the results of this research with the models proposed to interpret Natufian behavior. This integration shows that, while some aspects of these models explain why Natufian sites are located in certain areas of the study region, there are large gaps in their fit with the results. These gaps reflect an emphasis on ecological conditions dictating past human behavior. An alternative approach to assist in the understanding of past human behavior is to provide a model that examines the role of agency in the decisions humans make. These decisions, in turn, influence where one lives, who interacts with whom, and what information, knowledge and materials they exchange. It is also important to understand that these decisions also have a relationship with both social and ecological structures. The interactive agency model provides such an alternative approach that acknowledges the role agency plays in human life all the while recognizing that there are enabling and constraining features in both the social and ecological structure of an individual.

The interactive agency model illustrates a past human experience in which individuals and groups of individuals were aware of their surrounding as well as "the other." This model also shows that interaction with their surroundings and "the other" took place in three interrelated spheres – within-group interaction, between-group interaction and competitive interaction spheres.

CHAPTER 11

Conclusions

Bridging Theory and Method in Archaeology – Building Models

Archaeologists attempt to understand all aspects of human behavior through study of the material remains of past cultures. This study cannot occur without the assistance of certain *tools* – theory and method. The study of archaeology is continuously in flux. Theoretical perspectives and analytical methods tend to follow trend-like characteristics and, if not placed into an archaeological interpretive context, fall quickly out of fashion. While some theoretical and methodological tools withstand the test of time, many fall into disuse, either through revision or replacement. This is not to say that they are inadequate; rather the archaeologist's quest for improvement in research naturally leads to improvement in available tools.

The research presented in this dissertation looks to a particular theoretical perspective – social agency – as a *thinking toolkit*. Social agency demonstrates the duality of structure that is inescapable in human life, regardless of time period, mode of subsistence, demographic size, or geographical location. This duality shows the enabling and constraining nature of the structures that frame human existence. The domain of these structures is unlimited. Human actions and decisions influence these structures and the culmination of structure, action, and decision making form human social interaction through the communication of information, knowledge and materials. To this extent, social interaction of past human society is the focus of this research. Social agency has its roots in sociology but it has proven useful in other areas of the social sciences, including its recent venture into archaeology.

In keeping with the theme of using tools to discern past social interaction, social agency is also characterized as a temporary construct that takes shape for and by empirical work. In other words, social agency, if it is to be proven a useful tool, needs an analytical framework. This research uses cost-surface analysis, through the creation of least-cost-paths to shape the construct of social agency in order to understand past human interactions. Using cost-surface analysis, it is possible to include characteristics of social structure (perceived through the clustering of cultural materials on the basis of similarity) and ecological structure (perceived through the topographical variability of the ecological landscape). Applying a social agency perspective, framed by cost-surface analysis, results in the construction of a model that elucidates past social interaction for a culture in a specified geographical region.

Applying the model in this research indicates that there were three spheres of interaction for hunter-gatherers. These spheres correspond to within-group and between-group interactions. They also address different forms of interaction, including informal, daily, face-to-face interactions, formal, seasonal group-gathering interactions, and competitive interaction at both the informal and formal level.

Socializing the Natufian

The last 75 years of research on the Natufian culture reflect the flux in archaeological research. In chapter three, I discuss this flux in relation to *themes* that correspond to particular theoretical trends. These themes are identified as: (1) chronological, with an emphasis on the construction of time sequences; (2) cultural-ecological and evolutionary, where culture is framed, and evolves through its experience in the physical world, that being the ecological environment; and (3) use of a descriptive system to define the Natufian as a historical narrative.

The Natufian represents one of the final periods of archaeologically known hunter-gatherers in Southwest Asia and is of particular interest because these hunter-gatherers appear to have lived at the threshold of the emergence of cultivation and agriculture. The emergence of agriculture is the product of the convergence of several factors. The main factor of interest to researchers is the changing ecological landscape. Another factor, perhaps even a facilitator of the emergence of agriculture, is the sharing of knowledge on methods as well as plant species leading to cultivation. This sharing of knowledge is a direct result of interaction among groups and individuals. In this sense, re-examining the past themes and introducing an agency-centred approach to Natufian behaviour is fundamental.

To apply the interactive agency model to the Natufian data, an initial analysis of the material culture for each site is necessary. This is carried out through cluster analysis. The results of this analysis suggest that previous interpretation, focussing on distinct territorial-cultural groups, ignores the similarity in material culture. The non-lithic material culture illustrates this point most effectively. This similarity is not restricted to a particular territory, ecological biome, or time period. This result gives initial evidence that some form of interaction occurred among various Natufian social groups, but it does not suggest where or how this interaction occurred. The interactive agency model fulfils this objective.

According to the interactive agency model, there were three spheres, or levels, of interaction for the Natufian. At the within-group interactive level, interaction occurred within the groups that are identified in the cluster analysis. The size of the group primarily indicates the geographical extent as well as frequency of interaction within the individual groups. In this sphere, we see various level of interaction, from individual encounters to group gatherings. However, one common characteristic for all groups is the north-south direction of the interaction spheres. This north-south direction facilitated the exchange of materials that may not have been available throughout the region, such as marine shell specific to the Red or Mediterranean Sea, basalt and exotic materials (crystal, greenstone/malachite, opal, obsidian, etc).

The between-group interactive sphere illustrates the interaction that occurred among various Natufian social groups. At this level, there was a high degree of interaction, with a large volume of information and materials being exchanged. While there was individual, face-to-face interaction, the probability of large-scale exchange, in the form of multiple social group gatherings, is high. Materials are likely to have been exchanged, but exchange of knowledge and social structure predominated in these spheres. This exchange is evidenced in other forms of material culture, such as burials, architectural styles, and innovations, such as bedrock mortars.

The third sphere of interaction is the competitive sphere. Little is known about the Natufian competitive nature. There is preliminary evidence of conflict (Bocquentin & Bar-Yosef 2004) during the Early Natufian but it remains uncertain whether the competitive sphere was a factor in this conflict. At this point, the competitive sphere serves as a predictive tool showing where individual and group *chance encounters* are likely to have occurred.

The interactive agency model provides the opportunity to examine the Natufian culture from an anthropological stance. Accepting that cultures consider both social and ecological structures when making decisions on how to interact with others and what information and materials they will exchange provide a holistic approach to the understanding of past human activities. In this sense, the model fulfills the objectives of this research.

Implications of the Interactive Agency Model

The study of past hunter-gatherer societies is an exciting field of research in archaeology. The diversity of theoretical perspectives and analytical methods available for implementation of models in this area of research is impressive. The overwhelming focus of past hunter-gatherer studies has been on adaptive strategies and the ecological conditions in which these past cultures lived. The use of cultural historical and cultural ecology models to understand Natufian behavior provides excellent examples of this attention. Concentrating on these issues is appealing because hunter-gatherer societies, both present and past, have practiced various adaptive strategies to exploit the varied ecological environments in which they have lived. However, this focus tends to characterize these societies as at the mercy of their ecological environment in terms of where they live, whom they encounter, and what resources they use.

This is not to say that I do not agree that there are cultural and ecological factors that influence the decisions made by hunter-gatherers. I recognize the effectiveness of models that consider geographical location, ecological environment, mode of subsistence, and demographic size of the study population. However, while one model may prove effective for representing the behavior of one culture, it may be useless for another. For example, *optimal foraging models,* focusing on cognitive mechanisms that emphasize foraging strategies that provide maximum benefits or achieve optimal goals, proves to be an effective tool to understand some hunter-gatherer cultures living in areas of scarce resources or extreme climatic or ecological conditions (Foley 1985; Bettinger 1987; Winterhalter 1981). However, optimal foraging models do not apply to all hunter-gatherer cultures. The reason why this model is not effective is because it does not take into consideration other factors that affect the decisions individuals make in their settlement and subsistence choices. These factors include those characteristics that enable and constrain social structure. The interactive agent model addresses the shortcomings of these models because it directly confronts both ecological and social structures that are created and shaped through human interaction. Acknowledging both ecological and social characteristics of a culture, this model is not limited to the study of hunter-gatherers, nor is it restricted to a specific geographical location. In this sense, the interactive agent model follows what Myers (1988:274) categorizes as a humanistic approach to hunter-gatherer studies where, "humanistic accounts have in common an interest in exploring the cultural dimensions of hunter-gatherer life - the meaning through which they construct the world."

In a similar vein, the recent proliferation of predictive models in archaeology, models that attempt to illustrate potential patterns of settlement for past cultures, primarily employ dependent variables such as proximity to water, preference for a level ground, or a southern exposure. These variables may prove effective determinants of the location of some archaeological sites given a particular geographical location but, in certain geographical locations, these dependent variables are not the only desirable characteristics when deciding where to set up camp. Again, these models are not entirely effective because they do not take into consideration social factors that affect the decisions individuals make in their settlement choices. The interactive agent model also addresses the shortcomings of predictive models because it adds a social dimension to aid in the prediction of past human settlements. Acknowledging that interaction takes place in three different spheres makes it possible to predict where unknown archaeological sites may be located, as well as the possible reasons for the particular location of these sites. I acknowledge that lack of equality, or coverage, from previous surveys can have an impact on the least cost path analysis. However, the attractiveness of the interactive model is that one can update it at the onset of new information.

This research introduces the interactive agency model but, at this point, it is practical to consider the model as a work in progress. The interactive agency model effectively illustrates that there were defined social groups within the Natufian. The model also illustrates that these social groups did not live in a vacuum and that different spheres of social interaction tied the groups together. These spheres of interaction address the typological variability and technological similarity of material culture that defines the Natufian culture in the Levant.

REFERENCES CITED

Adams, W. Y. and E. W. Adams
1991   *Archaeological typology and practical reality: a dialectical approach to artifact classification and sorting.* Cambridge University Press, Cambridge.

Aldenderfer, M.
1998   *Montane Foragers: Asana and the South-Central Andean Archaic.* University of Iowa Press, Iowa City.

Aldenderfer, M. and R. Blashfield
1984   *Cluster Analysis.* Quantitative Applications in Social Sciences. Sage Publications, Beverly Hills.

Aldenderfer, M. and H. D. G. Maschner
1996   Introduction. In *Anthropology, Space and Geographic Information Systems*, edited by M. Aldenderfer and H. D. G. Maschner, pp. 4-18. Oxford University Press, New York.

Arnold, J. E.
1996   The archaeology of complex hunter-gatherers. Journal of Anthropological Method and Theory 3(2):77-126.

Banning, E. B.
2000   *The Archaeologist's Laboratory: The Analysis of Archaeological Data.* Klewer Academic, New York.

Barrett, J. C.
2000   Fields of discourse: reconstituting a social archaeology. In *Interpretive Archaeology: A Reader*, edited by J. Thomas. Leicester University Press, London.

Bar-Yosef, O.
1970   *The Epi-Paleolithic cultures of Palestine.* Doctoral Thesis, Hebrew University.

1981   The Epi-Palaeolithic complexes in the Southern Levant. In *Prehistoire du Levant*, edited by J. Cauvin and P. Sanlaville, pp. 389-408. CNRS, Paris.

1983   The Natufian of the southern Levant. In *The Hilly Flanks and Beyond, Studies in Ancient Oriental Civilization,* edited by P.E.L. Smith and P. Mortensen, pp. 11-42. vol. No 36. University of Chicago Press, Chicago: The Oriental Institute.

1989   Late Pleistocene adaptations in the Levant. In *The Pleistocene Old World: Regional Perspectives*, edited by O. Sofer, pp 219-236. Plenum Press, New York.

1998   The Natufian culture of the Levant, threshold to the origins of agriculture. *Evolutionary Anthropology* 6(5):159-177.

1999   Hayonim Cave. *Hadashot Arkheologyot: Excavations and Surveys in Israel* 110:9*-10*.

2001   From sedentary foragers to village hierarchies: the emergence of social institutions. In *The Origin of Human Social Institutions*, edited by W. G. Runciman, pp. 1-38. vol. 110. Published for the British Academy by Oxford University Press, New York.

Bar-Yosef, O. and A. Belfer-Cohen
1991   From Sedentary Hunter-Gatherers to Territorial Farmers in the Levant. In *Between Bands and States,* edited by S. A. Gregg, pp. 181-202, Illinois.

1992   From Foraging to Farming in the Mediterranean Levant. In *Transitions to Agriculture in Prehistory.*, edited by A. B. Gebauer and T. D. Price, pp. 21-48. Prehistory Press, Madison, Wisconsin.

1999   Encoding information: unique Natufian objects from Hayonim Cave, western Galilee, Israel. *Antiquity* 73(280):402-409.

2000   Nahal Ein Gev II: a Late Epipalaeolithic site in the Jordan Valley. *Journal of the Israel Prehistoric Society* 30:49-71.

Bar-Yosef, O., P. Goldberg and T. Levenson
1974   Late quaternary stratigraphy and prehistory in the lower Jordan valley. *Paleorient* 2(2):415-428.

Bar-Yosef, O. and F. R. Valla
1991   *The Natufian Culture in the Levant.* International Monographs in Prehistory, Ann Arbor.

Bar-Yosef, O., B. Vandermeersch, B. Arsenberg, A. Belfer-Cohen, P. Goldberg, H. Laville, L. Meignen, Y. Rak, J. D. Speth, E. Tchernov, A.-M. Tillier and S. Weiner
1992   The excavations in Kebara Cave, Mt. Carmel. *Current Anthropology* 33(5):497-550.

Bar-Yosef, O. and B. Vandermeersch
1989   Investigations in South Levantine Prehistory/ Prehistoire du Sud-Levant. *BAR International Series* 497:231-253.

Bar-Yosef, O. and J.C. Vogel
1987   Relative and absolute chronologies of the Epi-Palaeolithic in the southern Levant. In *Chronologies in the Near East, Relative and absolute chronology 16,000-4,000 B.P.*, edited by O.Aurenche, J. Even and F. Hours, pp. 219-245. BAR IS 79, Oxford.

Bartov, Y., M. Stein, Y. Enzel, A. Agnon, and Z. Reches
2002.   Lake Levels and Sequence Stratigraphy of Lake Lisan, the Late Pleistocene Precursor of the Dead Sea. *Quaternary Research* 57:9-21.

Baruch, U., and S. Bottema
1991. Palynological Evidence for Climatic Changes in the Levant ca. 17,000-9,000 BP.. In *The Natufian Culture in the Levant,* edited by O. Bar-Yosef and F. R. Valla, pp. 11-20. Ann Arbor: International Monographs in Prehistory.

Belfer-Cohen, A.
1989 The Natufian issue: A suggestion. In *Investigations in Southern Levantine Prehistory.*, edited by O. Bar-Yosef and B. Vandermeersch, pp. 297-308. vol. 497. BAR IS, Oxford.

1991a The Natufian in the Levant. *Annual Review of Anthropology* 20:167-186.

1991b Art items from layer B, Hayonim Cave: a case study of art in a Natufian context. In *The Natufian Culture in the Levant.*, edited by O. Bar-Yosef and F. Valla, pp. 569-587. International Monographs in Prehistory, Ann Arbor.

1995 Rethinking social stratification in the Natufian Culture: The evidence from burials. In *The Archaeology of Death in the Ancient Near East.*, edited by S. Campbell and A. Green, pp. 9-16. Oxbow Books, Oxford.

Bell, J.
1992 On capturing agency in theories about prehistory. In *Representations in Archaeology*, edited by J. C. Gardin and C. Peebles, pp. 30-55. Indiana University Press, Bloomington.

Bell, T. and G. Lock
2000 Topographic and cultural influences on walking the ridgeway in later prehistoric times. In *Beyond the Map: Archaeology and Spatial Technologies*, edited by G. Lock. IOS, Amsterdam.

Bell, T., A. Wilson and A. Wickham
2002 Tracking the Samnites: Landscape and communications routes in the Sangro valley, Italy. *American Journal of Archaeology* 106(2):169-186.

Bettinger, R. L.
1987 Archaeological Approaches to Hunter-Gatherers. *Annual Review of Anthropology* 16:121-142.

Bettinger, R. L. and M. A. Baumhoff
1982 The Numic spread: Great Basin cultures in competition. *American Antiquity* 47(3):485-503.

Betts, A.V.G.
1986 *The Prehistory of the Basalt Desert, Transjordan, an Analysis*, London University.

1988 The Black Desert survey. Prehistoric sites and subsistence strategies in eastern Jordan. In *The Prehistory of Jordan.*, edited by A. N. Garrard and H. G. Gebel, pp. 369-391. vol. 396. BAR IS, Oxford.

1998 The Epi-Palaeolithic Period. In *The Harra and the Hamad*, edited by A. V. G. Betts, pp. 11-35. vol. 9. Sheffield Archaeological Monographs, Sheffield.

Binford, L. R.
1980 Willow smoke and dogs tails: Hunter-gatherer systems in archaeological site formation. *American Antiquity* 45(1):4-20.

Bird-David, N.
1987 single persons and social cohesion in hunter-gatherer society. In *Dimensions of Social Life*, edited by P. Hocking, pp. 107-116. Mouton, Berlin.

Boaz, J. S. and E. Uleberg
1995 The Potential of GIS-Based Studies of Iron Age Cultural Landscapes in Eastern Norway. In *Archaeology and Geographical Information Systems: A European Perspective*, edited by G. Lock and Z. Stancic, pp. 249-259. Tatlor & Francis, London.

Bocquentin, F. and O. Bar-Yosef
2004 Early Natufian remains: Evidence for physical conflict from Mt. Carmel, Israel. In *Journal of Human Evolution*, vol. 27, no. 1-2, pp. 19-23.

Bourdieu, P.
1977 *Outline for a Theory of Practice.* Cambridge University Press, Cambridge.

Boyce, R. L. and P. C. Ellison
2001 Choosing the best similarity index when performing fuzzy set ordination on binary data. *Journal of Vegetation Science* 12:711-720.

Boyd, B.
1995 Houses and hearths, pits and burials: Natufian mortuary practices at Mallaha (Eynan), upper Jordan Valley. In *The Archaeology of Death in the Ancient Near East*, edited by S. Campbell and A. Green, pp. 17-23. vol. 51. Oxbow Monograph, Oxford.

2001 The Natufian burials from el-Wad, Mount Carmel: beyond issues of social differentiation. *Journal of the Israel Prehistoric Society* 31:185-200.

Braidwood, R. J.
1952 *The Near East and the foundations for civilization. an essay in appraisal of the general evidence.* Oregon State System of Higher Education, Eugene.

Burrough, P. A. and R. A. McDonnell
1998 *Principles of Geographical Information Systems.* Spatial Information Systems and Geostatistics. Oxford University Press, Oxford.

Byrd, B. F.
1987 *Beidha and the Natufian: Variability in Levantine settlement and subsistence.* Ph.D. thesis (unpublished), University of Arizona.

1989 *The Natufian encampment at Beidha: Late Pleistocene adaptation in the Southern Levant.* Jutland Archaeological Society Publications. 23. Aarhus University Press, Aarhus, Denmark.

1991 Beidha: An Early Natufian encampment in southern Jordan. In *The Natufian Culture in the Levant.*, edited by O. Bar-Yosef and F. R. Valla, pp. 245-264. International Monographs in Prehistory, Ann Arbor.

1994 Late quaternary hunter-gatherer complexes in the Levant between 20,000 and 10,000 BP. In *Late Quaternary Chronology and Paleoclimates of the Eastern Mediterranean*, edited by O. Bar-Yosef and R. S. Kra, pp. 205-226. Radiocarbon.

Byrd, B.F. and S. Colledge
1991 Early Natufian occupation along the edge of the southern Jordanian steppe. In *The Natufian Culture in the Levant.*, edited by O. Bar-Yosef and F. Valla, pp. 265-277. International Monagraphs in Prehistory, Ann Arbor.

Campana, D.
1991 Bone implements from Hayonim Cave: Some relevant issues. In *The Natufian Culture in the Levant.*, edited by O. Bar-Yosef and F. Valla, pp. 459-466. International Monographs in Prehistory, Ann Arbor.

Cauvin, M. C.
1991 Du Natoufien au Levant nord? Jayroud et Mureybet (Syrie). In *The Natufian Culture in the Levant*, edited by O. Bar-Yosef and F. Valla, pp. 295-314. International Monographs in Prehistory, Ann Arbor.

Cheetham, A. H. and J. E. Hazel
1969 Binary (presence-absence) similarity coefficients. *Journal of Paleontology* 43:113-136.

Christaller, W.
1933 *Central Places in Southern Germany*. Prentice-Hall, Englewood Cliffs.

Clark, J. E.
2000 Towards a better explanation of hereditary inequality: a critical assessment of natural and historic human agents. In *Agency in Archaeology*, edited by M.-A. Dobres and J. Robb, pp. 92-112. Routledge, London.

Clark, J. W.
1977 Time-distance Transformations of Transportation Networks. *Geographical Analysis* 9:195-205.

Cohen, M. N.
1985 Prehistoric hunter-gatherers: the meaning of social complexity. In *Prehistoric Hunter-Gatherers: The Emergence of Cultural Complexity*, edited by T. D. Price and J. Brown, pp. 99-119. Academic Press, Orlando.

Conard, N. J.
2002 An overview of the recent excavations at Baaz rockshelter, Damascus Province, Syria. In *Mauer Schau*, edited by R. Aslan, S. Blum, G. Kastl, F. Schweizer and D. Thumm. Verlag Bernhard Albert Greiner, Remshalden-Grunbach.

Conkey, M. W.
1980 The identification of prehistoric hunter-gatherer aggregation sites: The case of Altamira. *Current Anthropology* 21(5):609-630.

Copeland, L.
1991 Natufian sites in Lebanon. In *The Natufian Culture in the Levant.*, edited by O. Bar-Yosef and F. Valla, pp. 27-42. International Monographs in Prehistory, Ann Arbor.

Cordova, C. E., C. Foley, A. Nowell, and M. Bisson
2005 Landforms, Sediments, Soil Development, and Prehistoric Site Settings on the Madaba-Dhiban Plateau, Jordan. *Geoarchaeology* 20:29-56.

Cowgill, G. L.
1982 Clusters of objects and associations between variables: Two approaches to archaeological classification. In *Essays on Archaeological Typology*, edited by R. Whallon and J. Brown. Center for American Archeology Press, Evanston, Ill.

Crabtree, P., D. Campana, A. Belfer-Cohen and D. Bar-Yosef
1991 First results of the excavations at Salibiya I, lower Jordan valley. In *The Natufian Culture in the Levant.*, edited by O. Bar-Yosef and F. Valla, pp. 161-172. International Monographs in Prehistory, Ann Arbor.

Cunningham, K. M. and J. C. Ogilvie
1972 Evaluation of hierarchical grouping techniques: A preliminary study. *Computer Journal* 15:209-213.

Dean, D.
1996 Finding minimum-cost routes for access roads to single and multiple harvest sites. Paper presented at the Southern Forestry and GIS Conference, The University of Georgia, Athens.

Dincauze, D.
2000 *Environmental Archaeology: Principles and Practices*. Cambridge University Press, Cambridge.

Dobres, M.-A.
2000 *Technology and Social Agency: Outlining a Practice Framework for Archaeology*. Blackwell, Oxford.

Dobres, M.-A. and C. R. Hoffman
1999 *The Social Dynamics of Technology: Practice, Politics and World Views*. Smithsonian Institute Press, Washington D.C.

Dobres, M.-A. and J. Robb
2000 Agency in archaeology: paradigm or platitude? In *Agency in Archaeology*, edited by M.-A. Dobres and J. Robb, pp. 3-17. Routledge, London.

Dornan, J. L.
2002 Agency in archaeology: past, present and future directions. *Journal of Archaeological Method and Theory* 9(4):303-329.

Dunnell, R. C.
1971 *Systematics in Prehistory*. New York Free Press, New York.

Edwards, P.
1988 Natufian settlement in Wadi al-Hammeh. *Paleorient* 14(2):309-315.

1991 Wadi Hammeh 27: an Early Natufian site at Pella, Jordan. In *The Natufian Culture in the Levant.*, edited by O. Bar-Yosef and F. Valla, pp. 123-148. International Monographs in Prehistory, Ann Arbor.

1992 The Epipalaeolithic period. In *Pella in Jordan 2: The second interim report of the joint University of Sydney and College of Wooster excavations at Pella 1982-1985*, edited by A. E. McNicoll, J. Hanbury-Tenison, J. B. Hennessy, T. F. Potts, R. H. Smith, A. Walkmsley and P. Watson, pp. 1-16. Mediterranean Archaeological Supplement 2, Sydney.

ESRI
2003 *ESRI Maps and Data 2003*. Submitted to Electronic Report.

Everitt, B., S. Landau and M. Leese
1993 *Cluster Analysis*. 4th edition. Arnold, London.

Fisher, P. F.
1999 Geographical information systems: Today and tomorrow? In *Geographical Information Systems and Landscape Archaeology*, edited by M. Gillings, D. Mattingly and J. V. Dalen, pp. 5-11. The Archaeology of Mediterranean Landscapes, G. Barker and D. Mattingly, general editor. Oxbow Books, Oxford.

Foley, R.
1985 Optimality theory in anthropology. *Man* 20:222-242.

Foucault, M.
1986 Of Other Spaces, translated by Jay Miskowiec, *Diacritics* 16, 23.

Gaffney, V. and Z. Stančič
1991 *GIS Approaches to Regional Analysis: a Case Study of the Island of Hvar*. Znanstveni institute Filozofske Fakultete, University of Ljubljana, Ljubljana.

Gaffney, V., Z. Stančič and H. Watson
1996 Moving from catchments to cognition: tentative steps towards a larger archaeological context for GIS. In *Anthropology, Space and Geographic Information Systems*, edited by A. M. and H. Maschner, pp. 132-154. Oxford University Press, Oxford.

Gamble, C.
1986 *The Paleolithic Settlement of Europe*. Cambridge University Press, Cambridge.

1999 *The Paleolithic Societies of Europe*. Cambridge University Press, Cambridge.

Garrard, A. N.
1991 Natufian settlement in the Azraq basin, eastern Jordan. In *The Natufian Culture in the Levant.*, edited by O. Bar-Yosef and F. Valla, pp. 235-244. International Monographs in Prehistory, Ann Arbor.

Garrard, A. N. et al.
1987 An interim report on the 1985 excavation season. *Levant* XIX: 5-26.

Garrard, A. N., P. Harvey, F. Hivernel and B. Byrd
1985 The environmental history of the Azraq Basin. In *Studies in the History and Archaeology of Jordan*, edited by A. Hadidi, pp. 109-115. vol. 2. Routledge and Kegan Paul, London.

Garrard, A., A. Pirie, B. Schroeder and A. Wasse
2003 Survey of Nachcharini Cave and prehistoric settlement in the northern Anti-Lebanon Highlands. *Bulletin d'Archéologie et d'Architecture Libanaises* 7:15-48.

Garrard, A. and C. Yazbeck
2003 Qadisha Valley Prehistory Project, Northern Lebanon: Summary of first two seasons investigations. *Bulletin d'Archéologie et d'Architecture Libanaises* 7:7-14.

Garrod, D. A. E.
1932 A new Mesolithic industry: The Natufian of Palestine. *Journal of the Royal Anthropological Institute.* 62:257-270.

1957 The Natufian culture: The life and economy of a Meso-lithic people in the Near East. *Proceedings of the British Academy* 43:211-227.

Garrod, D. A. E. and D. M. A. Bate
1937 *The Stone Age of Mount Carmel: excavations at the Wady El-Mughara*. 1. Clarendon Press, Oxford.

Giddens, A.
1979 *Central Problems in Social Theory: Action, Structure, and Contradiction in Social Analysis*. University of California Press, Berkeley.

1984 *The Constitution of Society: Outline of the Theory of Structuration.* University of California Press, Berkeley.

Gillings, M. and A. Wise (editors)
1998 *GIS Guide to Good Practice.* Oxbow Books, Oxford.

Goldberg, P.
1981 Late Quaternary stratigraphy of Israel: and eclectic view. In *Prehistoire du Levant.*, edited by J. Cauvin and P. Sanlaville, pp. 55-66. C.N.R.S, Paris.

Gorenflo, L. and N. Gale
1990 Mapping regional settlement in information space. *Journal of Anthropological Archaeology* 9:240-274.

Goring-Morris, A. N.
1980 *Late Quaternary Sites in the Wadi Fazael, Lower Jordan Valley.* Unpublished MA Thesis, Hebrew University of Jerusalem.

1987 *At the Edge: Terminal Pleistocene Hunter-Gatherers in the Negev and Sinai.* B.A.R. Is 361.

1997 A Late Natufian campsite at Givat Hayil I, western Negev dunes, Israel. *Journal of the Israel Prehistoric Society* 27:43-61.

1998 Mobiliary art from the Late Epipalaeolithic of the Negev, Israel. *Rock Art Research* 15(2):81-88.

Goring-Morris, A. N. and O. Bar-Yosef
1987 A Late Natufian campsite from the western Negev, Israel. *Paleorient* 13(1):107-112.

Goring-Morris, A. N. and A. Belfer-Cohen
1998 The articulation of cultural processes and Late Quaternary environmental changes in Cisjordan. *Paleorient* 23(2):71-93.

Goring-Morris, N., P. Goldberg, Y. Goren, U. Baruch and D. E. Bar-Yosef
1999 Saflulim: a Late Natufian base camp in the central Negev highlands, Israel. *Palestine Exploration Quarterly* 131:36-64.

Goring-Morris, A. N. and S. A. Rosen
1987 *Prehistoric archaeology. Preliminary safety analysis report. Nuclear power plant - Shivta site.* Israel Electric Corporation. Copies available from Volume 9(1).

Gower, J. C.
1985 Measures of similarity, dissimilarity, and distance. In *Encyclopedia of Statistical Sciences*, edited by S. Kotz and N. L. Johnson, pp. 397-405. vol. 5. Wiley, New York.

Green, S. W.
1990 Approaching archaeological space: an introduction to this volume. In *Interpreting Space: GIS and Archaeology*, edited by K. M. S. Allen, S. W. Green and E. B. W. Zubrow, pp. 3-8. Taylor and Francis, London.

Grossman, L.
2003 Preserving cultural traditions in a period of instability: the Late Natufian of the hilly Mediterranean zone. *Current Anthropology* 44(4):571-580.

Grossman, L., A. Belfer-Cohen and O. Bar-Yosef
1999 A Final Natufian site: Fazael IV. *Journal of the Israel Prehistoric Society* 29:17-40.

Haggett, P.
1965 *Location Analysis in Human Geography.* Edward Arnold, London.

Hands, S. and B. Everitt
1987 A Monte Carlo study of the recovery of cluster structure in binary data by hierarchical clustering techniques. *Multivariate Behavioral Research* 22:235-243.

Hayden, B.
1995 Pathways to power: principles for creating socioeconomic inequalities. In *Foundations of Social Inequality*, edited by T. D. Price and G. Feinman, pp. 15-86. Plenum, New York.

Henry, D. O.
1973 *The Natufian of Palestine: Its material culture and ecology.* Unpublished Ph.D. thesis, Southern Methodist University.

1976 Rosh Zin: A Natufian settlement near Ein Avdat. In *Prehistory and Paleoenvironments in the Central Negev, Israel,* edited by A. E. Marks, pp. 317-347. vol. I. SMU Press, Dallas.

1976 The excavation of Hayonim Terrace: an interim report. *Journal of Field Archaeology*, 3(4) pp. 391-406.

1977 An examination of the artifactual variability in the Natufian of Palestine. *Eretz Israel* 3:229-240.

1981 An analysis of the settlement patterns and adaptive strategies of the Natufian. In *Prehistoire du Levant*, edited by A. N. Garrard and H. G. Gebel, pp. 421-431. CNRS, Paris.

1982 The prehistory of southern Jordan and relationships with the Levant. *Journal of Field Archaeology* 9(4):417-444.

1983 Adaptive evolution within the Epipaleolithic of the Near East. In *Advances in World Archaeology*, edited by F. Wendorf and A. Close, pp. 99-160. vol. 2. Academic Press, London.

1985 Preagricultural sedentism: The Natufian example. In *Prehistoric Hunter-Gatherers.*, edited by T. D. a. J. A. B. Price, pp. 365-384. Academic Press, Inc., Orlando, Florida.

1989 *From foraging to agriculture: the Levant at the end of the Ice Age*. University of Pennsylvania Press, Philadelphia.

1994 Prehistoric cultural ecology in southern Jordan. *Science* 265(5170):336-341.

1995 *Prehistoric Cultural Ecology and Evolution: Insights from Southern Jordan*. Plenum Press, New York.

1998 Prehistoric human ecology in the southern Levant east of the Rift from 20,000 - 6,000 BP. *Paleorient* 23(2):107-119.

Henry, D. and S. J. M. Davis
1974 The 1974 excavations of Hayonim Terrace (Israel), a brief report. *Paleorient* 2:195-197.

Heywood, I.
1990 Geographic information systems in the social sciences. *Environment and Planning* 22(1):849-852.

Higgs, E. S. and C. Vita-Finzi
1972 Prehistoric economies: a territorial approach. In *Papers in Economic Prehistory*, edited by E. S. Higgs, pp. 27-36. Cambridge University Press, Cambridge.

Hodder, I.
2000 Agency and individuals in long-term processes. In *Agency in Archaeology*, edited by M.-A. Dobres and J. Robb, pp. 21-33. Routledge, London.

Hodson, F. R.
1982 Some aspects of archaeological classification. In *Essays on Archaeological Typology*, edited by R. Whallon and J. Brown. Center for American Archeology Press, Evanston, Ill.

Ibrahim, M., J. Sauer and K. Yassine
1976 The east Jordan Valley survey 1975. *Bulletin of the American School of Oriental Research* 222:41-66.

Janetski, J. C. and M. Chazan
2002 Excavations at Wadi Mataha: A multi-component Epipalaeolithic site in southern Jordan. (unpublished document).

Jardine, N. and R. Sibson
1971 *Mathematical Taxonomy*. Wiley, New York.

Jenkins, R.
2002 *Pierre Bourdieu*. Routledge, London.

Jennings, J. and N. Craig
2001 Politywide analysis and imperial political economy: The relationship between valley political complexity and administrative centers in the Wari Empire of the central Andes. *Journal of Anthropological Archaeology* 20:479-502.

Jochim, M. A.
1976 *Hunter-Gatherer Subsistence and Settlement: A Predictive Model*. Academic Press, New York.

1998 *A Hunter-Gatherer Landscape: Southwest Germany in the Late Paleolithic and Mesolithic*. Plenum Press, New York.

Joyce, A. A.
2000 The founding of Monte Alban: sacred propositions and social practices. In *Agency in Archaeology*, edited by M.-A. Dobres and J. Robb, pp. 71-91. Routledge, London.

Joyce, A. A. and M. Winter
1996 Ideology, power and urban society in pre-Hispanic Oxaca. *Current Anthropology* 37(1):33-47.

Kaufman, D.
1992 Hunter-gatherers of the Levantine Epipaleolithic: the socioecological origins of sedentism. *Journal of Mediterranean Archaeology* 5(2):165-201.

Keeley, L. H.
1988 Hunter-gatherer economic complexity and "population pressure": A cross-cultural analysis. *Anthropological Archaeology* 7:373-411.

Kelly, R. L.
1995 *The Foraging Spectrum: Diversity in Hunter-Gatherer Lifeways*. Smithsonian Institution Press, Washington.

Korte, G. B.
1997 *The GIS Book*. Onward Press, Santa Fe, New Mexico.

Kuper, A.
1988 *The Invention of Primitive Society*. Routledge, London.

Kvamme, K. L.
1989 Geographic information systems in regional archaeological research and data management. In *Archeological Theory and Method*, edited by M. B. Schiffer, pp. 139-203. vol. 1. University of Arizona Press, Tucson.

Legendre, P. and L. Legendre
1998 *Numerical Ecology*. 2nd. English ed. Elsevier, Amsterdam.

Lévi-Strauss, C.
1966 *The Savage Mind*, University of Chicago Press, Chicago.

Llobera, M.
2000 Understanding movement: a pilot model towards the sociology of movement. In *Beyond the Map: Archaeology and Spatial Technologies*, edited by G. R. Lock, pp. 65-84. IOS Press, Amsterdam.

Lock, G. R. and T. M. Harris
1992 Visualizing spatial data: The importance of geographic information systems. In *Archaeology and the Information Age: A Global Perspective*, edited by P. Reilly and S. Rahtz, pp. 81-96. Routledge, London.

2000 Introduction: Return to Ravello. In *Beyond the Map: Archaeology and Spatial Technologies*, edited by G. Lock, pp. xiii-xxv. Series A: Life Sciences - Vol. 321 ed. NATO Science Series. IOS Press, Amsterdam.
Lösch, A.

1944 *The Economics of Location*. Yale University Press, New Haven.

Madry, S. and L. Rakos
1996 Line-of-sight and Cost Surface Techniques for Regional Archaeological Research in the Arroux River Valley. In *New Methods, Old Problems: Geographic Information Systems in Modern Archaeological Research*, edited by H. D. G. Maschner, pp. 104-126. Occasional Paper no. 23. Center for Archaeological Investigations.

Manly, B. F. J
1991 *Randomization and Monte Carlo methods in biology*. Chapman and Hall, London, UK.

Marble, D., Z. Gou, L. Liu and J. Saunders
1996 Recent advances in the exploratory analysis of interregional flows in space and time. In *Innovations in Geographic Information Systems*, edited by Z. Kemp. Taylor & Francis, London.

Marks, A. E. and P. A. Larson
1977 Test excavations at the Natufian site of Rosh Horesha. In *Prehistory and Paleoenvironments of the Central Negev, Israel*, edited by A. E. Marks, pp. 191-232. vol. II. Southern Methodist University Press, Dallas.

Martin, D.
1996 *Geographic Information Systems: Socioeconomic Applications*. Routledge, London.

Maschner, H. D. G.
1996 *New Methods, Old Problems: Geographic Information Systems in Modern Archaeological Research*. Center for Archaeological Investigations, Southern Illinois University, Carbondale.

McDonald, I.
1961 Statistical studies of recorded energy expenditure of man: Expenditure on walking related to weight, sex, age, height, speed, and gradient. *Nutrition Abstracts and Reviews* 31(3), pp. 739-762.

Milligan, G. W.
1996 Clustering validation: results and implications for applied analyses. In *Clustering and classification*, edited by P. Arabie, L. J. Hubert and G. D. Soete, pp. 341–375. World Scientific Publishers, River Edge, New Jersey.

Moore, A. M. T.
1991 Abu Hureyra 1 and the antecedents of agriculture on the Middle Euphrates. In *The Natufian Culture in the Levant*, edited by O. Bar-Yosef and F. Valla, pp. 277-294. International Monographs in Prehistory, Ann Arbor.

Moore, A. M. T., Legge A.J. and Hillman G.C.
2000 *Village on the Euphrates*. Oxford University Press, Oxford.

Muheisen, M., H. G. Gebel, C. Hannss and R. Neef
1988 Excavations at `Ain Rahub, a Final Natufian and Yarmoukian site near Irbid. In *The Prehistory of Jordan: The State of Research in 1986*, edited by A. N. Garrard and H. G. Gebel, pp. 472-502. vol. 396. BAR International Series, Oxford.

Myers, F.T.
1986 *Pintupi Country, Pintupi Self: Sentiment, Place, and Politics among western Desert Aborigines*. Smithsonian Institute and Australian Institute of Aborigines Studies, Washington/Canberra.

1988 Critical Trends in the Study of Hunter-Gatherers. *Annual Review of Anthropology* 17:261-282.

NIMA
2000 *Digital Terrain Elevation Data (DTED)*. Unpublished document, number MIL-PRF-89020B.

Nadel, D. Editor.
2002. *Ohalo II, A 23,000-Year-Old Fisher-Hunter-Gatherers' Camp on the Shore of the Sea of Galilee*. Haifa: Hecht Museum, Haifa University.

Noy, T.
1991 Art and decoration of the Natufian at Nahal Oren. In *The Natufian Culture in the Levant*, edited by O. Bar-Yosef and F. Valla, pp. 557-568. International Monographs in Prehistory, Ann Arbor.

Olszewski, D. I.
1988 The north Syrian late Epipalaeolithic and its relationship to the Natufian complex. *Levant* 20:127-137.

Openshaw, S.
1996 A view on the GIS crisis in geography. In *Human Geography: An Essential Anthology*, edited by J. Agnew, D. N. Livingstone and A. Rogers, pp. 675-685. Blackwell Publishers Ltd., Oxford.

Pandolf, K.B., B. Givoni and R.F. Goldman
1977 Predicting energy expenditure with loads while standing or walking very slowly. *Journal of Applied Physiology* 43, pp. 577-581.

Pauketat, T. R.
2000 The tragedy of the commoners. In *Agency in Archaeology*, edited by M.-A. Dobres and J. Robb, pp. 113-129. Routledge, London.

2001 Practice and history in archaeology. *Anthropological Theory* 1(1):73-98.

Perlés, C. and J. Phillips
1991 The Natufian conference - discussion. In *The Natufian Culture in the Levant*, edited by O. Bar-Yosef and F. Valla, pp. 637-644. International Monographs in Prehistory, Ann Arbor.

Pirie, A.
2004 Constructing Prehistory: Lithic Analysis in the Levantine Epipalaeolithic. *Journal of the Royal Anthropological Institute* 10:675-703.

Pred, A.
1986 *Place, Practice and Structure*. Polity Press, Oxford.

Price, T. D.
2003 Emerging ideas about complexity emerging. In *Theory, Method, and Practice in Modern Archaeology*, edited by R. J. Jeske and D. K. Clark, pp. 51-67. Praeger, Westport.

Price, T. D. and J. Brown
1985 Aspects of hunter-gatherer complexity. In *Prehistoric Hunter-Gatherers: The Emergence of Cultural Complexity*, edited by T. D. Price and J. Brown, pp. 3-20. Academic Press, Orlando.

Read, D. W.
1982 Toward a theory of archaeological classification. In *Essays on Archaeological Typology*, edited by R. Whallon and J. Brown. Center for American Archeology Press, Evanston, Ill.

Robb, J.
2001 *Social agency and anti-social agency: archaeology in the grey zone*. Paper presented at the 66th Annual Meeting of the Society for American Archaeology, New Orleans, LA.

Romesburg, H. C.
1990 *Cluster Analysis for Researchers*. Robert E. Krieger Publishing Company, Malabar.

Ronan, A. and M. Lechevallier
1991 The Natufian of Hatula. In *The Natufian Culture in the Levant*, edited by O. Bar-Yosef and F. R. Valla, pp. 149-160. International Monographs in Prehistory, Ann Arbor.

Rosen, S.A.
1991 Paradigms and politics in the terminal Pleistocene archaeology of the Levant. In *Perspectives on the past* edited by G.A. Clark, 309-21. Philadelphia: University of Pennsylvania Press.

Ruggles, A. J. and R. L. Church
1996 An Analysis of Late-Horizon Settlement Patterns in the Teotihuacan-Temascalapa Basins: A Location-Allocation and GIS-Based Approach. In *Anthropology, Space and Geographic Information Systems*, edited by M. Aldendefer and H. Maschner. Oxford University Press, Oxford.

Sahlins, M. D.
1972 *Stone Age Economics*. Aldine-Atherton, Chicago.

Salmon, M.
1982 *Philosophy in Archaeology*. Academic Press, New York.

Sassaman, K. E.
2000 Agents of change in hunter-gatherer technology. In *Agency in Archaeology*, edited by M.-A. Dobres and J. Robb, pp. 148-168. Routledge, London.

Savage, S.
1990 GIS in Archaeological Research. In *Interpreting Space: GIS and Archaeology*, edited by K. M. S. Allen, S. W. Green and E. B. W. Zubrow, pp. 22-33. Taylor & Francis, London.

Schiffer, M. B.
2000 Social theory in archaeology: building bridges. In *Social Theory in Archaeology*, edited by M. B. Schiffer, pp. 1-13. University of Utah Press, Salt Lake City.

Schroeder, H. B.
1976 Natufian and post-Natufian occupations in the interior of Lebanon. Paper presented at the Actes du 9e Congres International des Sciences Prehistorique et Protohistorique, Nice.

Schuldenrein, J., and G. A. Clark
2001 Prehistoric landscapes and settlement geography along the Wadi Hasa, west-central Jordan. Part I: geoarchaeology, human palaeoecology and ethnographic modeling. *Environmental Archaeology*, 6, pp. 23-38.

Sellars, J. R.
1998 The Natufian of Jordan. In *The Prehistoric Archaeology of Jordan*, edited by D. O. Henry, pp. 83-101. vol. 705. BAR International Series, Oxford.

Shanks, M. and C. Tilley
1992 *Reconstructing Archaeology: Theory and Practice*. 2nd ed. Routledge, London.

Sinclair, A.
2000   Constellations of knowledge: human agency and material affordance in lithic technology. In *Agency in Archaeology*, edited by M.-A. Dobres and J. Robb, pp. 196-212. Routledge, London.

Sneath, P. and R. Sokal
1973   *Numerical Taxonomy: The Principles and Practices of Numerical Classification*. W.H. Freeman and Company, San Francisco.

Spaulding, A. C.
1982   Structure in archaeological data: Nominal variables. In *Essays on Archaeological Typology*, edited by R. Whallon and J. Brown. Center for American Archeology Press, Evanston, Ill.

Stančič, Z., J. Dular, V. Gaffney and S. Tecco-Hvala
1995   A GIS-based analysis of Later Prehistoric settlement patterns in Dolenska, Slovenia. Paper presented at the Proceedings of the 1993 Conference on Computer Applications and Quantitative Methods in Archaeology.

Steward, J. H.
1936   The economic and social basis of primative bands. In *Essays in Anthropology Presented to A.L. Kroeber*, edited by R. Lowrie, pp. 331-345. University of California Press, Berkeley.

1937   *Ancient Caves of the Great Salt Lake Region*. Smithsonian Institute, Bureau of American Ethnology.

Stine, R. S. and D. P. Lanter
1990   Considerations for archaeological database design. In *Interpreting Space: GIS and Archaeology*, edited by K. M. S. Allen, S. W. Green and E. B. W. Zubrow, pp. 80-89. Taylor and Francis, London.

TAVO
1991   *Vorderen Orients. Sonderforschungsbereich*. Wiesbaden.

Tobler, W.
1993   *Three Presentations on Geographical Analysis and Modeling*. National Center for Geographic Information and Analysis. Copies available from Technical Report 93-1.

Tomlin, D. C.
1990   *Geographic Information Systems and Cartographic Modeling (.* Prentice-Hall, New Jersey.

Trigger, B. G.
1993   *A History of Archaeological Thought*. 2nd ed. Cambridge University Press, Cambridge.

Turville-Petre, F.
1932   Excavations at Mugharet El-Kebarah. *The Journal of the Royal Anthropological Institute of Great Britian and Ireland*, 62 (Jul. – Dec.), pp. 271-276.

Valdez, J. and D. Dean
2000   An efficient algorithm for reconstructing anisotropic spread cost surfaces after minimal change to unit cost structures. Paper presented at the Southern Forestry and GIS Conference, University of Georgia, Athens.

Valla, F. R.
1984   Les industries de silex de Mallaha (Eynan) et du Natoufien dans le Levant. *Memoires et Travaux de centre de Recherche Prehistoriques Francaises de Jerusalem.* 3.

1988   La fin de L'Epipaleolithique au Levant: les Industries a microlithes geometriques. *L'Anthropologie* 92(3):901-925.

1998   Natufian seasonality: a guess. In *Seasonality and Sedentism: Archaeological Perspectives from Old and New World Sites*, edited by T. R. Rocek and O. Bar-Yosef, pp. 93-108. Peabody Museum of Archaeology and Ethnology Harvard University Cambridge, Massachusetts.

1999   The Natufian: a coherent thought? In *Dorothy Garrod and the Progress of the Paleolithic Studies in the Prehistoric Archaeology of the Near East and Europe*, edited by W. Davis and R. Charles, pp. 225-241. Oxbow Books, Oxford.

Valla, F. R., Plisson, H. et R. Buxo
1989   Notes preliminaires sur les fouilles en cours sur la Terrace d'Hayonim. *Paleorient* 15(1):245-257.

Van Esch, S.
2001   ArcObjects Online. vol. 2005. ESRI.

Van Leusen, M.
1993   Cartographic modeling in a cell-based GIS. In *Computing the Past: Computer Applications and Quantitative Methods in Archaeology - CAA 92*, edited by J. Andresen, T. Madsen and I. Scollar. Aarhus University Press, Aarhus.

1999   Viewshed and Cost Surface Analysis Using GIS (Cartographic Modeling in a Cell-Based GIS II). In *Computer Applications and Quantitative Methods in Archaeology 1998*, edited by J. A. Barceló and A. Vila. vol. 757. BAR International Series.

2002   *Pattern to Process: Methodological Investigations into the Formation and Interpretation of Spatial Patterns in Archaeological Landscapes*. PhD, Rijksuniversiteit Groningen.

Van Pool, C. and T. V. Pool
2003   Introduction: method, theory and the essential tensions. In *Essential Tensions in Archaeological Method and Theory*, edited by T. Van Pool and C. Van Pool, pp. 1-4. University of Utah Press, Salt Lake City.

van Zeist, W., and S. Bottema
1982 Vegetation history of the Eastern Mediterranean and the Near east during the last 20000 years, in *Palaeoenvironments and Human Communities in the Eastern Mediterranean Region in Later Prehistory*, edited by J. L. Bintliff and W. v. Zeist, pp. 277-321. Oxford: BAR IS 133.

Vita-Finzi, C. and E. S. Higgs
1970 Prehistoric economy in the Mount Carmel area of Palestine: Site catchment analysis. *Proceedings of the Prehistoric Society* 36(1-42).

von Thunen, J. H.
1826 *Der Isolierte Staat in Beziehung auf Landwirtshaft und Nationalekonomie*, Hamburg.

Waechter, J.
1948 The excavations at Ala Safat, Transjordan. *Journal of the Palestine Oriental Society* 21:98-103.

Walsh, A. and J. C. Ollenburger
2001 *Essential Statistics for the Social and Behavioral Sciences*. Prentice Hall, Upper Saddle River, New Jersey.

Watson, P. J.
1986 Archaeological interpretation, 1985. In *American Archaeology Past and Future*, edited by D. J. Meltzer, D. D. Fowler and J. A. Sabloff, pp. 439-457. Smithsonian Institution Press, Washington D.C.

Weber, A.
1909 *Theory of the Location of Industries*. University of Chicago Press, Chicago.

Weinstein-Evron, M.
1998 *Early Natufian el-Wad Revisited* 77. ERAUL, Liege.

Whallon, R. and J. Brown
1982 *Essays on Archaeological Typology*. Center for American Archeology Press, Evanston, Ill.

Wheatley, D. and M. Gillings
2002 *Spatial Technology and Archaeology: The Archaeological Applications of GIS*. Taylor & Francis, London.

Willey, G. R. and P. Phillips
1958 *Method and Theory in American Archaeology*. University of Chicago Press, Chicago.

Williams, N.
1982 A boundary is to cross: observations on Yolngu boundaries and permissions. In *Resource Managers: North American and Australian Hunter-Gatherers*, edited by N. Williams and E. Hunn, pp. 131-154. Westview, Boulder.

Winterhalter, B.
1981 Optimal foraging strategies and hunter-gatherer research in anthropology: theory and models. In *Hunter-Gatherer Foraging Strategies*, edited by B. Winterhalter and E. A. Smith, pp. 13-35. University of Chicago Press, Chicago.

Wobst, H. M.
1999 Style in archaeology, or archaeologists in style. In *Material Meanings: Critical Approaches to Material Culture*, edited by E. S. Chilton, pp. 118-132. University of Utah Press, Salt Lake City.

2000 Agency in (spite of) material culture. In *Agency in Archaeology*, edited by M.-A. Dobres and J. Robb, pp. 40-50. Routledge, London.

Wright, D. W., M. F. Goodchild and J. D. Proctor
1997 Demystifying the persistent ambiguity of GIS as "tool" versus "science". *Annals of the Association of American Geographers* 87(2), pp. 346-362.

Wright, G. A.
1978 Social Differentiation in the Early Natufian. In *Social Archaeology: Beyond Subsistance and Dating.*, edited by C. L. Redman, M. J. Berman, E. V. Curtin, W. T. Langhorne, N. M. Versaggi and J. C. Wanser, pp. 201-223. Academic Press, New York.

Zohary, M.
1973 *Geobotanical Foundations of the Near East*. Stuttgart: Gustav Fischer Verlag.

APPENDIX A – Archaeological Data

1. Site Name
2. Phase
3. Site Size
4. Marine Shell (1 = Present; 0 = Absent)
5. Chipped-Stone Tools (Percentage of Total Tools)
6. Bone (1 = Present; 0 = Absent)
7. Basalt (1 = Present; 0 = Absent)
8. Groundstone (1 = Present; 0 = Absent)
9. Features (1 = Present; 0 = Absent)
10. Exotics (1 = Present; 0 = Absent)

Social Interaction in the Prehistoric Natufian

1. Site	2. Phase	3. Size	theo_jor	dent_m	dent_r	nerita_r	cowrie_r	conus_r	nassa_m	columb_m	conus_m	cerithi	vermetus
ain el-saratan	2	1	0	1	0	0	0	0	0	0	0	0	0
ain rahub	3	1	0	0	0	0	0	0	0	0	0	0	0
beidha	2	2	0	0	1	1	1	0	0	1	0	1	1
el wad	2	0	1	1	1	0	1	0	1	1	1	0	0
kebarah	2	0	0	1	0	0	0	0	0	0	0	0	0
fazael	3	1	0	1	1	0	1	0	1	1	0	0	0
givat hayil	3	0	0	1	0	0	0	0	1	0	0	0	0
hatoula	3	2	0	1	1	0	0	1	1	0	1	0	0
hayonim cave	2	0	0	1	1	0	0	0	0	1	1	0	0
hayonim cave	3	0	0	1	1	0	0	0	0	0	0	0	0
hayonim terrace	3	0	1	1	0	0	0	0	1	1	1	0	0
hilazon	3	0	0	1	0	0	0	0	0	0	0	0	0
khallat anaza	3	2	0	0	0	0	0	0	1	0	0	0	0
mallaha	2	2	1	1	0	0	1	0	0	0	1	0	0
mallaha	3	2	1	1	0	0	1	0	1	1	1	0	0
nahal ein gev	3	1	0	1	0	0	0	0	0	0	0	0	0
nahal oren	3	1	0	1	0	0	1	0	0	0	1	0	0
nahal sekher	3	0	0	1	0	0	0	0	1	0	0	0	0
rosh horesha	3	2	1	1	1	0	0	0	1	1	0	0	0
rosh zin	3	0	0	1	1	0	1	0	1	1	0	0	0
saflulim	3	1	0	1	1	0	1	0	1	1	0	0	0
salibiya	3	1	1	1	1	0	1	0	1	0	0	0	0
tabaqa	2	1	0	1	1	0	1	0	0	0	0	0	0
upper besor	2	1	0	1	1	0	0	0	0	0	0	0	0
wadi hammeh	2	2	0	1	0	0	0	0	0	0	0	0	0
wadi humeima	3	0	0	0	1	0	0	0	0	0	0	0	0
wadi judayid	2	0	0	0	1	0	0	0	0	0	0	0	0
wadi mataha	2	1	0	1	1	1	1	0	1	0	0	0	1

SITE	4. MARINE SHELL										5. CHIPPED-STONE TOOLS					
	murex	mitri	cerasto	pecten	pholas	cockle	arca	cardium	glycymer	donax	Scraper	Burin	Borer	Backed	Trunk
ain el-saratan	0	0	0	0	0	1	0	0	0	0	2.1	.4	.9	.0	4.2
ain rahub	0	0	0	0	0	0	0	0	0	0	2.6	1.2	1.5	4.5	3.3
beidha	0	0	0	1	0	0	0	0	0	0	11.6	3.9	1.1	12.9	6.5
el wad	0	0	1	0	0	0	1	1	1	1	1.4	6.7	1.2	3.5	3.4
kebarah	0	0	0	0	0	0	0	0	0	0	2.7	.4	.8	.0	.0
fazael	0	0	1	0	0	0	0	0	0	0	2.0	1.0	5.0	10.0	4.0
givat hayil	0	0	0	0	0	0	0	0	0	0	1.0	5.6	1.2	.0	10.4
hatoula	1	0	0	0	1	0	1	1	1	0	2.2	5.6	8.1	2.4	4.0
hayonim cave	0	0	0	0	0	1	0	0	0	0	8.6	27.6	3.4	2.3	2.3
hayonim cave	0	0	0	0	0	0	0	0	0	0	5.1	21.8	3.2	3.4	2.8
hayonim terrace	0	0	0	0	0	0	0	1	0	0	1.3	2.4	.6	3.2	2.3
hilazon	0	0	0	0	0	0	0	0	0	0	n/a	n/a	n/a	3.7	n/a
khallat anaza	0	0	1	0	0	0	0	0	0	0	n/a	4.1	7.8	9.2	2.6
mallaha	0	0	0	0	0	0	0	0	0	0	2.0	10.1	3.0	3.2	2.9
mallaha	0	0	1	0	0	0	0	1	1	0	1.2	7.5	2.1	3.1	3.8
nahal ein gev	0	0	0	0	0	0	0	0	0	0	3.1	4.2	23.3	3.5	4.2
nahal oren	0	0	0	0	0	1	0	0	1	0	.2	8.8	1.2	1.5	2.1
nahal sekher	0	0	0	0	0	0	0	0	0	0	.6	3.4	.0	.0	4.0
rosh horesha	0	1	0	0	0	0	0	0	0	0	2.7	12.4	1.5	9.6	7.7
rosh zin	0	0	0	0	0	0	0	0	1	1	6.6	8.1	1.4	8.5	7.9
saflulim	0	0	0	0	0	0	0	0	0	0	2.7	2.0	2.1	4.2	6.1
salibiya	0	0	0	0	0	0	1	0	0	0	3.9	4.7	3.7	4.2	2.7
tabaqa	0	0	0	0	0	0	0	0	0	0	9.6	7.0	1.6	17.1	2.7
upper besor	0	0	0	0	0	0	0	0	0	0	12.9	5.2	3.2	n/a	n/a
wadi hammeh	0	0	0	0	0	0	0	0	0	0	5.3	24.5	1.9	2.5	1.8
wadi humeima	0	0	0	0	0	0	0	0	0	0	2.2	.0	3.3	.0	3.3
wadi judayid	0	0	0	0	0	0	0	0	0	0	1.9	3.1	1.8	.6	5.2
wadi mataha	0	0	0	1	0	0	0	0	0	0	3.1	4.6	1.5	10.8	3.6

SOCIAL INTERACTION IN THE PREHISTORIC NATUFIAN

Site	5. Chipped-Stone Tools						6. Fauna/ Bone Tools								
	Notch	Retouch	Comp	Varia	Non-geo	Geo	Fauna	#fauna	Point	Haft	Awl	Needle	Worked	Spatu	Serrate
ain el-saratan	.9	4.7	.0	3.0	11.9	71.9	1	246	1	1	0	0	0	0	0
ain rahub	15.4	16.8	.5	.7	20.3	33.3	1	240	0	0	0	0	0	0	0
beidha	30.4	9.7	3.0	2.4	5.5	13.1	1	129	1	0	0	0	0	0	0
el wad	9.4	6.4	.7	7.1	21.7	13.0	1	2909	1	1	1	1	1	0	0
kebarah	.2	1.7	.4	1.3	49.8	42.6	1	232	1	1	1	0	1	1	0
fazael	6.0	12.0	.0	3.0	40.0	17.0	0	n/a	0	0	0	0	0	0	0
givat hayil	31.1	4.8	.2	4.8	7.7	32.8	1	0	0	0	0	0	0	0	0
hatoula	6.4	16.5	.1	.6	4.8	29.3	1	2389	1	0	1	1	1	1	0
hayonim cave	4.5	11.7	3.1	9.3	16.6	8.2	1	>10,000	1	1	1	1	1	1	0
hayonim cave	2.0	10.9	2.2	7.5	21.8	15.0	1	>10,000	1	1	1	1	1	1	0
hayonim terrace	6.6	7.0	.3	5.0	35.8	11.8	1	>10,000	1	0	1	0	0	0	0
hilazon	n/a	n/a	n/a	n/a	30.0	10.0	1	2109	1	0	1	1	1	0	0
khallat anaza	10.6	11.5	.0	2.3	14.8	15.7	1	33	0	0	0	0	1	0	0
mallaha	12.4	6.0	.6	10.9	39.0	6.9	1	1039	1	1	1	1	1	1	0
mallaha	15.4	7.2	.7	8.6	39.8	5.7	1	553	1	1	1	0	1	1	0
nahal ein gev	10.8	8.3	.7	14.2	16.3	6.2	1	56	1	0	1	0	1	0	0
nahal oren	14.9	7.6	.3	2.4	34.5	20.7	1	1846	1	1	0	0	0	0	0
nahal sekher	7.9	3.4	.0	2.3	13.6	65.0	1	<100	0	0	1	1	0	0	0
rosh horesha	16.3	13.7	.5	.2	13.4	30.3	1	1020	1	0	1	0	0	0	1
rosh zin	16.2	10.6	.4	.9	8.3	38.7	1	<100	0	0	0	0	0	0	0
saflulim	12.1	3.7	.5	4.3	10.2	53.3	1	<100	0	1	0	0	1	0	0
salibiya	4.1	14.7	.0	2.9	42.8	14.1	1	370	0	0	0	0	1	0	0
tabaqa	17.6	15.5	1.1	.5	3.7	23.5	1	<100	0	0	0	0	0	0	0
upper besor	n/a	n/a	n/a	n/a	17.5	11.0	1	<100	0	0	0	0	0	0	0
wadi hammeh	13.5	2.5	.5	7.4	28.3	16.2	1	273	1	1	1	0	1	1	0
wadi humeima	28.6	18.7	.0	.0	12.0	31.9	0	0	0	0	0	0	0	0	0
wadi judayid	9.5	14.0	.3	.2	2.9	60.5	1	196	0	0	0	0	0	0	0
wadi mataha	40.2	2.6	.5	12.9	5.2	14.4	1	244	0	0	0	0	1	0	0

Site	6. Fauna/ Bone Tools					7. Basalt									
	Pendant	Horn core	Raptor	Ostrich	Dog	Mortar	Pestle	Muller	Groove	Hammer	Anvil	Bowl	Plate	Incpl	incpe
ain el-saratan	0	1	0	0	1	0	1	1	0	0	0	0	0	0	0
ain rahub	0	0	0	0	0	0	0	0	0	0	0	0	0	0	0
beidha	0	1	0	0	0	0	0	0	0	0	0	0	0	0	0
el wad	1	1	0	0	0	1	1	1	1	1	0	1	0	0	0
kebarah	1	0	0	0	0	1	1	0	1	0	0	0	0	0	0
fazael	0	0	0	0	0	0	0	0	0	0	0	1	0	0	0
givat hayil	0	0	0	0	0	0	0	0	0	0	0	0	0	0	0
hatoula	1	0	1	0	1	0	0	0	0	0	0	0	0	0	0
hayonim cave	1	1	1	0	1	1	1	0	1	0	0	0	0	0	0
hayonim cave	1	1	1	0	0	1	1	1	1	0	0	0	0	0	0
hayonim terrace	1	0	1	0	0	0	0	0	0	0	0	0	0	0	0
hilazon	0	1	1	0	1	0	0	0	0	0	0	0	0	0	0
khallat anaza	0	0	0	0	0	1	0	1	0	1	0	0	0	0	1
mallaha	1	1	1	0	1	1	1	0	0	0	0	1	0	0	0
mallaha	1	1	1	0	1	1	1	1	1	1	0	0	0	0	1
nahal ein gev	0	0	0	0	0	1	1	1	1	0	0	0	0	0	0
nahal oren	1	1	0	0	1	0	0	0	0	0	0	0	0	0	0
nahal sekher	0	0	0	0	0	0	0	0	0	0	0	0	0	0	0
rosh horesha	0	0	0	1	0	0	0	0	0	0	0	0	0	0	0
rosh zin	0	0	0	1	0	0	0	0	0	0	0	0	0	0	0
saflulim	0	0	0	0	0	0	0	0	0	0	0	0	0	0	0
salibiya	1	0	1	0	0	0	0	0	0	0	0	0	0	0	0
tabaqa	0	0	0	0	0	1	1	1	0	0	0	1	0	0	0
upper besor	0	0	0	1	0	0	0	0	0	0	0	0	0	0	0
wadi hammeh	1	0	0	0	0	1	1	1	1	1	0	1	1	0	0
wadi humeima	0	0	0	0	0	0	0	0	0	0	0	0	0	0	0
wadi judayid	0	1	0	0	0	0	0	0	0	0	0	0	0	0	0
wadi mataha	0	1	1	0	0	0	0	0	1	0	0	0	0	0	0

Site	7. Basalt					8. Groundstone									
	Incpi	Quern	Fig	Pend	Frag	Mortar	Pestle	Muller	Groove	Hamm	Anvil	Bowl	Plate	Incpl	Incpe
ain el-saratan	1	0	0	0	0	0	0	0	1	0	0	0	0	0	0
ain rahub	0	0	0	0	0	0	0	0	0	0	0	0	0	0	0
beidha	0	0	0	0	0	0	1	1	1	0	0	0	0	0	0
el wad	0	1	1	1	0	0	1	0	0	0	0	0	0	0	1
kebarah	0	0	0	0	0	0	0	0	1	0	0	0	0	1	0
fazael	0	1	0	0	0	0	0	0	0	0	0	0	0	0	0
givat hayil	0	0	0	0	0	0	0	0	0	0	0	0	0	0	0
hatoula	0	0	0	0	0	0	1	1	1	0	0	0	0	0	0
hayonim cave	0	1	0	1	1	1	1	1	1	1	1	0	0	0	0
hayonim cave	0	1	0	1	1	1	1	1	0	1	1	0	0	0	0
hayonim terrace	0	0	0	0	0	1	0	0	0	0	0	0	0	0	0
hilazon	0	0	0	1	0	1	1	1	0	0	0	0	0	0	0
khallat anaza	0	0	0	0	1	0	0	0	0	0	0	0	0	0	0
mallaha	0	0	0	0	1	1	1	1	0	0	0	1	0	0	0
mallaha	0	0	0	1	1	0	0	0	0	0	0	0	0	0	1
nahal ein gev	0	0	0	0	1	0	0	1	0	1	0	0	1	0	0
nahal oren	0	0	0	0	0	1	0	0	0	0	0	1	0	0	1
nahal sekher	0	0	0	0	0	0	0	1	0	0	0	0	0	0	0
rosh horesha	0	0	0	0	0	0	0	0	1	0	0	0	0	0	0
rosh zin	0	0	0	0	0	0	1	1	1	0	0	0	0	0	0
saflulim	0	0	0	0	1	1	1	1	0	1	1	0	0	0	0
salibiya	0	0	0	0	0	0	0	0	0	0	0	0	0	0	0
tabaqa	0	1	0	0	0	1	1	1	0	0	0	1	0	0	0
upper besor	0	0	0	0	0	0	1	0	0	0	0	0	0	0	0
wadi hammeh	0	1	0	0	1	1	1	1	1	1	1	1	1	1	1
wadi humeima	0	0	0	0	0	1	0	0	0	0	0	0	0	0	0
wadi judayid	0	0	0	0	0	1	0	1	0	0	0	0	0	0	0
wadi mataha	1	0	0	0	1	1	1	0	0	0	0	0	0	0	0

Site	8. Ground Stone						9. Features						10. Exotics		
	Incpi	Quern	Fig	Pend	Frag	Wall	Circular	BedMor	Pave	Hearth	Pit	Burial	Crystal	Ochre	Ferrous
ain el-saratan	0	0	0	0	1	0	0	0	0	0	0	1	0	1	0
ain rahub	0	0	0	0	1	0	1	0	1	0	0	0	0	0	0
beidha	0	0	0	0	0	0	0	0	0	1	0	0	0	0	0
el wad	0	0	0	0	0	0	1	1	1	1	0	1	0	1	0
kebarah	0	0	1	1	0	0	0	0	0	0	1	1	0	0	0
fazael	0	0	0	1	0	0	0	0	0	0	0	0	0	0	0
givat hayil	0	0	0	0	1	0	0	0	0	1	0	0	0	0	0
hatoula	0	0	0	1	0	0	0	0	1	0	0	1	0	0	0
hayonim cave	1	1	0	1	1	1	1	1	0	1	0	1	0	1	0
hayonim cave	0	1	0	0	1	1	1	0	0	0	0	1	0	1	0
hayonim terrace	0	0	0	0	1	1	1	0	0	1	1	1	0	0	0
hilazon	0	0	0	0	0	0	1	0	0	0	0	1	0	1	0
khallat anaza	0	0	0	0	0	1	1	1	1	0	0	0	0	0	0
mallaha	0	1	0	0	0	0	1	0	0	1	1	1	0	0	0
mallaha	0	1	1	0	0	1	1	0	1	1	1	1	0	0	0
nahal ein gev	0	1	1	1	0	0	0	0	0	0	0	0	0	1	0
nahal oren	0	0	1	1	0	1	0	1	0	1	1	1	0	1	0
nahal sekher	0	0	0	0	0	0	0	0	0	1	0	0	0	1	0
rosh horesha	0	0	0	0	0	0	1	1	0	0	0	0	0	1	0
rosh zin	1	1	0	1	0	1	1	1	1	0	0	1	0	1	0
saflulim	0	1	0	0	1	1	0	1	1	0	1	0	0	1	0
salibiya	1	0	0	1	0	0	0	0	0	0	0	0	0	1	0
tabaqa	0	1	0	0	0	0	0	0	0	0	0	0	0	0	0
upper besor	0	0	0	0	0	0	1	1	1	1	0	0	0	0	0
wadi hammeh	1	1	1	1	1	1	1	0	0	0	0	1	1	1	1
wadi humeima	0	0	0	0	0	0	0	1	0	0	0	0	0	0	0
wadi judayid	0	0	0	0	0	0	0	0	0	0	0	0	0	0	0
wadi mataha	1	0	0	0	0	1	1	1	1	0	0	1	0	0	0

Site	10. Exotics						
	Agate	Malachit	Obsidian	feldspar	Gabbro	Quartz	Opal
ain el-saratan	0	0	0	0	0	0	0
ain rahub	0	0	0	0	0	0	0
beidha	0	0	0	0	0	0	0
el wad	0	1	0	0	0	0	0
kebarah	0	0	0	0	0	0	0
fazael	0	0	0	0	0	0	0
givat hayil	0	0	0	0	0	0	0
hatoula	0	0	0	1	1	0	0
hayonim cave	0	0	0	0	0	0	0
hayonim cave	0	0	0	0	0	1	0
hayonim terrace	0	0	0	0	0	0	0
hilazon	0	0	0	0	0	0	0
khallat anaza	0	1	0	0	0	0	0
mallaha	0	0	0	0	0	0	0
mallaha	0	1	1	0	0	0	1
nahal ein gev	0	0	0	0	0	0	0
nahal oren	0	0	0	0	0	0	0
nahal sekher	0	0	0	0	0	0	0
rosh horesha	0	1	0	0	0	0	0
rosh zin	0	0	0	0	0	1	0
saflulim	0	1	0	0	0	1	0
salibiya	0	0	0	0	0	0	0
tabaqa	0	0	0	0	0	0	1
upper besor	0	0	0	0	0	0	0
wadi hammeh	1	0	0	0	0	0	0
wadi humeima	0	0	0	0	0	0	0
wadi judayid	0	0	0	0	0	0	0
wadi mataha	0	0	0	0	0	0	0

APPENDIX B – Known radiocarbon dates for Natufian sites (note some sites are not included in this study)

Site	Lab #	Sample	^{14}C age (BP)	Calibrated after Stuiver & Reimer 1993
Wadi el-Hammeh	OxA-393	humic acids from seeds	11,920 ± 150	12170-11740
	OxA-394	charred seeds	12,200 ± 160	12280-11820
	OxA-507	charred seeds	11,950 ± 160	12220-11760
Beidha	AA-1463	charcoal	12,910 ± 250	13750-12900
	AA-1465	charcoal	12,450 ± 170	12950-12350
	AA-1464	charcoal	12,130 ± 190	12500-11900
	AA-1462	charcoal	10,910 ± 390	11600-10100
Wadi Judayid 2	SMU-805	charcoal	12,090 ± 800	13400-11200
	SMU-806	charcoal	12,750 ± 1000	14500-11800
	SMU-803	charcoal	12,780 ± 660	14100-12200
Wadi Mataha	N/A	humic acids from bone	11,200 ± 50	N/A
Ain Mallaha	Ly-1662	charcoal	11310 ± 880	12600-10000
	Ly-1661	charcoal	11,740 ± 570	12500-11100
	Ly-1660	charcoal	11,590 ± 540	12300-10900
el-Wad	UCLA-?	bone	11920 ± 660	12900-11100
	UCLA-?	bone	11,475 ± 650	12300-10700
	RT-1368	charcoal	12,950 ± 200	13750*13050
	Pta-5435	charcoal	12,620 ± 110	13100-12650
	RT-1367a	charcoal	10680 ± 190	10870-10420
	RT-1367b	charcoal	10,740 ± 200	10940-10480
Hayonim Cave	OxA-742	Lupinus seeds	12,360 ± 160	11510-11140
	OxA-743	Lupinus seeds	12,010 ± 180	12320-11810
Hayonim Terrace	OxA-2569	charred bone	11,220 ± 110	N/A
	OxA-1899	wild barley	10,000 ± 100	N/A
	OxA-2570	charred bone	11,820 ± 120	N/A
	OxA-2977	charred bone	11,720 ± 120	N/A
	OxA-2572	charred bone	11,460 ± 110	N/A
	OxA-2975	charred bone	11,790 ± 120	N/A
	OxA-2573	charred bone	10,100 ± 160	N/A
	SMU-231	charcoal	11,920 ± 90	12110-11790
Jericho	GL-70	charcoal	10,800 ± 180	10970-10580
	P-376	charcoal	11,166 ± 107	11250-11000
	BM-1407	charcoal	11,090 ± 90	11160-10950
Kebara Cave	UCLA-?	bone	11,150 ± 400	11600-10650
Nahal Oren Terrace	BM-764	bone collagen	10,046 ± 318	N/A
Rakefet Cave	I-7032	bone	10,980 ± 260	11250-10650
	I-7030	bone	10,580 ± 140	N/A
Rosh Horesha	SMU-9	charcoal	10,490 ± 430	N/A
	SMU-10	charcoal	10,880 ± 280	N/A
Salibiya I	RT-505a	charcoal	11,530 ± 550	N/A
Saflulim	OxA-2136	charcoal	10,930 ± 130	N/A
	OxA-2869	charcoal	11,150 ± 100	N/A

Site	Lab #	Sample	^{14}C age (BP)	Calibrated after Stuiver & Reimer 1993
Abu Hureyra	OxA-470	humic fraction	10,820 ± 160	N/A
	OxA-469	humic fraction	10,920 ± 140	N/A
	OxA-468	repeat of OxA-387	11,090 ± 150	N/A
	OxA-387	charred bone Tritcum boeoticum	11,070 ± 160	N/A
	OxA-172	seeds	10,900 ± 200	N/A
	OxA-431	humic fraction	10,680 ± 150	N/A
	OxA-430	charred bone Tritcum boeoticum	11,020 ± 150	N/A
	OxA-171	seeds	10,600 ± 200	N/A
	OxA-435	humic fraction	10,450 ± 180	N/A
	OxA-434	charred bone Tritcum boeoticum	10,490 ± 150	N/A
	OxA-397	seeds	10,420 ± 150	N/A
	OxA-474	bone	10,930 ± 150	N/A
	OxA-472	humic fraction	10,750 ± 170	N/A
	OxA-473	charred bone Tritcum boeoticum	10,000 ± 170	N/A
	OxA-386	seeds	10,800 ± 160	N/A
	OxA-471	humic fraction	10,620 ± 150	N/A
	OxA-408	humic fraction Tritcum boeoticum	10,300 ± 160	N/A
	OxA-170	seeds	10,600 ± 200	N/A
	BM-1718	charcoal	11,160 ± 110	N/A
Abu Hureyra (cont.)	BM-1121	charcoal	10,792 ± 82	N/A
	OxA-883	charred seeds	11,450 ± 300	N/A
Mureybet	MC-733	charcoal	10,030 ± 150	N/A
	MC-635	charcoal	10,170 ± 200	N/A
	MC-674	charcoal	10,090 ± 170	N/A
	MC-731	charcoal	10,230 ± 170	N/A
	MC-732	charcoal	10,230 ± 170	N/A
	MC-675	charcoal	10,350 ± 150	N/A
	Lv-607	charcoal	10,590 ± 140	N/A
	Lv-608	charcoal	10,590 ± 140	N/A
Hatoula	Gif A 91141	bone	11020 ± 180	N/A
Hilazon	n/a	charcoal	10750 ± 50	N/A
Nahal Seker VI	RT-1082N	charcoal	9460 ± 130	N/A

APPENDIX C – Cluster Analysis Output.

1. Simple Matching
2. Sörenson's
3. Phi 4-Point
4. Variance
5. Bray-Curtis
6. Kulczynski 2
7. Sokal and Sneath 4

Proximity matrix and cluster membership provided for each test.

Simple Matching – Proximity Matrix

Simple matching Measure

Case	1	2	3	4	5	6	7	8	9	10	11	12	13	14	15	16	17	18	19	20	21	22	23	24	25	26	27	28
1:ain el-saratan	1.0	.83	.75	.58	.79	.75	.83	.64	.65	.69	.72	.81	.70	.68	.57	.77	.77	.83	.74	.68	.65	.75	.74	.77	.59	.78	.80	.68
2:ain rahub	.83	1.0	.80	.56	.77	.85	.93	.67	.56	.64	.79	.81	.85	.65	.54	.77	.69	.90	.79	.75	.73	.83	.79	.91	.54	.90	.90	.75
3:beidha	.75	.80	1.0	.56	.69	.80	.83	.64	.58	.59	.69	.77	.68	.65	.49	.69	.64	.83	.74	.73	.68	.75	.77	.81	.47	.80	.88	.75
4:el wad	.58	.56	.56	1.0	.59	.63	.55	.59	.63	.64	.64	.62	.63	.65	.74	.57	.62	.58	.64	.60	.56	.60	.59	.62	.52	.56	.53	.58
5:kebarah	.79	.77	.69	.59	1.0	.74	.77	.70	.67	.70	.75	.73	.69	.74	.65	.83	.78	.77	.70	.64	.62	.77	.70	.73	.70	.74	.74	.64
6:fazael	.75	.85	.80	.63	.74	1.0	.88	.67	.56	.59	.74	.74	.78	.63	.54	.74	.67	.88	.79	.78	.73	.88	.84	.84	.52	.85	.85	.73
7:givat hayil	.83	.93	.83	.56	.77	.88	1.0	.67	.56	.59	.74	.74	.78	.63	.54	.74	.67	.88	.79	.73	.73	.85	.79	.89	.52	.90	.88	.73
8:hatoula	.64	.67	.64	.59	.70	.67	.67	1.0	.62	.60	.81	.79	.80	.65	.54	.77	.72	.95	.65	.67	.59	.72	.60	.68	.48	.67	.67	.62
9:hayonim cave	.65	.56	.58	.63	.67	.56	.56	.62	1.0	.86	.67	.72	.53	.75	.62	.63	.65	.58	.59	.63	.65	.60	.59	.59	.72	.56	.58	.63
10:hayonim cave	.69	.64	.59	.64	.70	.59	.62	.60	.86	1.0	.68	.78	.62	.77	.63	.67	.63	.64	.60	.62	.72	.64	.70	.63	.75	.62	.67	.67
11:hayonim terrace	.72	.79	.69	.64	.75	.74	.81	.70	.67	.68	1.0	.78	.69	.77	.70	.68	.78	.79	.75	.67	.69	.79	.65	.75	.56	.74	.74	.72
12:hilazon	.81	.81	.77	.62	.73	.74	.79	.73	.72	.78	.78	1.0	.69	.79	.58	.75	.75	.84	.74	.72	.67	.77	.72	.74	.58	.79	.84	.74
13:khallat anaza	.70	.85	.68	.63	.69	.78	.80	.59	.53	.62	.72	.69	1.0	.60	.67	.74	.64	.80	.74	.70	.73	.75	.72	.81	.54	.80	.78	.75
14:mallaha	.68	.65	.65	.65	.74	.63	.65	.67	.75	.77	.77	.79	.60	1.0	.72	.69	.74	.68	.62	.58	.63	.68	.74	.67	.64	.63	.68	.65
15:mallaha	.57	.54	.49	.74	.65	.54	.54	.56	.62	.63	.70	.58	.67	.72	1.0	.60	.65	.54	.53	.52	.54	.57	.53	.53	.53	.47	.49	.57
16:nahal ein gev	.77	.77	.69	.57	.83	.74	.77	.63	.67	.75	.68	.75	.74	.69	.60	1.0	.70	.81	.70	.67	.69	.77	.78	.73	.54	.74	.77	.64
17:nahal oren	.77	.69	.64	.62	.78	.67	.72	.65	.69	.63	.78	.75	.64	.74	.65	.70	1.0	.74	.65	.64	.64	.72	.63	.70	.60	.72	.72	.64
18:nahal sekher	.83	.90	.83	.58	.77	.88	.95	.69	.58	.64	.79	.84	.80	.68	.54	.81	.74	1.0	.81	.78	.75	.88	.81	.89	.54	.88	.78	.73
19:rosh horesha	.74	.79	.74	.64	.70	.79	.79	.65	.59	.60	.75	.78	.74	.62	.53	.70	.65	.81	1.0	.77	.69	.79	.68	.83	.48	.79	.77	.67
20:rosh zin	.68	.75	.73	.60	.64	.78	.73	.67	.63	.62	.67	.72	.70	.58	.52	.67	.64	.78	.77	1.0	.78	.78	.72	.81	.54	.73	.73	.75
21:saflulim	.65	.73	.68	.56	.62	.73	.73	.59	.65	.72	.69	.67	.73	.63	.54	.69	.64	.75	.69	.78	1.0	.73	.72	.74	.57	.73	.73	.73
22:salibiya	.75	.83	.75	.60	.77	.88	.85	.72	.60	.64	.79	.77	.75	.68	.57	.77	.72	.88	.79	.78	.73	1.0	.77	.81	.54	.83	.83	.78
23:tabaqa	.74	.79	.77	.59	.70	.84	.79	.60	.59	.70	.65	.75	.72	.74	.53	.78	.63	.81	.68	.72	.72	.77	1.0	.80	.63	.81	.84	.69
24:upper besor	.77	.91	.81	.62	.73	.84	.89	.68	.59	.63	.75	.80	.81	.67	.53	.73	.70	.89	.83	.81	.74	.81	.80	1.0	.51	.89	.86	.79
25:wadi hammeh	.59	.54	.47	.52	.70	.52	.52	.48	.72	.75	.56	.58	.54	.64	.47	.73	.60	.54	.48	.54	.57	.54	.63	.51	1.0	.49	.52	.52
26:wadi humeima	.78	.90	.80	.56	.74	.85	.90	.67	.56	.62	.74	.79	.80	.63	.47	.73	.72	.88	.79	.73	.73	.83	.81	.89	.49	1.0	.93	.75
27:wadi judayid	.80	.90	.88	.53	.74	.85	.88	.67	.58	.67	.74	.84	.78	.68	.49	.77	.72	.90	.77	.73	.73	.83	.84	.86	.52	.93	1.0	.78
28:wadi mataha	.68	.75	.75	.58	.64	.73	.73	.62	.63	.67	.72	.74	.75	.65	.57	.64	.64	.73	.67	.75	.73	.78	.69	.79	.52	.75	.78	1.0

Simple Matching - Cluster Membership

Case	5 Clusters	4 Clusters	3 Clusters	2 Clusters
1:ain el-saratan	1	1	1	1
2:ain rahub	1	1	1	1
3:beidha	1	1	1	1
4:el wad	2	2	2	2
5:kebarah	1	1	1	1
6:fazael	1	1	1	1
7:givat hayil	1	1	1	1
8:hatoula	3	3	1	1
9:hayonim cave	4	4	3	1
10:hayonim cave	4	4	3	1
11:hayonim terrace	1	1	1	1
12:hilazon	1	1	1	1
13:khallat anaza	1	1	1	1
14:mallaha	4	4	3	1
15:mallaha	2	2	2	2
16:nahal ein gev	1	1	1	1
17:nahal oren	1	1	1	1
18:nahal sekher	1	1	1	1
19:rosh horesha	1	1	1	1
20:rosh zin	1	1	1	1
21:saflulim	1	1	1	1
22:salibiya	1	1	1	1
23:tabaqa	1	1	1	1
24:upper besor	1	1	1	1
25:wadi hammeh	5	4	3	1
26:wadi humeima	1	1	1	1
27:wadi judayid	1	1	1	1
28:wadi mataha	1	1	1	1

Sörenson – Proximity Matrix

Dice (Czekanowski or Sorenson) Measure

Case	1	2	3	4	5	6	7	8	9	10	11	12	13	14	15	16	17	18	19	20	21	22	23	24	25	26	27	28
1:ain el-saratan	1.0	.22	.29	.35	.45	.17	.22	.29	.46	.44	.30	.48	.14	.38	.34	.39	.49	.30	.32	.28	.26	.23	.28	.17	.38	.00	.20	.28
2:ain rahub	.22	1.0	.11	.14	.10	.14	.25	.13	.14	.17	.26	.21	.33	.13	.14	.10	.07	.20	.19	.23	.21	.13	.11	.46	.14	.00	.20	.23
3:beidha	.29	.11	1.0	.31	.19	.33	.11	.29	.35	.27	.24	.34	.07	.33	.23	.19	.22	.30	.32	.39	.32	.23	.34	.35	.19	.11	.50	.44
4:el wad	.35	.14	.31	1.0	.40	.38	.14	.49	.61	.58	.49	.42	.42	.58	.73	.36	.49	.23	.47	.47	.42	.36	.38	.34	.49	.14	.14	.43
5:kebarah	.45	.10	.19	.40	1.0	.22	.10	.45	.51	.50	.44	.31	.19	.53	.50	.59	.55	.17	.29	.26	.24	.34	.25	.15	.57	.00	.09	.26
6:fazael	.17	.14	.33	.38	.22	1.0	.29	.27	.25	.20	.28	.16	.25	.21	.24	.22	.18	.38	.37	.44	.35	.55	.48	.32	.20	.14	.25	.31
7:givat hayil	.22	.25	.11	.14	.10	.29	1.0	.13	.14	.11	.35	.11	.11	.13	.14	.10	.15	.60	.19	.15	.21	.25	.11	.31	.09	.00	.00	.15
8:hatoula	.29	.13	.29	.49	.45	.27	.13	1.0	.52	.45	.48	.48	.20	.51	.45	.32	.44	.24	.36	.45	.35	.41	.24	.28	.36	.13	.18	.37
9:hayonim cave	.46	.14	.35	.61	.51	.25	.14	.52	1.0	.84	.53	.57	.27	.70	.60	.51	.59	.23	.40	.50	.55	.36	.38	.30	.70	.14	.23	.50
10:hayonim cave	.44	.17	.27	.58	.50	.20	.11	.45	.84	1.0	.48	.61	.31	.68	.57	.58	.44	.22	.33	.42	.58	.33	.48	.25	.71	.06	.27	.49
11:hayonim terrace	.30	.26	.24	.49	.44	.28	.35	.48	.53	.48	1.0	.47	.30	.60	.59	.28	.57	.32	.44	.34	.42	.45	.18	.29	.38	.09	.16	.44
12:hilazon	.48	.21	.34	.42	.31	.16	.11	.48	.57	.61	.47	1.0	.14	.60	.37	.38	.47	.38	.44	.38	.31	.30	.33	.33	.37	.11	.38	.43
13:khallat anaza	.14	.33	.07	.42	.19	.25	.11	.20	.27	.31	.30	.14	1.0	.24	.49	.32	.22	.20	.32	.33	.42	.23	.21	.35	.30	.11	.10	.44
14:mallaha	.38	.13	.33	.58	.53	.21	.13	.51	.70	.68	.60	.60	.24	1.0	.66	.44	.59	.24	.31	.32	.42	.35	.51	.27	.57	.06	.24	.44
15:mallaha	.34	.14	.23	.73	.50	.24	.14	.45	.60	.57	.59	.37	.49	.66	1.0	.43	.55	.18	.32	.36	.41	.31	.30	.21	.51	.00	.09	.43
16:nahal ein gev	.39	.10	.19	.36	.59	.22	.10	.32	.51	.58	.28	.38	.32	.44	.43	1.0	.40	.35	.29	.31	.39	.34	.44	.15	.61	.00	.17	.26
17:nahal oren	.49	.07	.22	.49	.55	.18	.15	.44	.59	.44	.57	.47	.22	.59	.55	.40	1.0	.28	.30	.36	.38	.34	.21	.25	.48	.15	.21	.36
18:nahal sekher	.30	.20	.30	.23	.17	.38	.60	.24	.23	.22	.32	.38	.20	.24	.18	.35	.28	1.0	.35	.36	.33	.44	.29	.40	.18	.00	.33	.21
19:rosh horesha	.32	.19	.32	.47	.29	.37	.19	.36	.40	.33	.44	.44	.32	.31	.32	.29	.30	.35	1.0	.51	.39	.41	.19	.46	.25	.19	.17	.31
20:rosh zin	.28	.23	.39	.47	.26	.44	.15	.45	.50	.42	.34	.38	.33	.32	.36	.31	.36	.36	.51	1.0	.61	.47	.38	.52	.39	.15	.21	.55
21:saflulim	.26	.21	.32	.42	.24	.35	.21	.35	.55	.58	.42	.31	.42	.42	.41	.39	.38	.33	.39	.61	1.0	.39	.41	.36	.44	.21	.27	.52
22:salibiya	.23	.13	.23	.36	.34	.55	.25	.41	.36	.33	.45	.30	.23	.35	.31	.34	.34	.44	.41	.47	.39	1.0	.30	.29	.27	.13	.22	.47
23:tabaqa	.28	.11	.34	.38	.25	.48	.11	.24	.38	.48	.18	.33	.21	.51	.30	.44	.21	.29	.19	.38	.41	.30	1.0	.33	.44	.21	.38	.32
24:upper besor	.17	.46	.35	.34	.15	.32	.31	.28	.30	.25	.29	.33	.35	.27	.21	.15	.25	.40	.46	.52	.36	.29	.33	1.0	.17	.31	.27	.45
25:wadi hammeh	.38	.14	.19	.49	.57	.20	.09	.36	.70	.71	.38	.37	.30	.57	.51	.61	.48	.18	.25	.39	.44	.27	.44	.17	1.0	.05	.13	.36
26:wadi humeima	.00	.00	.11	.14	.00	.14	.00	.13	.14	.11	.09	.11	.11	.06	.00	.00	.15	.00	.19	.15	.21	.13	.21	.31	.05	1.0	.40	.23
27:wadi judayid	.20	.20	.50	.14	.09	.25	.00	.18	.23	.27	.16	.38	.10	.24	.09	.17	.21	.33	.17	.21	.27	.22	.38	.27	.13	.40	1.0	.36
28:wadi mataha	.28	.23	.44	.43	.26	.31	.15	.37	.50	.49	.44	.43	.44	.44	.43	.26	.36	.21	.31	.55	.52	.47	.32	.45	.36	.23	.36	1.0

Sörenson's - Cluster Membership

Case	5 Clusters	4 Clusters	3 Clusters	2 Clusters
1:ain el-saratan	1	1	1	1
2:ain rahub	2	2	2	1
3:beidha	3	1	1	1
4:el wad	1	1	1	1
5:kebarah	1	1	1	1
6:fazael	1	1	1	1
7:givat hayil	4	3	2	1
8:hatoula	1	1	1	1
9:hayonim cave	1	1	1	1
10:hayonim cave	1	1	1	1
11:hayonim terrace	1	1	1	1
12:hilazon	1	1	1	1
13:khallat anaza	2	2	2	1
14:mallaha	1	1	1	1
15:mallaha	1	1	1	1
16:nahal ein gev	1	1	1	1
17:nahal oren	1	1	1	1
18:nahal sekher	4	3	2	1
19:rosh horesha	1	1	1	1
20:rosh zin	1	1	1	1
21:saflulim	1	1	1	1
22:salibiya	1	1	1	1
23:tabaqa	3	1	1	1
24:upper besor	2	2	2	1
25:wadi hammeh	1	1	1	1
26:wadi humeima	5	4	3	2
27:wadi judayid	3	1	1	1
28:wadi mataha	1	1	1	1

Phi 4-Point - Proximity Matrix

Fourfold Point Correlation

Case	1	2	3	4	5	6	7	8	9	10	11	12	13	14	15	16	17	18	19	20	21	22	23	24	25	26	27	28
1:ain el-saratan	1.0	.20	.14	.16	.33	.03	.20	.09	.36	.31	.13	.37	.04	.22	.15	.25	.36	.24	.17	.09	.06	.09	.12	.05	.21	.10	.12	.09
2:ain rahub	.20	1.0	.05	.13	.02	.09	.21	.08	.13	.17	.28	.18	.35	.07	.12	.02	.02	.15	.16	.25	.23	.07	.04	.46	.12	.05	.15	.25
3:beidha	.14	.05	1.0	.09	.02	.23	.05	.09	.16	.04	.06	.20	.12	.15	.05	.00	.00	.24	.17	.23	.13	.09	.20	.25	.11	.05	.49	.31
4:el wad	.16	.13	.09	1.0	.18	.32	.13	.17	.26	.28	.30	.25	.29	.31	.48	.12	.23	.21	.31	.20	.09	.23	.19	.30	.03	.13	.02	.15
5:kebarah	.33	.02	.09	.18	1.0	.08	.02	.28	.37	.34	.29	.14	.00	.39	.35	.48	.42	.09	.11	.03	.00	.21	.07	.01	.47	.12	.03	.03
6:fazael	.03	.09	.23	.32	.08	1.0	.26	.13	.10	.01	.15	.01	.13	.04	.09	.08	.01	.32	.27	.36	.25	.48	.40	.23	.01	.09	.18	.19
7:givat hayil	.20	.21	.05	.13	.02	.26	1.0	.08	.13	.05	.41	.04	.05	.07	.12	.02	.11	.59	.16	.12	.23	.23	.04	.28	.01	.05	.06	.12
8:hatoula	.09	.08	.09	.17	.28	.13	.08	1.0	.23	.14	.29	.34	.05	.26	.10	.09	.19	.20	.15	.22	.06	.29	.00	.17	.05	.08	.10	.10
9:hayonim cave	.36	.13	.16	.26	.37	.10	.13	.23	1.0	.74	.36	.51	.03	.51	.23	.37	.40	.21	.18	.26	.31	.23	.19	.22	.43	.13	.21	.26
10:hayonim cave	.31	.17	.04	.28	.34	.01	.05	.14	.74	1.0	.28	.54	.11	.50	.26	.47	.18	.17	.09	.15	.38	.17	.34	.13	.51	.05	.26	.26
11:hayonim terr.	.13	.28	.06	.30	.29	.15	.41	.29	.36	.28	1.0	.34	.13	.46	.46	.07	.43	.29	.29	.12	.22	.34	.04	.18	.11	.01	.07	.25
12:hilazon	.37	.18	.20	.25	.14	.01	.04	.34	.51	.54	.34	1.0	.05	.52	.18	.22	.33	.35	.30	.21	.11	.16	.18	.24	.18	.04	.35	.28
13:khallat anaza	.04	.35	.12	.29	.00	.13	.05	.05	.03	.11	.13	.05	1.0	.01	.41	.17	.00	.12	.17	.16	.28	.09	.03	.25	.08	.05	.00	.31
14:mallaha	.22	.07	.15	.31	.39	.04	.07	.26	.51	.50	.46	.52	.01	1.0	.44	.26	.41	.19	.07	.02	.15	.21	.39	.16	.29	.22	.19	.20
15:mallaha	.15	.12	.05	.48	.35	.09	.12	.10	.23	.26	.46	.18	.03	.44	1.0	.23	.32	.10	.05	.02	.08	.15	.05	.05	.06	.12	.08	.13
16:nahal ein gev	.25	.02	.00	.12	.48	.08	.02	.09	.37	.47	.07	.22	.11	.26	.23	1.0	.21	.32	.11	.09	.20	.21	.30	.01	.53	.22	.09	.03
17:nahal oren	.36	.02	.00	.23	.42	.01	.11	.19	.40	.18	.43	.33	.00	.41	.32	.21	1.0	.24	.08	.11	.13	.20	.02	.13	.22	.12	.14	.11
18:nahal sekher	.24	.15	.24	.21	.09	.32	.59	.20	.21	.17	.29	.35	.12	.19	.10	.32	.24	1.0	.32	.36	.33	.41	.23	.35	.10	.06	.28	.15
19:rosh horesha	.17	.16	.17	.31	.11	.27	.16	.15	.18	.09	.29	.30	.17	.07	.05	.11	.08	.32	1.0	.37	.20	.30	.01	.40	.07	.16	.09	.09
20:rosh zin	.09	.25	.23	.20	.03	.36	.12	.22	.26	.15	.12	.21	.16	.02	.02	.09	.11	.36	.37	1.0	.45	.37	.21	.49	.08	.12	.15	.38
21:saflulim	.06	.23	.13	.09	.00	.25	.23	.06	.31	.38	.22	.11	.28	.15	.08	.20	.13	.33	.20	.45	1.0	.26	.25	.29	.13	.23	.23	.33
22:salibiya	.09	.07	.09	.23	.21	.48	.23	.29	.23	.17	.34	.16	.09	.21	.15	.21	.20	.41	.30	.37	.26	1.0	.16	.18	.09	.07	.15	.37
23:tabaqa	.12	.04	.20	.19	.07	.40	.04	.00	.19	.34	.04	.18	.03	.39	.05	.30	.02	.23	.01	.21	.25	.16	1.0	.24	.30	.18	.35	.14
24:upper besor	.05	.46	.25	.30	.01	.23	.28	.17	.22	.13	.18	.24	.25	.16	.05	.01	.13	.35	.40	.49	.29	.18	.24	1.0	.03	.28	.20	.40
25:wadi hammeh	.21	.12	.11	.03	.47	.01	.01	.05	.43	.51	.11	.18	.08	.29	.06	.53	.22	.10	.07	.08	.13	.09	.30	.03	1.0	.11	.01	.02
26:wadi humeima	.10	.05	.05	.13	.12	.09	.05	.08	.13	.05	.01	.04	.05	.05	.22	.12	.11	.06	.16	.12	.23	.07	.18	.28	.11	1.0	.37	.25
27:wadi judayid	.12	.15	.49	.02	.03	.18	.06	.10	.21	.26	.07	.35	.00	.19	.08	.09	.14	.28	.09	.15	.23	.15	.35	.20	.01	.37	1.0	.36
28:wadi mataha	.09	.25	.31	.15	.03	.19	.12	.10	.26	.26	.25	.28	.31	.20	.13	.03	.11	.15	.09	.38	.33	.37	.14	.40	.02	.25	.36	1.0

Phi 4-Point - Cluster Membership

Case	5 Clusters	4 Clusters	3 Clusters	2 Clusters
1:ain el-saratan	1	1	1	1
2:ain rahub	2	2	2	2
3:beidha	3	3	3	2
4:el wad	4	4	1	1
5:kebarah	1	1	1	1
6:fazael	2	2	2	2
7:givat hayil	2	2	2	2
8:hatoula	5	1	1	1
9:hayonim cave	1	1	1	1
10:hayonim cave	1	1	1	1
11:hayonim terrace	1	1	1	1
12:hilazon	1	1	1	1
13:khallat anaza	4	4	1	1
14:mallaha	1	1	1	1
15:mallaha	4	4	1	1
16:nahal ein gev	1	1	1	1
17:nahal oren	1	1	1	1
18:nahal sekher	2	2	2	2
19:rosh horesha	2	2	2	2
20:rosh zin	2	2	2	2
21:saflulim	2	2	2	2
22:salibiya	2	2	2	2
23:tabaqa	3	3	3	2
24:upper besor	2	2	2	2
25:wadi hammeh	1	1	1	1
26:wadi humeima	3	3	3	2
27:wadi judayid	3	3	3	2
28:wadi mataha	2	2	2	2

Variance - Cluster

Variance Measure

Case	1	2	3	4	5	6	7	8	9	10	11	12	13	14	15	16	17	18	19	20	21	22	23	24	25	26	27	28
1:ain el-saratan	.00	.04	.06	.10	.05	.06	.04	.09	.09	.08	.07	.05	.07	.08	.11	.06	.06	.04	.06	.08	.09	.06	.06	.06	.10	.06	.05	.08
2:ain rahub	.04	.00	.05	.11	.06	.04	.02	.08	.11	.09	.05	.05	.04	.09	.11	.06	.08	.02	.05	.06	.07	.04	.05	.02	.11	.02	.02	.06
3:beidha	.06	.05	.00	.11	.08	.05	.05	.09	.10	.10	.08	.06	.08	.09	.13	.08	.09	.04	.06	.07	.08	.06	.06	.05	.13	.05	.03	.06
4:el wad	.10	.11	.11	.00	.10	.09	.11	.10	.09	.10	.09	.10	.09	.09	.06	.11	.10	.10	.09	.10	.11	.10	.10	.10	.12	.11	.12	.10
5:kebarah	.05	.06	.08	.10	.00	.06	.06	.07	.08	.07	.06	.07	.09	.09	.09	.04	.06	.06	.07	.09	.10	.06	.07	.07	.07	.06	.06	.09
6:fazael	.06	.04	.05	.09	.06	.00	.03	.08	.11	.10	.06	.06	.06	.09	.11	.06	.08	.03	.05	.06	.07	.03	.04	.04	.12	.04	.04	.07
7:givat hayil	.04	.02	.05	.11	.06	.03	.00	.08	.11	.10	.05	.05	.05	.09	.11	.06	.07	.01	.05	.07	.07	.04	.05	.03	.12	.02	.03	.07
8:hatoula	.09	.08	.09	.10	.07	.08	.08	.00	.10	.10	.07	.07	.10	.06	.11	.09	.09	.08	.09	.08	.10	.07	.10	.08	.13	.08	.08	.10
9:hayonim cave	.09	.11	.10	.09	.08	.11	.11	.10	.00	.03	.08	.07	.12	.06	.10	.08	.08	.10	.10	.09	.09	.10	.10	.10	.07	.11	.10	.09
10:hayonim cave	.08	.09	.10	.09	.07	.10	.10	.10	.03	.00	.08	.06	.10	.06	.09	.06	.09	.09	.10	.10	.07	.09	.07	.09	.06	.10	.08	.08
11:hayonim terrace	.07	.05	.08	.09	.06	.06	.05	.07	.08	.08	.00	.06	.07	.06	.07	.08	.06	.05	.06	.08	.08	.05	.09	.06	.11	.06	.06	.07
12:hilazon	.05	.05	.06	.10	.07	.06	.05	.07	.07	.06	.06	.00	.08	.05	.10	.06	.06	.04	.06	.07	.08	.06	.06	.05	.10	.05	.04	.06
13:khallat anaza	.07	.04	.08	.09	.08	.06	.05	.10	.12	.10	.07	.08	.00	.10	.08	.06	.09	.05	.06	.07	.07	.06	.07	.05	.11	.05	.06	.06
14:mallaha	.08	.09	.09	.09	.06	.09	.09	.08	.06	.06	.06	.05	.10	.00	.07	.08	.06	.08	.10	.10	.09	.08	.06	.08	.09	.09	.08	.09
15:mallaha	.11	.11	.13	.06	.09	.11	.11	.11	.10	.09	.07	.10	.08	.07	.00	.10	.09	.11	.12	.12	.11	.11	.12	.12	.12	.13	.13	.11
16:nahal ein gev	.06	.06	.08	.11	.04	.06	.06	.09	.08	.06	.08	.06	.06	.08	.10	.00	.07	.05	.07	.08	.08	.06	.06	.07	.07	.06	.06	.09
17:nahal oren	.06	.08	.09	.10	.06	.08	.07	.09	.08	.09	.06	.06	.09	.06	.09	.07	.00	.06	.09	.09	.09	.07	.09	.07	.10	.07	.07	.09
18:nahal sekher	.04	.02	.04	.10	.06	.03	.01	.08	.10	.09	.05	.04	.05	.08	.11	.05	.06	.00	.05	.06	.06	.03	.05	.03	.11	.03	.02	.07
19:rosh horesha	.06	.05	.06	.09	.07	.05	.05	.09	.10	.10	.06	.06	.06	.10	.12	.07	.09	.05	.00	.06	.08	.05	.08	.04	.13	.05	.06	.08
20:rosh zin	.08	.06	.07	.10	.09	.06	.07	.08	.09	.10	.08	.07	.07	.10	.12	.08	.09	.06	.06	.00	.06	.06	.07	.05	.11	.07	.07	.06
21:saflulim	.09	.07	.08	.11	.10	.07	.07	.10	.09	.07	.08	.08	.07	.09	.11	.08	.09	.06	.08	.06	.00	.07	.07	.06	.11	.07	.07	.07
22:salibiya	.06	.04	.06	.10	.06	.03	.04	.07	.10	.09	.05	.06	.06	.08	.11	.06	.07	.03	.05	.06	.07	.00	.06	.05	.11	.04	.04	.06
23:tabaqa	.06	.05	.06	.10	.07	.04	.05	.10	.10	.07	.09	.05	.07	.06	.12	.06	.09	.05	.08	.07	.07	.06	.00	.05	.09	.05	.04	.08
24:upper besor	.06	.02	.05	.10	.07	.04	.03	.08	.10	.09	.06	.05	.05	.08	.12	.07	.07	.03	.04	.05	.06	.05	.05	.00	.12	.03	.03	.05
25:wadi hammeh	.10	.11	.13	.12	.07	.12	.12	.13	.07	.06	.11	.10	.11	.09	.12	.07	.10	.11	.13	.11	.11	.11	.09	.12	.00	.13	.12	.12
26:wadi humeima	.06	.02	.05	.11	.06	.04	.02	.08	.11	.10	.06	.05	.05	.09	.13	.06	.07	.03	.05	.07	.07	.04	.05	.03	.13	.00	.02	.06
27:wadi judayid	.05	.02	.03	.12	.06	.04	.03	.08	.10	.08	.06	.04	.06	.08	.13	.06	.07	.02	.06	.07	.07	.04	.04	.03	.12	.02	.00	.06
28:wadi mataha	.08	.06	.06	.10	.09	.07	.07	.10	.09	.08	.07	.06	.06	.09	.11	.09	.09	.07	.08	.06	.07	.06	.08	.05	.12	.06	.06	.00

Variance - Cluster Membership

Case	5 Clusters	4 Clusters	3 Clusters	2 Clusters
1:ain el-saratan	1	1	1	1
2:ain rahub	1	1	1	1
3:beidha	1	1	1	1
4:el wad	2	2	2	2
5:kebarah	1	1	1	1
6:fazael	1	1	1	1
7:givat hayil	1	1	1	1
8:hatoula	3	3	1	1
9:hayonim cave	4	4	3	1
10:hayonim cave	4	4	3	1
11:hayonim terrace	1	1	1	1
12:hilazon	1	1	1	1
13:khallat anaza	1	1	1	1
14:mallaha	4	4	3	1
15:mallaha	2	2	2	2
16:nahal ein gev	1	1	1	1
17:nahal oren	1	1	1	1
18:nahal sekher	1	1	1	1
19:rosh horesha	1	1	1	1
20:rosh zin	1	1	1	1
21:saflulim	1	1	1	1
22:salibiya	1	1	1	1
23:tabaqa	1	1	1	1
24:upper besor	1	1	1	1
25:wadi hammeh	5	4	3	1
26:wadi humeima	1	1	1	1
27:wadi judayid	1	1	1	1
28:wadi mataha	1	1	1	1

SOCIAL INTERACTION IN THE PREHISTORIC NATUFIAN

Bray & Curtis - Proximity Matrix

Bray & Curtis Nonmetric Measure

Case	1	2	3	4	5	6	7	8	9	10	11	12	13	14	15	16	17	18	19	20	21	22	23	24	25	26	27	28
1:ain el-saratan	.00	.78	.71	.65	.55	.83	.78	.71	.54	.56	.70	.52	.86	.62	.66	.61	.51	.70	.68	.72	.74	.77	.72	.83	.62	1.0	.80	.72
2:ain rahub	.78	.00	.89	.86	.90	.86	.75	.87	.86	.83	.74	.79	.67	.88	.86	.90	.93	.80	.81	.77	.79	.88	.89	.54	.86	1.0	.80	.77
3:beidha	.71	.89	.00	.69	.81	.67	.89	.71	.65	.73	.76	.66	.93	.67	.77	.81	.78	.70	.68	.61	.68	.77	.66	.65	.81	.89	.50	.56
4:el wad	.65	.86	.69	.00	.60	.63	.86	.51	.39	.42	.51	.58	.58	.42	.27	.64	.51	.77	.53	.53	.58	.64	.62	.66	.51	.86	.86	.57
5:kebarah	.55	.90	.81	.60	.00	.78	.90	.55	.49	.50	.56	.69	.81	.47	.50	.41	.45	.83	.71	.74	.76	.66	.75	.85	.43	1.0	.91	.74
6:fazael	.83	.86	.67	.63	.78	.00	.71	.73	.75	.80	.72	.84	.75	.79	.76	.78	.82	.63	.63	.56	.65	.45	.52	.68	.80	.86	.75	.69
7:givat hayil	.78	.75	.89	.86	.90	.71	.00	.87	.86	.89	.65	.89	.89	.88	.86	.90	.85	.40	.81	.85	.79	.75	.89	.69	.91	1.0	1.0	.85
8:hatoula	.71	.87	.71	.51	.55	.73	.87	.00	.48	.55	.52	.52	.80	.49	.55	.68	.56	.76	.64	.55	.65	.59	.76	.72	.64	.87	.82	.63
9:hayonim cave	.54	.86	.65	.39	.49	.75	.86	.48	.00	.16	.47	.43	.73	.30	.40	.49	.41	.77	.60	.50	.45	.64	.62	.70	.30	.86	.77	.50
10:hayonim terrace	.56	.83	.73	.42	.50	.80	.89	.55	.16	.00	.52	.39	.69	.32	.43	.42	.56	.78	.67	.58	.42	.67	.52	.75	.29	.89	.73	.51
11:hayonim cave	.70	.74	.76	.51	.56	.72	.65	.52	.47	.52	.00	.53	.70	.40	.41	.72	.43	.68	.56	.66	.58	.55	.82	.71	.62	.91	.84	.56
12:hilazon	.52	.79	.66	.58	.69	.84	.89	.52	.43	.39	.53	.00	.86	.40	.63	.63	.53	.62	.56	.62	.69	.70	.67	.71	.63	.89	.62	.57
13:khallat anaza	.86	.67	.93	.58	.81	.75	.89	.80	.73	.69	.70	.86	.00	.76	.51	.68	.78	.80	.68	.67	.58	.77	.79	.65	.70	.89	.90	.56
14:mallaha	.62	.88	.67	.42	.47	.79	.88	.49	.30	.32	.40	.40	.76	.00	.34	.56	.41	.76	.69	.68	.58	.65	.49	.73	.43	.94	.76	.56
15:mallaha	.66	.86	.77	.27	.50	.76	.86	.55	.40	.43	.41	.63	.51	.34	.00	.57	.45	.82	.68	.64	.59	.69	.70	.79	.49	1.0	.91	.57
16:nahal ein gev	.61	.90	.81	.64	.41	.78	.90	.68	.49	.42	.72	.63	.68	.56	.57	.00	.60	.65	.71	.69	.61	.66	.56	.85	.39	1.0	.83	.74
17:nahal oren	.51	.93	.78	.51	.45	.82	.85	.56	.41	.56	.43	.53	.78	.41	.45	.60	.00	.72	.70	.64	.62	.66	.79	.75	.52	.85	.79	.64
18:nahal sekher	.70	.80	.70	.77	.83	.63	.40	.76	.77	.78	.68	.62	.80	.76	.82	.65	.72	.00	.65	.64	.67	.56	.71	.60	.82	1.0	.67	.79
19:rosh horesha	.68	.81	.68	.53	.71	.63	.81	.64	.60	.67	.56	.56	.68	.69	.68	.71	.70	.65	.00	.49	.61	.59	.81	.54	.75	.81	.83	.69
20:rosh zin	.72	.77	.61	.53	.74	.56	.85	.55	.50	.58	.66	.62	.67	.68	.64	.69	.64	.64	.49	.00	.39	.53	.62	.48	.61	.85	.79	.45
21:saflulim	.74	.79	.68	.58	.76	.65	.79	.65	.45	.42	.58	.69	.58	.58	.59	.61	.62	.67	.61	.39	.00	.61	.59	.64	.56	.79	.73	.48
22:salibiya	.77	.88	.77	.64	.66	.45	.75	.59	.64	.67	.55	.70	.77	.65	.69	.66	.66	.56	.59	.53	.61	.00	.70	.71	.73	.88	.78	.53
23:tabaqa	.72	.89	.66	.62	.75	.52	.89	.76	.62	.52	.82	.67	.79	.49	.70	.56	.79	.71	.81	.62	.59	.70	.00	.67	.56	.79	.62	.68
24:upper besor	.83	.54	.65	.66	.85	.68	.69	.72	.70	.75	.71	.67	.65	.73	.79	.85	.75	.60	.54	.48	.64	.71	.67	.00	.83	.69	.73	.55
25:wadi hammeh	.62	.86	.81	.51	.43	.80	.91	.64	.30	.29	.62	.63	.70	.43	.49	.39	.52	.82	.75	.61	.56	.73	.56	.83	.00	.95	.87	.64
26:wadi humeima	1.0	1.0	.89	.86	1.0	.86	1.0	.87	.86	.89	.91	.89	.89	.94	1.0	1.0	.85	1.0	.81	.85	.79	.88	.79	.69	.95	.00	.60	.77
27:wadi judayid	.80	.80	.50	.86	.91	.75	1.0	.82	.77	.73	.84	.62	.90	.76	.91	.83	.79	.67	.83	.79	.73	.78	.62	.73	.87	.60	.00	.64
28:wadi mataha	.72	.77	.56	.57	.74	.69	.85	.63	.50	.51	.56	.57	.56	.56	.57	.74	.64	.79	.69	.45	.48	.53	.68	.55	.64	.77	.64	.00

Bray & Curtis - Cluster Membership

Case	5 Clusters	4 Clusters	3 Clusters	2 Clusters
1:ain el-saratan	1	1	1	1
2:ain rahub	2	2	2	1
3:beidha	3	1	1	1
4:el wad	1	1	1	1
5:kebarah	1	1	1	1
6:fazael	1	1	1	1
7:givat hayil	4	3	2	1
8:hatoula	1	1	1	1
9:hayonim cave	1	1	1	1
10:hayonim cave	1	1	1	1
11:hayonim terrace	1	1	1	1
12:hilazon	1	1	1	1
13:khallat anaza	2	2	2	1
14:mallaha	1	1	1	1
15:mallaha	1	1	1	1
16:nahal ein gev	1	1	1	1
17:nahal oren	1	1	1	1
18:nahal sekher	4	3	2	1
19:rosh horesha	1	1	1	1
20:rosh zin	1	1	1	1
21:saflulim	1	1	1	1
22:salibiya	1	1	1	1
23:tabaqa	3	1	1	1
24:upper besor	2	2	2	1
25:wadi hammeh	1	1	1	1
26:wadi humeima	5	4	3	2
27:wadi judayid	3	1	1	1
28:wadi mataha	1	1	1	1

Kulczynski 2 – Proximity Matrix

Case	1	2	3	4	5	6	7	8	9	10	11	12	13	14	15	16	17	18	19	20	21	22	23	24	25	26	27	28
1:ain el-saratan	1.0	.32	.29	.44	.46	.17	.32	.33	.59	.52	.31	.48	.14	.43	.44	.39	.52	.36	.33	.29	.28	.23	.28	.18	.49	.00	.24	.29
2:ain rahub	.32	1.0	.16	.41	.15	.18	.25	.29	.41	.42	.45	.32	.48	.29	.41	.15	.15	.21	.31	.44	.44	.17	.16	.54	.41	.00	.21	.44
3:beidha	.29	.16	1.0	.39	.20	.34	.16	.33	.44	.31	.25	.35	.07	.38	.29	.20	.23	.36	.33	.41	.34	.23	.35	.37	.24	.16	.60	.47
4:el wad	.44	.41	.39	1.0	.47	.57	.41	.51	.61	.59	.55	.51	.54	.59	.73	.43	.52	.48	.55	.50	.44	.49	.46	.55	.49	.41	.29	.47
5:kebarah	.46	.15	.20	.47	1.0	.24	.15	.48	.60	.55	.45	.31	.20	.57	.59	.59	.56	.23	.29	.26	.25	.36	.25	.17	.68	.00	.11	.26
6:fazael	.17	.18	.34	.57	.24	1.0	.35	.34	.38	.26	.31	.17	.26	.27	.38	.24	.22	.40	.40	.51	.43	.55	.50	.32	.31	.18	.27	.36
7:givat hayil	.32	.25	.16	.41	.15	.35	1.0	.29	.41	.28	.61	.16	.16	.29	.41	.15	.29	.63	.31	.30	.44	.33	.16	.36	.28	.00	.00	.30
8:hatoula	.33	.29	.33	.51	.48	.34	.29	1.0	.54	.45	.49	.52	.22	.51	.47	.34	.44	.41	.38	.45	.35	.48	.26	.37	.38	.29	.31	.37
9:hayonim cave	.59	.41	.44	.61	.60	.38	.41	.54	1.0	.85	.59	.70	.34	.71	.60	.60	.63	.48	.47	.54	.58	.49	.46	.48	.70	.41	.48	.54
10:hayonim cave	.52	.42	.31	.59	.55	.26	.28	.45	.85	1.0	.51	.69	.36	.68	.58	.64	.45	.40	.36	.43	.59	.40	.54	.36	.72	.28	.50	.51
11:hayonim terrace	.31	.45	.25	.55	.45	.31	.61	.49	.59	.51	1.0	.48	.31	.62	.67	.28	.58	.44	.45	.34	.42	.48	.18	.33	.43	.15	.22	.44
12:hilazon	.48	.32	.35	.51	.31	.17	.16	.52	.70	.69	.48	1.0	.14	.67	.46	.38	.50	.47	.44	.39	.33	.30	.33	.36	.46	.16	.47	.45
13:khallat anaza	.14	.48	.07	.54	.20	.26	.16	.22	.34	.36	.31	.14	1.0	.27	.63	.33	.23	.24	.33	.35	.45	.23	.21	.37	.39	.16	.12	.47
14:mallaha	.43	.29	.38	.59	.57	.27	.29	.51	.71	.68	.62	.67	.27	1.0	.67	.47	.59	.40	.33	.32	.43	.42	.56	.37	.58	.14	.40	.45
15:mallaha	.44	.41	.29	.73	.59	.38	.41	.47	.60	.58	.67	.46	.63	.67	1.0	.51	.59	.38	.38	.39	.44	.44	.37	.34	.51	.00	.19	.46
16:nahal ein gev	.39	.15	.20	.43	.59	.24	.15	.34	.60	.64	.28	.38	.33	.47	.51	1.0	.41	.45	.29	.31	.40	.36	.44	.17	.72	.00	.23	.26
17:nahal oren	.52	.15	.23	.52	.56	.22	.29	.44	.63	.45	.58	.50	.23	.59	.59	.41	1.0	.42	.31	.36	.38	.38	.22	.31	.52	.29	.32	.36
18:nahal sekher	.36	.21	.36	.48	.23	.40	.63	.41	.48	.40	.44	.47	.24	.40	.38	.45	.42	1.0	.45	.53	.52	.50	.35	.42	.38	.31	.33	.32
19:rosh horesha	.33	.31	.33	.55	.29	.40	.31	.38	.47	.36	.45	.44	.33	.33	.38	.29	.31	.45	1.0	.52	.40	.43	.19	.51	.30	.31	.23	.31
20:rosh zin	.29	.44	.41	.50	.26	.51	.30	.45	.54	.43	.34	.39	.35	.32	.39	.31	.36	.53	.52	1.0	.61	.52	.39	.63	.43	.30	.32	.55
21:saflulim	.28	.44	.34	.44	.25	.43	.44	.35	.58	.59	.42	.33	.45	.43	.44	.40	.38	.52	.40	.61	1.0	.44	.43	.46	.47	.44	.42	.52
22:salibiya	.23	.17	.23	.49	.36	.55	.33	.48	.49	.40	.48	.30	.23	.42	.44	.36	.38	.50	.43	.52	.44	1.0	.30	.29	.38	.17	.25	.52
23:tabaqa	.28	.16	.35	.46	.25	.50	.16	.26	.46	.54	.18	.33	.21	.56	.37	.44	.22	.35	.19	.39	.43	.30	1.0	.36	.55	.32	.47	.34
24:upper besor	.18	.54	.37	.55	.17	.32	.36	.37	.48	.36	.33	.36	.37	.37	.34	.17	.31	.42	.51	.63	.46	.29	.36	1.0	.27	.36	.28	.55
25:wadi hammeh	.49	.41	.24	.49	.68	.31	.28	.38	.70	.72	.43	.46	.39	.58	.51	.72	.52	.38	.30	.43	.47	.38	.55	.27	1.0	.14	.29	.39
26:wadi humeima	.00	.00	.16	.41	.00	.18	.00	.29	.41	.28	.15	.16	.16	.14	.00	.00	.29	.00	.31	.30	.44	.17	.32	.36	.14	1.0	.42	.44
27:wadi judayid	.24	.21	.60	.29	.11	.27	.00	.31	.48	.50	.22	.47	.12	.40	.19	.23	.32	.33	.23	.32	.42	.25	.47	.28	.29	.42	1.0	.53
28:wadi mataha	.29	.44	.47	.47	.26	.36	.30	.37	.54	.51	.44	.45	.47	.45	.46	.26	.36	.32	.31	.55	.52	.52	.34	.55	.39	.44	.53	1.0

Kulczynski 2 - Cluster Membership

Case	5 Clusters	4 Clusters	3 Clusters	2 Clusters
1:ain el-saratan	1	1	1	1
2:ain rahub	2	1	1	1
3:beidha	3	2	2	1
4:el wad	1	1	1	1
5:kebarah	1	1	1	1
6:fazael	4	3	1	1
7:givat hayil	4	3	1	1
8:hatoula	1	1	1	1
9:hayonim cave	1	1	1	1
10:hayonim cave	1	1	1	1
11:hayonim terrace	1	1	1	1
12:hilazon	1	1	1	1
13:khallat anaza	2	1	1	1
14:mallaha	1	1	1	1
15:mallaha	1	1	1	1
16:nahal ein gev	1	1	1	1
17:nahal oren	1	1	1	1
18:nahal sekher	4	3	1	1
19:rosh horesha	4	3	1	1
20:rosh zin	2	1	1	1
21:saflulim	2	1	1	1
22:salibiya	4	3	1	1
23:tabaqa	3	2	2	1
24:upper besor	2	1	1	1
25:wadi hammeh	1	1	1	1
26:wadi humeima	5	4	3	2
27:wadi judayid	3	2	2	1
28:wadi mataha	2	1	1	1

Sokal & Sneath 4 - Proximity Matrix

Sokal and Sneath Measure 4

Case	1	2	3	4	5	6	7	8	9	10	11	12	13	14	15	16	17	18	19	20	21	22	23	24	25	26	27	28
1:ain el-saratan	1.0	.61	.57	.58	.66	.51	.61	.55	.68	.66	.57	.69	.48	.61	.58	.62	.68	.63	.58	.54	.53	.54	.56	.52	.61	.44	.56	.54
2:ain rahub	.61	1.0	.53	.59	.51	.55	.61	.55	.59	.62	.67	.61	.70	.55	.58	.51	.49	.58	.60	.66	.65	.54	.52	.75	.58	.47	.58	.66
3:beidha	.57	.53	1.0	.55	.50	.61	.53	.55	.58	.52	.53	.60	.44	.58	.47	.50	.50	.63	.58	.62	.57	.54	.60	.63	.44	.53	.76	.66
4:el wad	.58	.59	.55	1.0	.59	.68	.59	.59	.63	.64	.65	.63	.65	.65	.74	.56	.62	.63	.66	.60	.55	.62	.60	.66	.52	.59	.51	.57
5:kebarah	.66	.51	.50	.59	1.0	.54	.51	.64	.69	.67	.64	.57	.50	.70	.68	.74	.71	.55	.55	.51	.50	.61	.53	.51	.74	.43	.48	.51
6:fazael	.51	.55	.61	.68	.54	1.0	.64	.57	.55	.51	.58	.51	.56	.52	.55	.54	.51	.67	.64	.69	.63	.74	.70	.61	.51	.55	.59	.60
7:givat hayil	.61	.61	.53	.59	.51	.64	1.0	.55	.59	.54	.75	.52	.53	.55	.58	.51	.57	.80	.60	.57	.65	.63	.52	.65	.51	.47	.47	.57
8:hatoula	.55	.55	.55	.59	.64	.57	.55	1.0	.61	.57	.65	.67	.48	.63	.55	.54	.60	.62	.58	.61	.53	.65	.50	.59	.47	.55	.56	.55
9:hayonim cave	.68	.59	.58	.63	.69	.55	.59	.61	1.0	.87	.68	.76	.51	.76	.62	.69	.70	.63	.59	.63	.66	.62	.60	.62	.72	.59	.63	.63
10:hayonim cave	.66	.62	.52	.64	.67	.51	.54	.57	.87	1.0	.64	.78	.56	.75	.63	.74	.59	.60	.55	.57	.69	.59	.68	.57	.76	.54	.66	.63
11:hayonim terrace	.57	.67	.53	.65	.64	.58	.75	.65	.68	.64	1.0	.67	.57	.73	.73	.54	.71	.66	.64	.56	.61	.67	.48	.59	.55	.51	.54	.63
12:hilazon	.69	.61	.60	.63	.57	.51	.52	.67	.76	.78	.67	1.0	.48	.77	.59	.61	.67	.69	.65	.61	.55	.58	.59	.62	.59	.52	.69	.64
13:khallat anaza	.48	.70	.44	.65	.50	.56	.53	.48	.51	.56	.57	.48	1.0	.51	.71	.58	.50	.56	.58	.58	.64	.54	.52	.63	.54	.53	.50	.66
14:mallaha	.61	.55	.58	.65	.70	.52	.55	.63	.76	.75	.73	.77	.51	1.0	.72	.63	.70	.61	.54	.51	.58	.61	.70	.58	.64	.47	.61	.60
15:mallaha	.58	.58	.47	.74	.68	.55	.58	.55	.62	.63	.73	.59	.71	.72	1.0	.62	.66	.56	.53	.51	.54	.58	.53	.53	.53	.35	.45	.57
16:nahal ein gev	.62	.51	.50	.56	.74	.54	.51	.54	.69	.74	.54	.61	.58	.63	.62	1.0	.61	.67	.55	.55	.60	.61	.65	.51	.77	.43	.55	.51
17:nahal oren	.68	.49	.50	.62	.71	.51	.57	.60	.70	.59	.71	.67	.50	.70	.66	.61	1.0	.64	.54	.55	.57	.60	.49	.57	.61	.57	.58	.55
18:nahal sekher	.63	.58	.63	.63	.55	.67	.80	.62	.63	.60	.66	.69	.56	.61	.56	.67	.64	1.0	.67	.70	.69	.72	.62	.68	.56	.47	.64	.58
19:rosh horesha	.58	.60	.58	.66	.55	.64	.60	.58	.59	.55	.64	.65	.58	.54	.53	.55	.54	.67	1.0	.68	.60	.65	.49	.70	.46	.60	.55	.55
20:rosh zin	.54	.66	.62	.60	.51	.69	.57	.61	.63	.57	.56	.61	.58	.51	.51	.55	.55	.70	.68	1.0	.73	.69	.61	.76	.54	.57	.58	.69
21:saflulim	.53	.65	.57	.55	.50	.63	.65	.53	.66	.69	.61	.55	.64	.58	.54	.60	.57	.69	.60	.73	1.0	.64	.63	.65	.57	.65	.63	.67
22:salibiya	.54	.54	.54	.62	.61	.74	.63	.65	.62	.59	.67	.58	.54	.61	.58	.61	.60	.72	.65	.69	.64	1.0	.58	.59	.55	.54	.58	.69
23:tabaqa	.56	.52	.60	.60	.53	.70	.52	.50	.60	.68	.48	.59	.52	.70	.53	.65	.49	.62	.49	.61	.63	.58	1.0	.62	.66	.61	.69	.57
24:upper besor	.52	.75	.63	.66	.51	.61	.65	.59	.62	.57	.59	.62	.63	.58	.53	.51	.57	.68	.70	.76	.65	.59	.62	1.0	.49	.65	.60	.71
25:wadi hammeh	.61	.58	.44	.52	.74	.51	.51	.47	.72	.76	.55	.59	.54	.64	.53	.77	.61	.56	.46	.54	.57	.55	.66	.49	1.0	.43	.51	.51
26:wadi humeima	.44	.47	.53	.59	.43	.55	.47	.55	.59	.54	.51	.52	.53	.47	.35	.43	.57	.47	.60	.54	.65	.54	.61	.65	.43	1.0	.69	.66
27:wadi judayid	.56	.58	.76	.51	.48	.59	.47	.56	.63	.66	.54	.69	.50	.61	.45	.55	.58	.64	.55	.58	.63	.58	.69	.60	.51	.69	1.0	.70
28:wadi mataha	.54	.66	.66	.57	.51	.60	.57	.55	.63	.63	.63	.64	.66	.60	.57	.51	.55	.58	.55	.69	.67	.69	.57	.71	.51	.66	.70	1.0

Sokal and Sneath 4 - Cluster Membership

Case	5 Clusters	4 Clusters	3 Clusters	2 Clusters
1:ain el-saratan	1	1	1	1
2:ain rahub	2	2	2	1
3:beidha	3	3	3	2
4:el wad	4	4	2	1
5:kebarah	1	1	1	1
6:fazael	2	2	2	1
7:givat hayil	2	2	2	1
8:hatoula	5	1	1	1
9:hayonim cave	1	1	1	1
10:hayonim cave	1	1	1	1
11:hayonim terrace	1	1	1	1
12:hilazon	1	1	1	1
13:khallat anaza	4	4	2	1
14:mallaha	1	1	1	1
15:mallaha	4	4	2	1
16:nahal ein gev	1	1	1	1
17:nahal oren	1	1	1	1
18:nahal sekher	2	2	2	1
19:rosh horesha	2	2	2	1
20:rosh zin	2	2	2	1
21:saflulim	2	2	2	1
22:salibiya	2	2	2	1
23:tabaqa	3	3	3	2
24:upper besor	2	2	2	1
25:wadi hammeh	1	1	1	1
26:wadi humeima	3	3	3	2
27:wadi judayid	3	3	3	2
28:wadi mataha	2	2	2	1